Eng[d] by A.H. Ritchie.

Alice Cary

A MEMORIAL

OF

ALICE AND PHŒBE CARY,

WITH SOME OF THEIR LATER POEMS.

BY

MARY CLEMMER AMES.

ILLUSTRATED BY TWO PORTRAITS ON STEEL.

TWELFTH THOUSAND.

NEW YORK:
PUBLISHED BY HURD AND HOUGHTON.
Cambridge: The Riverside Press.
1875.

RIVERSIDE, CAMBRIDGE:
STEREOTYPED AND PRINTED BY
H. O. HOUGHTON AND COMPANY.

TO

ALICE CARY CLYMER

(LITTLE ALICE),

WHO, TO THEIR LAST EARTHLY HOUR, GAVE TO HER AUNTS A
DAUGHTER'S TENDEREST LOVE AND DEVOTION, THIS
MEMORIAL OF THEIR LIVES

Is Affectionately Dedicated,

BY HER FRIEND AND THEIRS,

MARY CLEMMER AMES.

THE HOME OF THE CARY SISTERS.

"In my younger days I lived near by and was acquainted with Alice and Phœbe Cary, the poet sisters; and now, after so many years, as I visit the old Cary homestead, in fancy I again see the little house where they were born,

'Little and low, and black and old,
With children as many as it could hold.'

Close beside where it once stood I yet find the well,

'The deep old well
Where the spring was never dry.'

It is now covered over with boards, and never more do little children, as Alice and Phœbe had often done, look down into its clear pure water to see their happy faces reflected back to their wondering eyes. The old barn where they once played, and watched the swallows fly in and out, is still standing as is also the majestic oak by the roadside, under the shade of which they wrote some of their sweetest songs. But it is many, many years since, moved by a longing to better their condition, they left 'Clover Nook,' their once happy home with its running brooks and fields of clover and shady groves; the little graveyard on the hillside where their loving mother lay at rest; and, standing farther down the road, the little brick schoolhouse where they had learned their first lessons, and at best, had obtained but a limited knowledge of books. All these, and their venerable father, were left behind—and the two sisters started out in the world among entire strangers, to battle with—they knew not what. But the songs that flowed from their hearts soon led them to heights of poetic fame. The sisters both wrote unceasingly—Alice, alone, in the space of twenty years sending out eleven volumes, besides numerous articles for the press, every thought and word written out by her own tireless hand; and when that busy hand had written down her last thoughts, her body was laid in the grave, in the presence of many of the prominent literary men of that day. After the death of Alice, Phœbe, who had given the world many beautiful pen pictures, soon finished her work and the sisters were laid side by side, resting from their labor in that silent city of the dead, Greenwood, far from their own beloved Clover Nook."

O. W. GOGIN, Mt. Healthy, Ohio.

—— Clovernook, near Cincinnati and the home of Alice and Phœbe Cary, has been bought by their lifelong friend, Mrs. M. Louise Thomas, and is to be restored as far as possible and preserved as a Cary Memorial.

PREFACE.

WHEN, at the request of the brothers of Alice and Phœbe Cary, I sat down to write a Memorial of their lives, and, looking through the entire mass of their papers, found not a single word of their own referring in any personal way to themselves, every impulse of my heart impelled me to relinquish the task. To tell the story of any human life, even in its outward incidents, wisely and justly, is not an easy thing to do. But to attempt a fit memorial of two women whose lives must be chiefly interpreted by inward rather than outward events, and solely from personal knowledge and remembrance, was a responsibility that I was unwilling to assume. With the utter absence of any data of their own, it seemed to me that the lives of the Cary sisters could only be produced from the combined reminiscences of all their more intimate personal friends. Months were consumed in writing to, and in waiting for replies from, long-time friends of the sisters. All were willing, but alas! they "had destroyed all letters," had forgotten "lots and lots of things that would have been interesting;" they were preoccupied, or sick; and, after months of waiting,

I sat where I began, with the mass of Alice's and Phœbe's unedited papers before me, and not an added line for their lives, with a new request from their legatees and executors, that I should go on with the Memorial.

Here it is.

It has cost me more than labor. Every day I have buried my friends anew. Every line wrung from memory has deepened the wound of irreparable loss.

From beginning to end my one purpose has been, not to write a eulogy, but to write justly. In depicting their birthplace and early life in Ohio, I have quoted copiously from Phœbe's sketch of Alice, and Ada Carnahan's sketch of her Aunt Phœbe, both published in the (Boston) "Ladies' Repository," believing that that which pertained exclusively to their early family life could be more faithfully told by members of the family than by any one born outside of it. Save where full credit is given to others, I, alone, am responsible for the statements of this Memorial. Not a line in it has been recorded from "hearsay." Not a fact is given that I do not know to be true, either from my own personal knowledge, or from the lips of the women whose lives and characters it helps to represent. I make this statement as facts embodied by me before, in a newspaper article, have been publicly questioned. One writer went so far as to say in a public journal, that, "As she would not willingly misrepresent her, Mrs. Ames must have misunderstood

Alice Cary." I *never* misunderstood Alice Cary. She never uttered a word to me that I did not perfectly understand. I have never recorded a word of her that I did not know to be true, nor with any purpose but to do absolute justice to my dearest friend. This is a full and final reply to any query or doubt which this Memorial may suggest or call forth. All who read have a perfect right to criticise and to question; but I shall not feel any obligation to make further reply. Life is too short and too precious to spend it in privately answering persons who "wish to be assured that the Cary sisters were not Universalists," or who cultivate original theories concerning their character or life.

The poems following the Memorial have, with but three or four exceptions, never before been gathered within the covers of a book. The exceptions are Alice's "The Sure Witness," "One Dust," and "My Creed," all published before in the volume of her poems brought out by Hurd and Houghton, in 1865, and reproduced here as special illustrations of her character, faith, and death.

In parting with a portion of the treasures and "pictures of memory," it has been difficult sometimes to decide which to give and which to retain. Many, too precious for any printed page, were nevertheless such a part of the true souls from whom they emanated, that to withhold them seemed like defrauding the living for the sake of the dead. Thus some inci dents are given solely because they are necessary to the perfect portrayal of the nature which they concern. No fact has been told which has not this significance. No line has been written for the sake of writing it. But as I cease, I feel more keenly even than when I began, how inadequate is any one hand, however conscientious, to trace two lives so delicately and variously tinted, to portray two souls so finely veined with a many-shaded deep humanity.

M. C. A.

October, 1872.

CONTENTS

CHAPTER XI.

CHAPTER XII.

LATER POEMS BY ALICE CARY.

BALLADS AND LOVE SONGS

POEMS OF THOUGHT.

POEMS OF NATURE AND HOME.

FOR THE LOST.

RELIGIOUS POEMS.

LAST POEMS.

LATER POEMS BY PHŒBE CARY.

BALLADS

RELIGIOUS POEMS

LOVE POEMS.

LAST POEMS.

A MEMORIAL

OF

ALICE AND PHŒBE CARY.

CHAPTER I.

THE HOUSE OF THEIR BIRTH. — THEIR FATHER AND MOTHER. — ANCESTRY, CHILDHOOD, AND EARLY YOUTH.

IN a brown house, "low and small," on a farm in the Miami Valley, eight miles north of Cincinnati, Ohio, Alice Cary was born on the 26th day of April, 1820. In the same house, September 4, 1824, was born her sister and life-long companion, Phœbe.

This house appeared and reappeared in the verse of both sisters, till their last lines were written. Their affection for it was a deep and life-long emotion. Each sister, within the blinds of a city house, used to shut her eyes and listen till she thought she heard the rustle of the cherry-tree on the old roof, and smelled again the sweet-brier under the window. You will realize how perfectly it was daguerreotyped on Phœbe's heart when you follow two of the many pictures which she has left of it. Phœbe says: "The house was small, unpainted, without the slightest pretensions to architectural beauty. It was one story and a half in height, the front looking toward the west and separated from the high road by a narrow strip of dooryard grass. A low porch ran across the north of the house, and from the steps of this a path of blue flagstones led to a cool, unfailing well of water a few yards distant. Close to the walls, on two sides, and almost pushing their strong, thrifty boughs through the little attic window, flourished several fruitful apple and cherry trees; and a luxuriant sweet-brier, the only thing near that seemed designed solely for ornament, almost covered the other side of the house. Beyond the door-yard, and sloping toward the south, lay a small garden, with two straight rows of currant bushes dividing its entire length, and beds of vegetables laid out on either side. Close against the fence nearest the yard grew several varieties of roses, and a few hardy and common flowers bordered the walks. In one corner a thriving peach tree threw in summer its shade over a row of bee-hives, and in another its withered mate was supported and quite hidden by a fragrant bower of hop vines. A little in the rear of the dwelling stood the ample, weather-beaten barn, the busy haunt of the restless swallows and quiet, comfortable doves, and in all seasons the never-failing resort of the children. A stately and symmetrical oak, which had been kindly spared from the forest when the clearing for the house was made, grew near it, and in the summer threw its thick, cool shadow over the road, making a grateful shade for the tired traveller, and a pleasant playground for the children, whose voices, now so many of them stilled, once made life and music there through all the livelong day."

OUR HOMESTEAD.

Our old brown homestead reared its walls
  From the wayside dust aloof,
Where the apple-boughs could almost cast
  Their fruit upon its roof;
And the cherry-tree so near it grew
  That, when awake I've lain
In the lonesome nights, I've heard the limbs
  As they creaked against the pane;
And those orchard trees! O, those orchard trees!
  I've seen my little brothers rocked
In their tops by the summer breeze.

The sweet-brier under the window-sill,
  Which the early birds made glad,
And the damask rose by the garden fence,
  Were all the flowers we had.
I've looked at many a flower since then,
  Exotics rich and rare,
That to other eyes were lovelier,
  But not to me so fair;
For those roses bright! O, those roses bright!
  I have twined them in my sister's locks
That are hid in the dust from sight.

We had a well — a deep, old well,
  Where the spring was never dry,
And the cool drops down from the mossy stones
  Were falling constantly:
And there never was water half so sweet
  As the draught which filled my cup,
Drawn up to the curb by the rude, old sweep,

That my father's hand set up;
And that deep, old well! O, that deep, old well!
I remember now the plashing sound
Of the bucket as it fell.

Our homestead had an ample hearth,
Where at night we loved to meet;
There my mother's voice was always kind,
And her smile was always sweet;
And there I've sat on my father's knee,
And watched his thoughtful brow,
With my childish hand in his raven hair —
That hair is silver, now!
But that broad hearth's light! O, that broad hearth's light!
And my father's look, and my mother's smile,
They are in my heart, to-night!

In her "Order for a Picture," which was her favorite among all the poems she had ever written, Alice has given us another reflection of her first home upon earth, and its surroundings: —

"O, good painter, tell me true,
Has your hand the cunning to draw
Shapes of things that you never saw?
Aye? Well, here is an order for you.

"Woods and cornfields, a little brown —
The picture must not be over-bright —
Yet all in the golden and gracious light
Of a cloud, when the summer sun is down.
Alway and alway, night and morn,
Woods upon woods, with fields of corn

Lying between them, not quite sere,
  And not in the full, thick, leafy bloom,
  When the wind can hardly find breathing-room
Under their tassels, — cattle near,
Biting shorter the short, green grass,
And a hedge of sumach and sassafras,
With bluebirds twittering all around, —
(Ah, good painter, you can't paint sound!) —
These, and the house where I was born,
Low and little, and black and old,
With children many as it can hold,
All at the windows open wide, —
Heads and shoulders clear outside:
And fair young faces all ablush:
  Perhaps you may have seen, some day,
  Roses crowding the self-same way,
Out of a wilding, wayside bush."

In such a home were born Alice and Phœbe Cary; Alice, the fourth, and Phœbe, the sixth child of Robert Cary and Elizabeth Jessup, his wife.

Phœbe, in her precious memorial of Alice, gives this picture of their father and mother: "Robert Cary was a man of superior intelligence, of sound principles, and blameless life. He was very fond of reading, especially romances and poetry; but early poverty and the hard exigencies of pioneer life had left him no time for acquiring anything more than the mere rudiments of a common school education; and the consciousness of his want of culture, and an invincible diffidence born with him, gave him a shrinking, retiring manner, and a want of confidence in his own judgment, which was inherited to a large measure by his offspring. He was a tender, loving father, who sang his children to sleep with holy hymns, and habitually went about his work repeating the grand old Hebrew poets, and the sweet and precious promises of the New Testament of our Lord." Ada Carnahan, the child of Robert and Elizabeth Cary's oldest daughter, who inherits in no small degree the fine mental gifts of her family, in her admirable sketch of her Aunt Phœbe, published in the Boston "Ladies' Repository," says of this father of poets: "When he had no longer children in his arms, he still went on singing to himself, and held in his heart the words that he had so often repeated. For him the common life of a farmer was idealized into poetry; springtime and harvest were ever recurring miracles, and dumb animals became companionable. Horses and cattle loved him, and would follow him all over the farm, sure to receive at least a kind word or gentle pat, and perhaps a few grains of corn, or a lump of salt or sugar; and there was no colt so shy that would not eat out of his hand, and rub its head caressingly against his shoulder. Of his children, Alice the most resembled him in person, and all the tender and close sympathy with nature, and with humanity, which in her found expression, had in him an existence as real, if voiceless. In his youth he must have been handsome. He was six feet in height, and well proportioned, with curling black hair, bright brown eyes, slightly aquiline nose, and remarkably beautiful teeth." Those who saw him in New York, in the home of his daughters, remember him a silver-haired, sad-eyed, soft-voiced patriarch, remarkable for the gentleness of his manners, and the emotional tenderness of his temperament. Tears rose to his eyes, smiles flitted across his face, precisely as they did in the face of Alice. He was the prototype of Alice. In her was reproduced not only his form and features, but his mental, moral, and emotional nature. To see father and daughter together, one would involuntarily exclaim, "How alike!" They loved to be together. It was a delight to the father to take that long journey from the Western farm to the New York home. Here, for the first time, he found reproduced in reality many of the dreams of his youth. Nothing gave greater delight to his daughters than "to take father" to see pictures, to visit friends, and to join in evening receptions. In the latter he took especial pleasure, when he could sit in an arm-chair and survey the bright scene before him. He had poet eyes to see, and a poet's heart to feel the beauty of woman. Alice had a friend whom he never mentioned save as "your friend the pretty woman." He was informed, one evening, at a small party, that the beautiful young lady whom he was admiring, and who looked about twenty-five, was a happy matron and the mother of a grown-up son. His look of childlike amazement was irresistible. "Well, well," he exclaimed, "mothers of grown-up sons never looked as young as that in my day!"

The wife of this man, the mother of Alice and Phœbe Cary, was blue-eyed and beautiful. Her children lived to rise up and call her blessed. Alice said of her: "My mother was a woman of superior intellect and of good, well-ordered life. In my memory she stands apart from all others, wiser, purer, doing more, and living better than any other woman." And this is her portrait of her mother in her "Order for a Picture:"

" A lady, the loveliest ever the sun
Looked down upon, you must paint for me :
O, if I only could make you see
The clear blue eyes, the tender smile,
The sovereign sweetness, the gentle grace,
The woman's soul, and the angel's face
That are beaming on me all the while,
I need not speak these foolish words :
Yet one word tells you all I would say,
She is my mother : you will agree
That all the rest may be thrown away."

Phœbe said of her : " She was the wonder of my childhood. She is no less a wonder to me as I recall her now. How she did so much work, and yet did it well ; how she reared carefully, and governed wisely, so large a family of children, and yet found time to develop by thought and reading a mind of unusual strength and clearness, is still a mystery to me. She was fond of history, politics, moral essays, biography, and works of religious controversy. Poetry she read, but cared little for fictitious literature. An exemplary housewife, a wise and kind mother, she left no duty unfulfilled, yet she found time, often at night, after every other member of the household was asleep, by reading, to keep herself informed of all the issues of the day, political, social, and religious." When we remember that the woman who kept herself informed of all the issues of the day, political, social, and religious, was the mother of nine children, a housewife, who performed the labor of her large household with her own hands ; that she lived in a rural neighborhood, wherein personal and family topics were the supreme subjects of discussion, aloof from the larger interests and busy thoroughfares of men, we can form a juster estimate of the superiority of her natural powers, and the native breadth of her mind and heart.

Such were the father and mother of Alice and Phœbe Cary. From their father they inherited the poetic temperament, the love of nature, and of dumb creatures, their loving and pitying hearts, which were so large that they enfolded all breathing and unbreathing things. From their mother they inherited their interest in public affairs, their passion for justice, their devotion to truth and duty as they saw it, their clear perceptions, and sturdy common sense.

Blended with their personal love for their father and mother, was an ingenuous pride and delight in their ancestry. They were proud of their descent. This was especially true of Phœbe. With all her personal modesty, which was very marked, pride of race was one of Phœbe Cary's distinguishing traits. She was proud of the Cary coat-of-arms, which hung framed in the little library in Twentieth Street; prouder still to trace her name from the true and gentle father who gave it to her, to the John Cary who taught the first Latin school in Plymouth, and from him to the gallant Sir Robert Cary, who vanquished a chevalier of Aragon, in the reign of Henry V., in Smithfield, London. A friend, in a former biographical sketch of the two sisters, referring to this knight, said that the genealogy which connected him with the American Cary family "is at best unverified." In private, Phœbe often referred to this published doubt with considerable feeling.

"Why do you care?" asked a friend. "The con queror of the Knight of Aragon cannot make you more or less."

"But I *do* care," she said. "He was *my* ancestor it has been proved. He bore the same name as my own father. I don't like to have any doubt cast upon it It is a great comfort to me to know that we sprung from a noble, not an ignoble race." This fact was so much to her in life, it seems but just that she should have the full benefit of it in death. Thus is given the entire story of the Knight of Aragon, as printed in Burke's "Heraldry," with the complete genealogy of the branch of the American Cary family to which Alice and Phœbe belong: —

John Cary, a lineal descendant of Sir Thomas Cary, (a cousin of Queen Elizabeth), came to the Plymouth Colony in 1630, was prominent and influential among the Pilgrim Fathers. He was thoroughly educated — taught the first Latin class, and held important offices in the town and church. He married Elizabeth, a daughter of Francis Godfrey, in 1644. He died in Bridgewater, in 1681, aged 80 years.

SECOND GENERATION.

Joseph, the ninth child of John, born in Plymouth, in 1665, emigrated to Connecticut, and was one of the original proprietors of the town of Windham. At the organization of the first church in Windham, in the year 1700, he was chosen deacon. He was a useful and very prominent man. He died in 1722.

THIRD GENERATION.

John, the fourth child of Joseph, born in Windham, Connecticut, June 23, 1695, married Hannah Thurston, resided in Windham, was a man of wealth and influence in the church and in public affairs. He died in 1776, aged 81 years.

FOURTH GENERATION.

Samuel, the ninth child of John, born June 13, 1734, graduated at Yale College in the class of 1755, was a physician, eminent in his profession; married Deliverance Grant, in Bolton, Connecticut, and emigrated to Lyme, New Hampshire, among the first colonists, where he died in 1784.

FIFTH GENERATION.

Christopher, the eldest child of Samuel, born February 25, 1763, joined the army at an early age, under Colonel Waite of New Hampshire; was taken prisoner by the British, and suffered great hardships. He married Elsie Terrel, at Lyme, New Hampshire, in 1784, removed with his family to Cincinnati, Ohio, in 1802, died at College Hill, Ohio, in 1837.

SIXTH GENERATION.

Robert, the second child of Christopher, born January 24, 1787, emigrated with his father to the Northwest Territory, in 1802, settled upon a farm near Mount Healthy, Hamilton County, Ohio, married Elizabeth Jessup in 1814, was a soldier in the war of 1812, and was at Hull's surrender. He died in 1866. Their children were:—

1. Rowena, born 1814, married Carnahan, died 1869.
2. Susan, born 1816, married Alex. Swift, died 1852.
3. Rhoda, born 1818, died 1833.
4. Alice, born 1820, died 1871.
5. Asa, born 1822, living at Mount Pleasant, Ohio.

6. Phœbe, born 1824, died 1871.
7. Warren, born 1826, living near Harrison, Ohio
8. Lucy, born 1829, died 1833.
9. Elmina, born 1831, married Alex. Swift, and died 1862.

"In the beginning of the reign of Henry V., a certain knight-errant of Aragon, having passed through divers countries and performed many feats of arms, to his high commendation, arrived here in England, where he challenged any man of his rank and quality to make trial of his valor and skill in arms. This challenge Sir Robert Cary accepted, between whom a cruel encounter and a long and doubtful combat was waged in Smithfield, London. But at length this noble champion vanquished the presumptuous Aragonois, for which King Henry V. restored unto him a good part of his father's lands, which, for his loyalty to Richard II., he had been deprived by Henry IV., and authorized him to bear the arms of the Knight of Aragon, which the noble posterity continue to wear unto this day; for, according to the laws of heraldry, whoever fairly in the field conquers his adversary, may justify the wearing of his arms."

Phœbe had the Cary coat of arms engraved on a seal ring, which was taken from her finger after death

You see that it happened to the Cary family, as to many another of long descent, that it emerged from the vicissitudes of time and toil, poor, possessing no finer weapon to vanquish hostile fate than the intrinsic temper of its inherited quality, the precious metal of honesty, industry, integrity, bravery, honor —

in fine, true manhood. The great-grandfather of Alice and Phœbe, Samuel Cary, was graduated from Yale. A physician by profession, in Lyme, New Hampshire, he seems to have been the last of the manifold "Cary boys" who possessed the advantages of a liberal education. His eldest son, Christopher, entered the army of the Revolution at the age of eighteen. When peace was won, the young man received not money, but a land grant, or warrant, in Hamilton County, Ohio, as his recompense. The necessity of poverty probably compelled Christopher to the lot of a tiller of the soil.

And even Phœbe, if she thought of it, must have acknowledged that this grandsire of hers, who went into the army of freedom to fight the battles of his country at eighteen, who, when liberty was won, went to struggle with the earth, to wrest from the wilderness a home for himself and his children, was an ancestor more worthy of her admiration and pride than even the doughty Sir Robert, who fought with and overcame the Knight of Aragon. The editor of the "Central Christian Advocate," in writing of the death of Alice, says: —

"We remember well her grandfather, and the house at the foot of the great hill, where his land grant was located. In early boyhood we often climbed the hills, and sometimes listened to the conversation of the somewhat rough and rugged soldier, whom we all called 'Uncle Christopher.'"

Robert Cary came with his father, Christopher, from New Hampshire to the wilderness of Ohio in 1803, at the age of fifteen. Says his granddaughter, Ada Carnahan: "They travelled in an emigrant wagon to

Pittsfield, and descending the river on a flat-boat, arrived at Fort Washington. This was a thriving settlement, though its people had hardly ceased to depend on its fort for protection from the savages, who still infested the surrounding forests and made occasional incursions into its immediate neighborhood." Here, for several years, the family remained, before making a purchase of lands some eight miles north of the settlement, on what is still known as the Hamilton Road.

Robert Cary and Elizabeth Jessup were married January 13, 1814, and began their married life upon a quarter section of the original Cary purchase, the same land which will be remembered for many generations as the Clovernook of Alice Cary's stories. Again says Ada Carnahan: "In the comparatively short time that had elapsed, there had been most marvelous changes in all this vicinity. The red-man had disappeared. Log cabins and their surrounding clearings were scattered all over the region, while here and there might be seen a more pretentious frame dwelling. One of the latter Robert Cary reared for his home, which it continued to be for eighteen years, during which his nine children were born. The farm upon which Robert and Elizabeth Cary began life was not, however, a gift, and it was the work of many laborious years to clear it from the incumbrance of debt — years which could not but make their impression upon their rising family, and inculcate those lessons of perseverance, industry, and economy, which are the very foundations of success." . . . .

"As is almost always the case in large families, the Cary children divided themselves into groups and couples, as age and disposition dictated. In this grouping, Alice and Phœbe, afterwards to be brought into such close communion of life and thought, were separated. Alice's passionate devotion in life and death to the sister next older than herself is well known, while Phœbe, standing between her two brothers, turned toward the younger of these, whom she made her constant playfellow. . . . . The children were much together in the open air, and were intimately acquainted with every nook and corner of their father's farm. They gathered wild flowers in May-time, and nuts in October, and learned to love the company of trees and blossoms, birds and insects, and became deeply imbued with the love of nature. They were sensitive and imaginative, and it may well be that they, at least two of them, saw more beauty, and heard more melody in nature than every eye is open to perceive. As they grew older, this kind of holiday life was interrupted by occasional attendance upon the district school, and by instruction in such household employments as were deemed indispensable — in knitting, sewing, spinning, cooking, churning, etc. Of all these, Phœbe only became proficient in the first two. In both these she took pleasure up to the time of her last illness, and in both she was unusually dexterous and neat, as well as in penmanship, showing in these respects a marked contrast to Alice. The school-house in which they gained the rudiments of an English education was distant a mile and a quarter from their home. The plain, one story, brick building is still used for school purposes. This distance was always walked. Upon her last visit to this vicinity, in 1867, Phœbe Cary pointed out to me a goodly forest tree, growing at one side, but in the highway, and told how, when they were returning from school, one day, Alice found lying in the road a freshly cut switch, and picked it up, saying, 'Let us stick it in the ground and see if it will grow;' and immediately acting on her own suggestion, she stuck it in the ground; and there, after more than thirty-five years, it stood, a graceful and fitting monument to the gracious and tender nature which bade it live.

"In the autumn of 1832, by persevering industry and frugal living, the farm was at last paid for, and a new and more commodious dwelling erected for the reception of the family, grown too large to be longer sheltered by the old roof-tree. This new dwelling, which is still standing, is no more than the plainest of farm-houses, built at a time when the family were obliged to board the builders, and the bricks were burned on the spot; yet it represents a degree of comfort only attained after a long struggle."

"It cost many years of toil and privation — the new house. We thought it the beginning of better times. Instead, all the sickness and death in the family dates from the time that it was finished. It seems as if nothing but trouble and sorrow have come since," said Alice Cary, late in the autumn of 1869, to a friend, as her starry eyes shone out from her pallid face, amid the delicate laces of her pillow, in the chamber on Twentieth Street.

"Before that time I had two sources of unalloyed happiness: the companionship of my sister Rhoda, and the care of my little sister Lucy. I shall always think Rhoda was the most gifted of all our family. The stories that she used to tell me on our way home from school had in them the germ of the most wonderful novels — of better novels than we read nowadays. When we saw the house in sight, we would often sit down under a tree, that she might have more time to finish the story. My anxiety concerning the fate of the people in it was often so great I could not possibly wait to have it continued. At another time it would take her days together to tell one story. Rhoda was very handsome; her great, dark eyes would shine with excitement as she went on. For myself, by the time she had finished, I was usually dissolved in tears over the tragic fate of her heroes and heroines. Lucy was golden-haired and blue-eyed, the only one who looked like our mother. I was not fourteen when she died — I'm almost fifty, now. It may seem strange when I tell you that I don't believe that there has been an hour of any day since her death in which I have not thought of her and mourned for her. Strange, isn't it, that the life and death of a little child not three years old could take such a hold on another life? I have never lost the consciousness of the presence of that child.

"That makes me think of our ghost story. Almost every family *has* a ghost story, you know? Ours has more than one, but *the* one foreshadowed all the others."

"Do tell it to me," said the friend sitting by her bed.

"Well, the new house was just finished, but we had not moved into it. There had been a violent shower; father had come home from the field, and everybody had come in out of the rain. I think it was about four in the afternoon, when the storm ceased and the sun shone out. The new house stood on the edge of a ravine, and the sun was shining full upon it, when some one in the family called out and asked how Rhoda and Lucy came to be over in the new house, and the door open. Upon this all the rest of the family rushed to the front door, and there, across the ravine, in the open door of the new house, stood Rhoda with Lucy in her arms. Some one said, 'She must have come from the sugar camp, and has taken shelter there with Lucy from the rain.' Upon this another called out, 'Rhoda!' but she did not answer. While we were gazing and talking and calling, Rhoda herself came down-stairs, where she had left Lucy fast asleep, and stood with us while we all saw, in the full blaze of the sun, the woman with the child in her arms slowly sink, sink, sink into the ground, until she disappeared from sight. Then a great silence fell upon us all. In our hearts we all believed it to be a warning of sorrow — of what, we knew not. When Rhoda and Lucy both died, then we knew. Rhoda died the next autumn, November 11; Lucy a month later, December 10, 1833. Father went directly over to the house and out into the road, but no human being, and not even a track, could be seen. Lucy has been seen many times since by different members of the family, in the same house, always in a red frock, like one she was very fond of wearing; the last time by my brother Warren's little boy, who had never heard the story. He came running in, saying that he had seen 'a little girl up-stairs, in a red dress.' He is dead now, and such a bright boy. Since the apparition in the door, never for one year has our family been free from the shadow of death. Ever since, some one of us has been dying." . . . .

"I don't like to think how much we are robbed of in this world by just the conditions of our life. How much better work I should have done, how much more success I might have won, if I had had a better opportunity in my youth. But for the first fourteen years of my life, it seemed as if there was actually nothing in existence but work. The whole family struggle was just for the right to live free from the curse of debt. My father worked early and late; my mother's work was never done. The mother of nine children, with no other help than that of their little hands, I shall always feel that she was taxed far beyond her strength, and died before her time. I have never felt myself to be the same that I was before Rhoda's death. Rhoda and I pined for beauty; but there was no beauty about our homely house, but that which nature gave us. We hungered and thirsted for knowledge; but there were not a dozen books on our family shelf, not a library within our reach. There was little time to study, and had there been more, there was no chance to learn but in the district school-house, down the road. I never went to any other — not very much to that. It has been a long struggle. Now that I can afford to gather a few beautiful things about me, it is too late. My leisure I must spend here" (turning toward her pillow). "Do you know." (with a pathetic smile) "I seem to myself like a worn-out old ship, laid up from further use. I may be repaired a little; but I'll never be seaworthy again."

The friend, looking into her face, saw the dark eyes drowned in tears.

CHAPTER II.

EARLY STRUGGLES AND SUCCESS.

THE deaths of Rhoda and Lucy Cary were followed by the decline and passing away of their mother, who died July 30, 1835. In 1837, Robert Cary married again. His second wife was a widow, suitable in years, and childless. Had her temperament been different, her heart must have gone out in tenderness to the family of young, motherless girls toward whom she was now called to fill a mother's place. The limitations of her nature made this impossible. Such a mental and spiritual organism as theirs she could not comprehend, and with their attempted pursuits she had no sympathy. All time spent in study she considered wasted.

Alice, now seventeen, and Phœbe, thirteen, were beginning to write down in uncertain lines the spontaneous songs which seemed to sing themselves into being in their hearts and brains. A hard, uncultured, utilitarian woman, to whom work for work's sake was the ultimatum of life, could not fail to bring unhappiness to two such spirits, nor fail to sow discord in a household whose daily toil from birth had been lightened and brightened by an inborn idealism, and the unconscious presence of the very spirit of song. Ada Carnahan says: "Alice kept busily at work during the day, prosecuting her studies at night. This was a fruitful source of dissension between herself and stepmother, who could not believe that burning candles for this purpose was either proper or profitable, that reading books was better than darning socks, or writing poems better than making bread. But the country girls, uncultured in mind and rustic in manners, not needing to be told the immense distance which separated them from the world of letters they longed to enter, would not be discouraged. If they must darn and bake, they would also study and write, and at last publish: if candles were denied them, a saucer of lard with a bit of rag for wick could and did serve instead, and so, for ten long years, they studied and wrote and published without pecuniary recompense; often discouraged and despondent, yet never despairing; lonely and grown over-sensitive, prone to think themselves neglected and slighted, yet hugging their solitude in unconscious superiority; looking out to the graveyard on the near hillside with a regret for the past, and over and beyond it into the unknown distance with hope for the future." Phœbe, speaking of the Cary sisters as if merely acquaintances, says: "They saw but few books or newspapers. On a small shelf of the cottage lay all the literary treasures of the family. These consisted of a Bible, Hymn Book, the 'History of the Jews,' 'Lewis and Clark's Travels,' 'Pope's Essays,' and 'Charlotte Temple,' a romance founded on fact. There might have been one or two more, now forgotten, and there was, I know, a mutilated novel by an unknown hand, called the 'Black Penitents,' the mystery of whose fate (for the closing pages of the work were gone) was a life-long regret to Alice'

Robert and Elizabeth Cary were early converts to Universalism, and the "Trumpet," says Phœbe, "read by them from the publication of its first numbers till the close of their lives, was for many years the only paper seen by Alice, and its Poet's Corner the food of her fancy, and source of her inspiration." Yet with such ill selected and scanty food for the mind, and early trained to be helpful in a household where great needs and small resources left little time for anything but the stern, practical part of life, these children began very early to see visions and to dream dreams. "At the age of fifteen Alice was left motherless, and, in one sense, companionless, her yet living sisters being too old or too young to fill the place left vacant in her life. The only sins of writing of which she seemed to have been guilty up to this time were occasional efforts to alter and improve the poetry in her school reader, and a few pages of original rhymes which broke the monotony of her copy-books. All ambition, and all love of the pursuits of life, seemed for a time to have died with her beloved sister. Her walks, which were now solitary, generally terminated at the little family burial-place, on a green hill that rose in sight of home." All these conditions and influences in her life must be considered in measuring her success, or in estimating the quality of her work. One of the severest criticisms passed on her early poems was that they were full of graves. Remembering the bereaved and lonely girl whose daily walk ended in the graveyard on the hill-side, where her mother and sisters slept, how could her early song escape the shadow of death and the vibration of sorrow? With her, it was the utterance of actual loss, not the morbid sentimentalism of poetic youth. In after years, Phœbe often spoke of the new keen sensation of delight which she felt when, for the first time, she saw her own verses in print. "O, if they could only look like that now," she said to me within a year of her death; "if they only could look like that now, it would be better than money." She was but fourteen when, without consulting even Alice, she sent a poem in secret to a Boston newspaper, and knew nothing of its acceptance, till to her astonishment she saw it copied in a home (Cincinnati) paper. She laughed and cried over it. "I did not care any more if I were poor, or my clothes plain. Somebody cared enough for my verses to print them, and I was happy. I looked with compassion on my schoolmates. You may know more than I do, I thought, but you can't write verses that are printed in a newspaper; but I kept my joy and triumph to myself."

Meanwhile Robert Cary built a new house on the farm, to which he removed with his second wife, leaving Alice and Phœbe, their two brothers, and young sister Elmina, to live together in the old home. By this time newspapers and magazines, with a few new books, including the standard English poets, were added to the cottage library, while several clergymen and other persons of culture coming into the rural neighborhood, brought new society and more congenial associations to the sisters. Alice had begun to publish, and without hope of present reward was sending her verses through the land astray, they chiefly finding shelter in the periodicals and journals of the Universalist Church, with which she was most familiar, and in the daily and weekly journals of Cincinnati. The Boston "Ladies' Repository," the "Ladies' Repository" of Cincinnati, and "Graham's Magazine," were among the leading magazines which accepted and published her earlier verses. Phœbe says: "Alice's first literary adventure appeared in the 'Sentinel' (now 'Star of the West'), published in Cincinnati. It was entitled 'The Child of Sorrow,' and was written in her eighteenth year. The 'Star,' with the exception of an occasional contribution to some of the dailies of the same city, was for many years her only medium of publication. After the establishing of the 'National Era' at Washington in 1847, she wrote poetry regularly for its columns, and here she first tried her hand at prose, in a series of stories under a fictitious name. From Dr. Bailey of the 'Era' she received the first money ever earned by her pen — ten dollars sent as a gratuity, when she had written for him some months. She afterwards made a regular engagement to furnish him with contributions to his paper for a small stipulated sum." Even now the real note of a natural singer will penetrate through all the noise of our day, and arrest the step and fix the ear of many a pilgrim amid the multitude. This was far more strikingly the fact in 1850–51. Poets, so called, then were not so plenty as now; the congregation of singers so much smaller, any new voice holding in its compass one sweet note was heard and recognized at once. There had come a lull in the national struggles. The tremendous events which have absorbed the emotion and consumed the energies of the nation for the last decade were only just beginning to show their first faint portents. Men of letters were at leisure, and ready to listen to any new voice in literature. Indeed, they were anxious and eager to see take form and substance in this country an American literature which should be acknowledged and honored abroad. Judging by the books of American authors which he has left behind, no one at that time could have been quite so much on the alert for new American poets and poetesses as Dr. Rufus W. Griswold. He generously set amid his "American Female Writers" names which perished like morning-glories, after their first outburst of song. He could not fail, then, to hear with delight those sweet strains of untutored music breaking from that valley of the West, heard now across all the land. The ballads and lyrics written by that saucer of lard with its rag flame, in the hours when others slept, were bringing back at last true echoes and sympathetic responses from kindred souls, throbbing out in the great world of which as yet these young singers knew nothing. Alice's "Pictures of Memory" had already been pronounced by Edgar Allan Poe to be one of the most musically perfect lyrics in the English language. The names of Alice and Phœbe Cary in the corners of newspapers and magazines, with the songs which followed, had fixed the attention and won the affection of some of the best minds and hearts in the land. Men of letters, among them John G. Whittier, had written the sisters words of appreciation and encouragement. In 1849, the editor of the "Tribune," Horace Greeley, visited them in their own home, and thus speaks of the interview: "I found them, on my first visit to Cincinnati, early in the summer of 1849; and the afternoon spent in their tidy cottage on 'Walnut Hills,' seven miles out of the city, in the company of congenial spirits, since departed, is among the greenest oases in my recollection of scenes and events long past."

In May, 1849, Phœbe writes: "Alice and I have been very busy collecting and revising all our published poems, to send to New York. Rev. R. W. Griswold, quite a noted author, is going to publish them for us this summer, and we are to receive for them a hundred dollars. I don't know as I feel better or worse, as I don't think it will do us much good, or any one else. This little volume, entitled "Poems of Alice and Phœbe Cary," published by Moss and Brother, of Philadelphia, was the first condensed result of their twelve years of study, privation, aspiration, labor, sorrow, and youth.

To the year 1850, Alice and Phœbe had never met any of their Eastern friends save Mr. Greeley. But after the publication of their little book, they went forth together to the land of promise, and beheld face to face, for the first time, the sympathetic souls who had sent them so many words of encouragement and praise. They went first to New York, from thence to Boston, and from Boston these women minstrels took their way to Amesbury, and all unknown, save by name, knocked at the door of the poet Whittier. Mr. Whittier has commemorated that visit by his touching poem of "The Singer," published after the death of Alice.

Years since (but names to me before),
Two sisters sought at eve my door;
Two song-birds wandering from their nest,
A gray old farm-house in the West.

Timid and young, the elder had
Even then a smile too sweetly sad;
The crown of pain that all must wear
Too early pressed her midnight hair.

Yet, ere the summer eve grew long,
Her modest lips were sweet with song,
A memory haunted all her words
Of clover-fields and singing-birds.

Her dark, dilating eyes expressed
The broad horizons of the West;
Her speech dropped prairie flowers; the gold
Of harvest wheat about her rolled.

Fore-doomed to song she seemed to me;
I queried not with destiny:
I knew the trial and the need,
Yet all the more, I said, God speed!

What could I other than I did?
Could I a singing-bird forbid?
Deny the wind-stirred leaf? Rebuke
The music of the forest brook?

She went with morning from my door;
But left me richer than before:
Thenceforth I knew her voice of cheer,
The welcome of her partial ear.

Years passed; through all the land her name
A pleasant household word became;
All felt behind the singer stood
A sweet and gracious womanhood.

Her life was earnest work, not play;
Her tired feet climbed a weary way;
And even through her lightest strain
We heard an undertone of pain.

Unseen of her, her fair fame grew,
The good she did she rarely knew,
Unguessed of her in life the love
That rained its tears her grave above.

The friendship thus sympathetically begun between these tender, upright souls never waned while human life endured. To their last hour, Alice and Phœbe cherished for this great poet and good man the affection and devotion of sisters. Of this first visit Alice wrote: "I like him very much, and was sorry to say good-by." After an absence of three months the sisters returned to the West, which was nevermore to be their home.

In November of the same year (1850), Alice Cary, broken in health, sad in spirit, with little money, but with a will which no difficulty could daunt, an energy and patience which no pain or sorrow could overcome, started alone to seek her fortune, and to make for herself a place and home in the city of New York. Referring to this the year before her death, she said: "Ignorance stood me in the stead of courage. Had I known the great world as I have learned it since, I should not have dared; but I didn't. Thus I came."

The intellectual life of neither man nor woman can be justly judged without a knowledge of the conditions which impelled that life and gave to it shape and substance. Alice Cary felt within her soul the divine impulse of genius, but hers was essentially a feminine soul, shy, loving, full of longings for home, overburdened with tenderness, capable of an unselfish, lifelong devotion to one. Whatever her mental or spiritual gifts, no mere ambition could ever have borne such a woman out into the world to seek and to make her fortune alone. Had Alice Cary married the man whom she then loved, she would never have come to New York at all, to coin the rare gifts of her brain and soul into money for shelter and bread. Business interests had brought into her western neighborhood a man at that time much her superior in years, culture, and fortune. Naturally he sought the society of a young, lovely woman so superior to her surroundings and associations. To Alice he was the man of men. It is doubtful if the most richly endowed man of the world whom she met afterwards in her larger sphere, ever wore to her the splendor of manhood which invested this king of her youth. Alice Cary loved this man, and in the profoundest sense she never loved another. A proud and prosperous family brought all their pride and power to bear on a son, to prevent his marrying a girl to them uneducated, rustic, and poor. "I waited for one who never came back," she said. "Yet I believed he would come, till I read in a paper his marriage to another. *Can* you think what life would be — loving one, waiting for one who would *never* come!"

He did come at last. His wife had died. Alice was dying. The gray-haired man sat down beside the gray-haired woman. Life had dealt prosperously with him, as is its wont with men. Suffering and death had taken all from her save the lustre of her wondrous eyes. From her wan and wasted face they shone upon him full of tenderness and youth. Thus they met with life behind them — they who parted plighted lovers when life was young. He was the man whom she forgave for her blighted and weary life, with a smile of parting as divine as ever lit the face of woman.

Alice Cary's was no weak nature. All its fine feminine gold was set in a will of iron. All its deep wells of tenderness were walled and held in by justice, common sense, and unyielding integrity. She outlived that sorrowful youth to speak of it with pity, to drop a silent tear upon its memory as if it were the youth of another person. She lived to become preëminently one of the world's workers. She had many and flattering offers of marriage, but she never entered into a second engagement. With all her capacity for affection, hers was an eclectic and solitary soul. He who by the very patent of his nature was more to her than any other being could be, passed out from her life, but no other one ever took his place.

It was in this desolation of her youth that Alice Cary resolved to go to New York, and make a home and life-work for herself. Many sympathetic souls had sent back answering echoes to her songs. We may believe that to her lonely heart the voice of human praise was sweet. If it could not recall the first promise of her morning, at least it foretold that hers would be a busy, workful, and successful day. It cannot be said that she found herself alone in New York, for, from the first, her genius and true womanliness gathered around her a small circle of devoted friends. Women loved her,

> "And men, who toiled in storm and sun,
> Found her their meet companion."

In the spring of 1851, she wrote to her sisters to join her, and in April, Phœbe and her lovely young sister, then scarcely twenty years of age, left Cincinnati and came to Alice. Of this departure of the three from the home nest, Phœbe says: "Without advice or counsel of any but themselves, they resolved to come to New York, and after the manner of children in the story-book, seek their fortune. Many sad and trying changes had come to the family, and home was not what it had been. They had comparative youth, though they were much older in years than in experience and knowledge of the world; they had pleasant visions of a home and name that might be earned by literary labor, and so the next spring the bold venture was made.

"Living in a very economical and humble way, writing for whatever papers would accept their contributions, and taking any remuneration that was offered, however small, they did from the first somehow manage to live without debt, and with little obligation." To appreciate more perfectly the industry and frugality which enabled them to do this, we must know how much smaller, at that time, was the reward for all literary labor, than it is now. Speaking of their coming to make New York their home, in his sketch of the sisters in the "Eminent Women of the Age," Horace Greeley says: —

"I do not know at whose suggestion they resolved to migrate to this city, and attempt to live here by literary labor; it surely was not mine. If my judgment was ever invoked, I am sure I must have responded that the hazard seemed to me too great, the inducements inadequate. And, before you dissent from this opinion, be pleased to remember that we had then scarcely any periodical literature worthy of the name outside of the political and commercial journals. I doubt that so much money was paid, in the aggregate, for contributions to *all* the magazines and weeklies issued from this city, as were paid in 1870 by the 'Ledger' alone. Our magnificent system of dissemination by means of railroad trains and news companies was then in its infancy; when I started 'The New Yorker,' fifteen years earlier, it had no existence. It impeaches neither the discrimination, the justice, nor the enterprise, of the publishers of 1850, to say that they hardly paid for contributions a tithe of the prices now freely accorded to favorite writers; they paid what they could. I remember seeing Longfellow's grand 'Endymion' received in manuscript at the office of a popular and successful weekly, which paid fifteen dollars for it; a hundred such would now be quickly taken at one hundred and fifty dollars each, and the purchasers would look anxiously about them for more.

"Alice and Phœbe came among us, as I have said, in 1850. They hired two or three modest rooms, in an unfashionable neighborhood, and set to work resolutely to earn a living by the pen."

The secret of the rare material success which attended them from the beginning is to be found in the fact that from the first they began to make a home: also in the fact that they possessed every attribute of character and habit necessary to the making of one. They had an unfeigned horror of "boarding." Any friend of theirs ever compelled to stay in a boarding house was sure of an extra portion of their commiseration and sympathy. A home they must have, albeit it was up two flights of stairs. To the maintenance of this home they brought industry, frugality, and a hatred of debt. If they had money but to pay for a crust, then a crust must suffice. With their inflexible integrity they believed that they had no right to more, till they had money to pay for that more. Thus from the beginning to the end they always lived within their income. They never wore or had anything better than they could afford. With true feminine instinct, they made their little "flat" take on at once the cosiest look of home. A man-genius seeking the city, as they did, of course would have taken refuge in a boarding-house attic, and "enjoyed himself" in writing poems and leaders amid dirt and forlornity. Not so these women-poets. I have heard Alice tell how she papered one room with her own hands, and Phœbe how she painted the doors, framed the pictures, and "brightened up" things generally. Thus from the first they had a home, and by the very magnetism that made it bright, cheery, in truth a home, they drew around them friends who were their friends no less till they breathed their last sigh. One of these was Mr. Greeley. He always cherished for these sisters three the respect and affection which every true man instinctively feels for the true women who have their being within the circle of his life. In their friendship one religious faith, kindred pursuits, mutual friends, and long association strengthened and cemented the fraternal bond to the last. Mr. Greeley himself thus refers to their early tea-parties.

"Being already an acquaintance, I called on the sisters soon after they had set up their household gods among us, and met them at intervals thereafter at their home or at the houses of mutual friends. Their parlor was not so large as some others, but quite as neat and cheerful; and the few literary persons, or artists, who occasionally met at their informal invitation, to discuss with them a cup of tea and the newest books, poems, and events, might have found many more pretentious, but few more enjoyable gatherings.

I have a dim recollection that the first of these little tea-parties was held up two flights of stairs, in one of the less fashionable sections of the city; but good things were said there that I recall with pleasure yet; while of some of the company, on whom I have not since set eyes, I cherish a pleasant and grateful remembrance. As their circumstances gradually, though slowly improved, by dint of diligent industry and judicious economy, they occupied more eligible quarters; and the modest dwelling they have for some years owned and improved, in the very heart of this emporium, has long been known to the literary guild, as combining one of the best private libraries with the sunniest drawing-room (even by gas-light) to be found between King's Bridge and the Battery."

Thus began in 1850–51 the life and work of Alice and Phœbe Cary in New York. The next year saw the coming out of Alice's first series of "Clovernook Papers." They were full of the freshness and fragrance of her native fields; full of simple, original, graphic pictures of the country life, and the men and women whom she knew best; full of the exquisite touches of a spontaneous, child-like genius, and they were gathered up as eagerly by the public as the children gather wild flowers. Their very simplicity and freshness won all hearts. They sold largely in this country and in Great Britain. English critics bestowed on them the highest and most discriminating praise, as pure products of American life and genius, while the press of this country universally acknowledged their delicious simplicity and originality. Alice published a second series in 1853, with unabated success, while in 1854, Ticknor and Fields published the "Clovernook Children," which were as popular with younger readers, as the "Papers" had been with their elders. In 1853, "Lyra and Other Poems, by Alice Cary," were published by Redfield. This volume called out some severe criticisms on the uniform sadness of its tone; one especially in "Putnam's Monthly," which caused Alice much pain. Nevertheless it was a successful book, and was brought out a second time complete, with the addition of "The Maiden of Tlascala," a narrative poem of seventy-two pages, by Ticknor and Fields, in 1855. Alice's first novel, "Hagar, a Story of To-Day," was written for and appeared in the "Cincinnati Commercial," and was afterwards brought out by Redfield in 1852. "Married, Not Mated," appeared in 1856. "Pictures of Country Life, by Alice Cary," were published by Derby and Jackson in 1859. This book reproduced much of the freshness, the exquisite grace and naturalness, of her "Clovernook Papers." She was free on her native heath, when she painted rural scenery and rural life. These Papers were translated into French in Paris, and "The Literary Gazette" (London), which is not accustomed to flatter American authors, said: "Every tale in this book might be selected as evidence of some new beauty or unhackneyed grace. There is nothing feeble, nothing vulgar, and, above all, nothing unnatural or melodramatic. To the analytical subtlety and marvelous naturalness of the French school of romance she has added the purity and idealization of the home affections and home life belonging to the English, giving to both the American richness of color and vigor of outline, and her own individual power and loveliness."

"Lyrics and Hymns," with portrait, beautifully bound and illustrated, which still remain the standard selection of her poems, were issued by Hurd and Houghton, in 1866. In 186–, "The Lover's Diary," in exquisite form, and "Snow Berries, A Book for Young Folks," were bought by Ticknor and Fields. The same year a novel, "The Bishop's Son," which first appeared in the "Springfield (Mass.) Republican," was published by Carleton, New York. "The Born Thrall," a novel in which Alice hoped to embody her deepest thoughts and maturest convictions concerning the sorrows and wrongs of woman, was interrupted by her last sickness, while passing through the "Revolution," and never finished. She left, beside, a completed novel in manuscript, not yet published. Thus, beside writing constantly for "Harper's Magazine," the "Atlantic Monthly," "Riverside Magazine," "New York Ledger," "New York Weekly," "New York Independent," "Packard's Monthly," and chance periodicals innumerable, which entreated her name for their pages, the active brain and soul of Alice Cary in twenty years produced eleven volumes, every word and thought of which was wrought from her own being, and every line of which was written by her own hand. In the same number of years, Phœbe, beside aiding in the editing of several books, the most important of which was "Hymns for All Christians," published by Hurd and Houghton in 1869, brought out "Poems and Parodies," published by Ticknor and Fields, 1854, and "Poems of Faith, Hope, and Love," issued by Hurd and Houghton in 1868. Beside, Alice and Phœbe left, at their death, poems enough uncollected to give each name two added volumes, one of each a book of

Child-Poems. The disparity in the actual intellectual product of the two sisters, in the same number of years, is very striking. It is the result, not so much of mental inequality, as of the compelling will, energy, industry, and the patience of labor of the elder sister.

CHAPTER III.

THEIR HOME. — HABITS OF LIFE AND OF LABOR. — THE SUMMER OF 1869.

Before 1856, Alice and Phœbe had removed to the pretty house in Twentieth Street, which was destined to be their last earthly home. Within a short time Alice bought this house, and was its sole owner at the time of her death. An English writer has said: "Single women can do little to form a circle; they can but adorn one when found." This certainly was never true of the two single women whose earthly days we are tracing. From the beginning, the house in Twentieth Street became the centre of one of the choicest and most cosmopolitan circles in New York. The two sisters drew about them not only the best, but the most genial minds. True men and women equally found in each, companion, counselor, and friend. They met every true woman that came to them with sympathy and tenderness, feeling that they shared with her all the mutual toils and sorrows of womanhood. They met every true man, as brother, with an open, honest, believing gaze. Intensely interested in all great public questions, loving their country, devoted to it, devoted to everything good and true; alive to everything of interest in politics, religion, literature, and society; the one pensive and tender, the other witty and gay, men of refinement, culture, and heart found in them the most delightful companions. Beside (which was much), no man welcome, was afraid to go to their house. Independent in their industry and resources, they asked few favors. They had no "designs," even the most harmless, cn any living man. Men the most marriageable, or unmarriageable, could visit the Carys without fear or question. The atmosphere of the house was transparent as the sunshine. They loved women, they delighted in the society of agreeable men, and fearlessly said so. The weekly refreshment of the house was hospitality, its daily habit, labor. I have never known any other woman so systematically and persistently industrious as Alice Cary. Hers was truly the genius of patience. No obstacle ever daunted it, no pain ever stilled it, no weariness ever overcame it, till the last weariness of death. As Phœbe said, "The pen literally fell from her hand at last," and only then, because in the valley of the shadow of death, which she had already entered, she could no longer see to trace the trembling, uncertain lines. But few men or women could look back upon fifty years of more persistent industry. I doubt if she ever kept a diary, or wrote down a rule for her life. She did not need to do so; her life itself was the rule. There was a beautiful, yet touching uniformity in her days. Her pleasure was her labor. Of rest, recreation, amusement, as other women sought these, she knew almost nothing. Her rest and recreation were the intervals from pain, in which she could labor. It was not always the labor of writing. No, sometimes it was making a cap, or trimming a bonnet, or rummaging to the depths of feminine boxes; yet no less it was work of some sort, never play. The only hour of rest any day brought, was the hour after dinner, the twilight hour, when one sister always came to the other's room, and with folded hands and low voices they talked over, almost always, the past, the friends loved, scattered, or gone before.

The morning might be for mirth, but the evening belonged to memory. All Alice's personal surroundings were dainty and womanly. It was no dreary den, in which she thought and wrought. It was a sunny room over the library, running the depth of the house, with windows at both ends. A carpet of woody tints, relieved with scarlet flowers, covered the floor. On the pale walls, tinted a delicate green, hung pictures, all of which had to her some personal association. Over the mantel hung an oil painting, called "Early Sorrow," the picture of a poor, wind-beaten young girl, her yellow hair blown about her face, and the rain of sorrow in her eyes, painted by a struggling, unfortunate artist, whom Alice had done more to help and encourage, than all other persons in the world.

Autumn leaves and sea-mosses imprisoned in frames, with rich Bohemian vases, adorned the black marble mantel. Beside the back window, within the alcove for which it had been expressly made, stood the bed, her couch of suffering and musing, and on which she died. The bedstead was of rosewood traced with a band of coral, and set with arabesques of gilt; its white coverlet and pillow-cases edged with delicate lace. Above it hung an exquisite engraving of Cupid, the gift of Mrs. Greeley, brought by her from Paris. At the foot of the bed hung a colored engraving of Rosa Bonheur's "Oxen," a farmer ploughing down the furrows of a rolling field. "It rests me," she would say; "I look at it, and live over my youth." Often in the afternoon, while taking her half hour's rest from work, as she leaned back among the pillows, the dark eyes were lifted and fixed upon this picture. In the winter, curtains of fawn-colored satin, edged and tasseled with soft red, shaded this alcove from the front room. The front windows were hung with the same. Between them, a mirror reached from floor to ceiling.

Beside one of these windows stood Alice's desk. It was of rosewood, finely finished and commodious, a bureau, desk, and book-case combined. The drawers below were the receptacle of her beloved India shawls, for which she had the same love that some women have for diamonds, and others for rare paintings. The drawer of her desk contained her manuscript papers; the shelves above, the books that she was reading, and her books of reference; while above all hung a favorite landscape in water-colors. On the other side of the mantel-piece stood corresponding bureau and shelves, filled with books. Here were copies of her own and Phœbe's works, which never appeared in the library or drawing-room below. Above these book-shelves, hung an autumn landscape. On one side of the alcove there was an engraving of Correggio's "Christ;" on the other, a copy of "The Huguenot Lovers." Beside the hall door, opposite her desk, there hung a portrait in oil of their father, by the hand which painted "Early Sorrow;" on the other side of the door there was at one time a portrait of Phœbe. Easy chairs and foot-stools completed the furniture of this room, in which Alice Cary lived for fifteen years, the room in which she slowly and sadly relinquished life, and in which at last she died.

At the opposite end of the hall was a room which cor responded exactly with that of Alice, the room which had been Elmina's, in which she died, and which from her death was "Phœbe's room." Rich purple curtains used to hang from the alcove, shading the face of the lovely sufferer, and curtains of the same hue draped the windows. But Phœbe eschewed all draperies, and, summer or winter, nothing denser than white shades and the thinnest of lace curtains hung between her and the strongest sunshine. A bright red carpet, relieved by small medallions, covered the floor. Over the mantel-piece for a long time hung a superb copy of "The Huguenot Lovers," in a gilt frame. This was replaced at last by a copy of Turner, in oil, a resplendent Venetian scene. Beside the alcove hung the chromo of Whittier's "Barefoot Boy," which was a great favorite with Phœbe, while clusters of flowers in lithograph and water-colors, added to the bright cheerfulness of the room. Between the windows was a full length mirror; on one side of the room was Phœbe's desk, of the same form and wood, though of a smaller size than that of Alice. In its appointments it was a perfect model of neatness. It was always absolutely in order; while, beside books, its shelves were ornamented with vases and other pretty trinkets. On the opposite side of the room stood a table, the receptacle of the latest newspapers, magazines, and novels, that, like the desk, was ever in order, and in addition to its freight of literature always made room for a work-basket well stocked with spools, scissors, and all the implements of an accomplished needlewoman.

Both sisters always retained their country habit of

retiring and rising early; they were rarely out of bed after ten at night, and more rarely in it after six of the morning. Till the summer of 1869, Alice always rose and went to market, Phœbe getting up as early and going to her sewing. From that time till her death, Phœbe did the marketing, and the purchases of the day were all made before breakfast. From that date, though not equal to the exertion of dressing and going out, Alice arose no less early.

She was often at her desk by five o'clock A. M., rarely later than six. Not a week that she did not more than once tell us at the breakfast table that she had already written a poem that morning, sometimes more than one. Waking in the night, or before light, it was often her solace to weave her songs while others slept; and the first thing she did on rising was to write them down from memory. During Elmina's decline it had been the custom of Alice and Phœbe to meet the first thing in the morning by her bed, to ask the dear one how she had rested, and to begin the communion of the day. From her death it was the habit of Phœbe to go directly to Alice as soon as she arose. Sitting down on the edge of the bed, each would tell the story of her night, though it was Alice who, being very wakeful, really had a story of pains and thoughts and dreams to tell. I spent the summer, autumn, and a part of the winter of 1869 with them, and the memories of those days are as unique as they are precious. "We three" met each morning at the breakfast table, in that pleasant, pictured dining-room, which so many remember. The same dainty china which made the Sunday evening teas so appetizing, made the breakfast table beautiful; often with the addition of a vase full of fresh flowers, brought by Phœbe from market. If Alice was able to be there at all, she had been able before coming down to deck her abundant locks with a dainty morning cap, brightened with pink ribbons, and, in her white robe and breakfast shawl, with its brilliant border, never looked lovelier than when pouring coffee for two ardent adorers of her own sex. She was always her brightest at this time. She had already done work enough to promise well for the rest of her day. She was glad to see us, glad to be able to be there, ready to tell us each our fortune anew, casting our horoscope afresh in her teacup each morning. Phœbe, in her street dress, just home from market, "had seen a sight," and had something funny to tell. More, she had any amount of funny things to tell. The wittiest Phœbe Cary that ever made delightful an evening drawing-room was tame, compared with this Phœbe Cary of the breakfast table, with only two women to listen to her, and to laugh till they cried and had strength to laugh no longer, over her irresistible remarks, which she made with the assumed solemnity of an owl. Then came the morning journals and the mail; and with discussing the state of the nation, growing "wrought up" over wrong and injustice everywhere, sharing the pleasant gossip of friends, the breakfast was often lengthened to a nearly two hours' sitting. Alice then went to the kitchen to order her household for the day, when each of the three went to the silence and labor of her own room, seeing no more of each other, unless meeting over a chance cup of tea at lunch, till they reassembled at the dinner table, each to tell the pleasant part of the story of her day, and to repeat the delightful intercourse of the morning. After dinner there was a general adjournment to Alice's or Phœbe's room, as it might happen. It was at this time, usually, that each sister read to the other the poem that she had written or corrected and copied that day. I can see Phœbe now, softly opening the door with her neat manuscript in her hand. Sitting down beside Alice's couch, in a shy, deprecating, modest fashion, most winsome to behold, she would read in low voice the poem. We never criticised it. The appealing tones of our reader made the very thoughts of criticism impossible. If it was funny, we laughed; if it was sad, we cried, and our reader with us; and in either case she was entirely satisfied with the appreciation of her audience. Then Alice would slowly go to her desk, draw forth tumbled sheets of manuscript, the opposite of Phœbe's in their chirography, and, settling in her easy-chair, begin in a low, crooning tone, one of those quaint, wild ballads of hers, which long before had made her preeminently the balladist of America. Many of these I cannot see now without seeming to hear again the thrilling vibration of her voice, as we heard it when she read the song herself the very day that it flowed from heart and pen. Any time or anywhere, if I listen, I can hear her say, —

"In the stormy waters of Gallaway
My boat had been idle the livelong day,
Tossing and tumbling to and fro,
For the wind was high and the tide was low.

"The tide was low and the wind was high,
And we were heavy, my heart and I,
For not a traveller, all the day,
Had crossed the ferry of Gallaway."

Phœbe's lays, when grave or sad, almost always savored of her native soil and home life; but Alice, on the rhythm of her lyric, would bear us far out from the little room and the roaring streets, into the very land of romance, to the days of chivalry and "flowery tapestrie." The knight and lady, the crumbling castle, the tumbling and rushing sea, became for the moment as real to us as to her.

The house below was as attractive as above.

A small, richly stained window at the head of the stairs flooded the small hall with gorgeous light. This hall was frescoed in panels of oak; floor and stairs covered with Brussels carpet of oak and scarlet tints. On its walls hung colored engravings of oxen, cows, and horses ploughing a field.

To the right of the front entrance stood, wide open, the door of the spacious parlor, within whose walls for more than fifteen years gathered weekly so many gifted and congenial souls. This parlor was a large square room with five windows, two back and two front, with a deep bay-window between. These windows were hung with lace, delicately embroidered, from which were looped back curtains of pale green brocatelle lined with white silk. On either embrasure of the bay-window, in Gothic, gold illuminated frames, stood two altar pieces, about three feet high, from an old church in Milan, each bearing on a field of gold an angel in azure and rosy vestments, one playing on a dulcimer, the other holding a golden palm. In antique letters in black, beneath, was written on one tablet Psalm cl. 3, and on the other, the succeeding verse of the same. A large oil-painting of sheep lying on a hillside hung at one time over the white marble mantel; later, a fine

Venetian scene from Turner, while on either side, very tall vases of ruby glass threw a wine-like hue on the silvery wall. On one side of the mantel there was a rosewood étagère, lined with mirrors, and decorated with vases and books. On the other side there was an exquisite copy in oil of Guido's "Aurora," brought by a friend from Italy. Opposite the bay-window a very broad mirror rose from floor to ceiling.

Lovely Madonnas and other rare paintings covered the walls, some of which had been placed there by friends who had no proper room for them. The carpet was of velvet in deep crimson and green; the chairs and sofas, which were luxurious, were also cushioned in velvet of various blending hues.

The most remarkable article in the room was the large centre table, made of many thousand mosaics of inlaid wood, each in its natural tint. Clusters of pansies, of the most perfect outline and hue, formed the border of the table, while the extreme edge was inlaid in tints scarce wider than a thread. It was a work of endless patience, and of the finest art. It was made by a poor Hungarian artist, who used nearly a whole lifetime in this work of his hands. He brought it to this country hoping to realize for it a large sum, but was compelled by necessity, at last, to part with it for a small amount. It passed from various owners before it was bought by Alice Cary and placed in her parlor as its central shrine, around which gathered her choicest friends. Among the few books lying on a small stand within the bay-window was "Ballads of New England," written and presented by Whittier, with this inscription: —

TO ALICE AND PHŒBE CARY,

Who from the farm-field singing came,
The song whose echo now is fame,
And to the great false city took
The honest hearts of Clovernook,
And made their home beside the sea
The trysting-place of Liberty.

From their old friend,
JOHN G. WHITTIER.

Christmas, 1869.

Another was a dainty book in green and gold, entitled "The Golden Wedding," presented "To Phœbe Cary, with the kind regards of Joseph and Rebecca W. Taylor," the parents of Bayard Taylor.

Across the hall, opposite the parlor, was the library, which so many will remember as the very penetrale of this home, in which "the precious few" were so wont to gather for converse and choice communion. These words recall one wild night of rain and storm, which had hindered everybody else from coming but Mr. Greeley, when he said, in the hour before church, "Come, girls, let us read 'Morte d'Arthur;'" and, taking Tennyson from the book-case, read from beginning to end aloud, "The Passing of Arthur." Mr. Greeley's tones, full of deep feeling, I shall hear while memory endures, as he read: —

"Ah! my Lord Arthur, whither shall I go?
Where shall I hide my forehead and my eyes?
For now I see the true old times are dead,
When every morning brought a noble chance,
And every chance brought out a noble knight.

. . . .

But when the whole ROUND TABLE is dissolved,
Which was an image of the mighty world;

And I, the last, go forth companionless,
And the days darken round me, and the years,
Among new men, strange faces, other minds."
  And slowly answered Arthur from the barge:
"The old order changeth, yielding place to new,
And God fulfills Himself in many ways,
Lest one good custom should corrupt the world.
Comfort thyself: what comfort is in me?
I have lived my life, and that which I have done
May He within Himself make pure! but thou,
If thou shouldst never see my face again,
Pray for my soul. More things are wrought by prayer
Than this world dreams of. Wherefore, let thy voice
Rise like a fountain for me night and day.
For what are men better than sheep or goats
That nourish a blind life within the brain,
If, knowing God, they lift not hands of prayer,
Both for themselves and those who call them friend?
For so the whole round earth is every way
Bound by gold chains about the feet of God.
But now farewell. I am going a long way —
With these thou seëst — if indeed I go —
(For all my mind is clouded with a doubt)
To the island-valley of Avilion;
Where falls not hail, or rain, or any snow,
Nor ever wind blows loudly; but it lies
Deep-meadowed, happy, fair with orchard lawns
And bowery hollows crown'd with summer sea,
Where I will heal me of my grievous wound."

Alice settled far back in her easy-chair, listening with eloquent eyes. Phœbe sat on a low hassock, playing with the long necklace on her neck, every bead of which marked a friend's remembrance. Dear sisters! passed forever beyond the storm, we whom the storm even here has parted, may at least recall that hour of peace shared together!

This little library was furnished in oak, its walls

frescoed in oak with panels of maroon shaded to crimson. Two windows faced the street, the opposite end being nearly taken up by a large window of stained glass in which gold and sapphire lights commingled. Opposite the hall door was a black marble mantel surmounted by a mirror set in ebony and gold. On either side, covering the entire length of the room, were open oaken book-shelves, filled with over a thousand volumes, the larger proportion handsome library editions of the standard books of the world. The windows were hung with satin curtains of an oaken tinge edged with maroon. Between them was a copy of the Cary coat-of-arms, of which Phœbe was so fond, richly framed. Below, a little gem in oil, of a Northampton (Massachusetts) scene, hung over a small table covered with a crimson cloth, on which lay a very large Family Bible. To the left of the front windows hung an oil portrait of Madame Le Brun, the famous French artist, from an original painting by herself, now hanging in the Florentine Museum. On the other side of the door hung, in oval frames, the portraits of Alice and Phœbe, painted not long after their arrival in New York. The marble-topped table before the stained glass window was piled with costly books, chiefly souvenirs from friends. Two deep arm-chairs were near, one cushioned in green, the other in blue velvet; the green, Alice's chair; the blue, Phœbe's. The Brussels carpet was the exact counterpart of the walls, shaded in oak, maroon, and crimson. You have discovered before now, that the Cary home was never furnished by an upholsterer? Its furniture, its trinkets and treasures, were the combined accumulation of twenty years. It was filled with keepsakes from friends, and some of its choicest articles had been bought at intervals, as she could afford to do so, by Alice at Marley's shop for antique furniture on Broadway, which she took extreme pleasure in visiting. Here, also, she could gratify her taste for old exquisite china, in which she took the keenest delight. Many who drank tea with her have not forgotten the delicate, egg-like cups out of which they drank it. She had a china tea-set in her possession over a hundred years old. Many have the impression that Phœbe was the housekeeper of this home. Until the summer of 1869, this was in no sense true. Beyond the occasional spontaneous preparation of a favorite dish, Phœbe had no care of the house. For nearly twenty years Alice arose, went to market, and laid out the entire household plan of the day, before Phœbe appeared at breakfast.

Alice Cary managed her house with quiet system and without ado. Her home was beautifully kept, the kitchen and garret as perfect in their appointments and as perfect in their order as her parlor. She was an indulgent mistress, respecting the rights of every person in her household as much as her own, and two servants (sisters) who were with her when she died, one of whom closed Phœbe's eyes in death, lived with her many years.

Phœbe did not "take to housework," but was a very queen of the needle. Over work-basket and cutting-board she reigned supreme, and here held Alice at disadvantage. Alice could trim a bonnet or make a cap to perfection; with these, the creative quality of her needle ended. A dress subdued her, and brought her a humble suppliant to the sewing-throne of Phœbe.

There were at least two weeks in early spring, and two in the autumn, which were called "Miss Lyon's weeks," when Alice was literally under the paw of a lion. Miss Lyon was the dressmaker. She was quiet, kindly, artistic, and necessary; therefore, in her kingdom, an unmitigated tyrant. Literature did not dare to peep in on Miss Lyon's weeks, or if it did, it was before she came, or while she was at breakfast. Books and papers she would not suffer in her sight after work began. She was always wanting "half a yard more" of something. She was always sending us out for "trimmings," and, as we rarely found the right ones, was continually sending us again. Poor Alice! she went out six times one hot morning to find a stick of braid, which Miss Lyon insisted should have a peculiar kink. Once back, we had to sit down beside her, to "try on" and to assist. If we did not, "we could not have our new frocks, that was all," for Miss Lyon "could not possibly go through them alone, and she had not another day, not one, before winter." Thus, while purgatory reigned on Alice's side of the house, Phœbe in hers sat enthroned in serene satisfaction. She was no slave to Miss Lyon, not she. On the contrary, while Miss Lyon snubbed us, she crossed the hall to consult Phœbe in a tone of deference, which (professionally) she never condescended to bestow on her victims. In Miss Lyon's days, nobody would have suspected that the house held a blue-stocking. Dry goods, shreds, and tags prevailed above stairs, and Alice's room looked like a first-class dressmaker's shop, in which Miss Lyon ruled between two forlorn apprentices. It is not easy to see Alice Cary in a comical light, and yet Alice Cary in Phœbe's door, holding up an unfin ished sacque, in which she had sewed a sleeve upside down, and made one an inch shorter than the other, with her look of blended consternation and despair, *was* a comical sight. Phœbe was her only refuge in such a plight, and to rip the sleeve, trim it, right it, and baste it in again, was the work of a very few minutes for her deft fingers. Sacques, dresses, cloaks, and hats, all cut, and fitted, and made, came out from her hands absolutely perfect, to the wonder and envy of the unfortunates across the hall. Miss Lyon, always leaving her sceptre up-stairs, at the table was a sorrowful, communicative woman, who poured the story of her troubles, her loneliness, and poor health into sympathizing ears. She tormented us, but we liked her, and were sorry for her. We comforted her when she was sick, and cried when she died, and remembered her with a sigh. It was a weary woman's poor little life after all! She too had her dream of future, home, and rest; but the money that she worked so hard to earn, and denied herself the necessities of life to save, she saved to will to a well-to-do relative who had neglected and forsaken her while she lived. By July, Miss Lyon's reign was over, but the kingdoms she had conquered were all visible, marked by the new dresses lying in a row on the bed in the little attic chamber. Alas! on that same bed some of them lay after Alice's death, untouched. The poor hand that made them, and knotted their dainty ribbons, and the lovely form that was to have worn them, both alike locked from all device in the fastness of the grave!

The only shadow resting on the house was that of sickness and hovering death. Nothing could have been more absolutely harmonious than the daily abiding intercourse of these sisters. This was not because they always thought alike, nor because they never in any way crossed each other, nor was it based on their devoted affection and perfect faith in each other alone. Persons may believe in each other, and love each other dearly, and yet live in a constant state of friction. It was chiefly because each cherished a most conscientious consideration for the peculiarities of the other, and because in the minutest particular they treated each other with absolute politeness. There is such an expression used as "society manner." These sisters had no manner for society more charming in the slightest particular, than they had for each other. No pun ever came into Phœbe's head too bright to be flashed over Alice, and Alice had no gentleness for strangers which she withheld from Phœbe. The perfect gentlewomen which they were in the parlor, they were always, under every circumstance. There was not a servant in the house, who, in his or her place, was not treated with as absolute a politeness as a guest in the parlor. This spirit of perfect breeding penetrated every word and act of the household. What Alice and Phœbe Cary were in their drawing-room, they were always in the absolute privacy of their lives. Each obeyed one inflexible law. Whatever she felt or endured, because of it she was not to inflict any suffering upon her sister; no, not even if that sister had inadvertently been the cause of it. If she was "out of sorts," she went into her own room, shut her door and "had it out" by herself. Whatever shape her Apollyon might take, she fought with him, and slew him, alone. When she appeared outside, it might strike one that a new line of pain had for the moment lit upon her face; that was the only sign of the foe routed. The bright sally, the quiet smile, the perfection of gentle breeding were all there, undimmed and indestructible.

The first of July, Phœbe went to Waldemere, Bridgeport, Conn., to visit the family of Mr. P. T. Barnum, and then to Cambridge, to see Mr. and Mrs. H. O. Houghton; from thence to visit the family of Rev. Dr. B. F. Tefft in Bangor, Maine. Early in June, Alice had been persuaded to visit a beloved niece in the mountain region of Pennsylvania. She remained a week, and on her return told how the sweet country air and the smell of the woods had brought back her girlhood. "But I could not stay," she said; "I had so much to do." Nor would she be induced to go again, though loving friends urged, indeed entreated her to leave her desk, and the heat and turmoil of the city.

Physically and mentally she needed change and respite from the overstrain of too long continued toil. A summer in the country, at this crisis in her health, could not have failed to renovate, if not to restore life. But she clung to her home, her own room and surroundings, and to her work, and reluctantly Phœbe went forth to the kind friends awaiting her, alone. That was a mystical month that followed, that month of July. The very walls of the houses seemed changed into burning brass. The sun, uncooled by showers, rose and set, tracking all his course with a consuming fire. Everybody who could escape, had fled the city. During the entire month I do not remember that one person, not of the small household, crossed the threshold. We closed blinds and doors, and *were alone.* Apart at work all day, we spent our evenings together.

In those summer nights, with the blinds opened to let in a stray breeze from the bay, with no light but the fitful flicker of the lamp across the street, in the silence and dimness, feeling the whole world shut out and far away; then it was that the flood-gates of memory opened, and one received into her soul, with a depth and fullness and sacredness never to be expressed, that which was truly Alice Cary's life.

In August, Alice wrote to me at Newport: "Phœbe is still away, and I alone in the house; but busy as a bee from morning till night. I often hear it said that people, as they grow older, lose their interest in things around them; but this is not true of me. I take more interest in life, in all that concerns it, and in human beings, every year I live. If I fail of bringing something worthy to pass, I don't mean that it shall be for lack of energy or industry. I'm putting the house in order, and have such new and pleasant plans for the winter. Do hasten back, that I may tell you all about them." In two weeks I returned, and, going at once to her familiar room, she met me on the threshold without a word. As she kissed me, her tears fell upon my face; and, looking up, I saw the change in hers. The Indian summer of youth, which had made it so fair, four little weeks before, had now gone from it forever; the shadow of the grave reached it already.

"Since I wrote you," she said, "my only sister, save Phœbe, has died; and look at me!" She moved, and I saw that the graceful, swaying movement, so especially hers, was gone—that she was hopelessly lame.

Thus that first of September began the last, fierce

struggle between life and death, which was to continue for seventeen months. Only God and his ministering angels know with what pangs that soul and body parted. I cannot think of it without a shudder and a sigh — a shudder for the agony, a sigh for that patient and tender and loving heart, so full of life and yearning amid the anguish of dissolving nature. At first it seemed impossible that she could remain lame. Each day we said: "To morrow you *must* come down-stairs again." But, save with crutches, she never walked again. In the beginning it seemed impossible for her to adjust her mind or habits to this fact, or to realize that she was not able to join the familiar circle around the Sunday evening tea-table. Yet the more impossible it became for her to participate personally, the more eager she became for the happiness of others. She would have us dress in her room, that she might refresh her eyes with bright colors; and leave the door of her room open, that she might hear the tones of dear, familiar voices coming up from below. When tea was cheering, and speech and laughter flowing freest, there was something inexpressibly touching in the thought of the woman who provided this cheer for so many, sitting by herself in a darkened room, sick and alone. Once, in going up to her, I found her weeping. "You should not have left the others," she said "My only pleasure is in thinking that you are all happy down-stairs. But it makes me cry to think that I am done with it all; that in one sense I am as far away from you in health, as if I were already in eternity."

In the early dawn of a wintry morning, I went in to her bedside to say good-by. The burning hands outstretched, the tearful, beseeching eyes, the low voice burdened with loving farewell, are among the most precious and pathetic of all the treasures which faithful memory bears on to her in the land where she now is.

CHAPTER IV.

THEIR SUNDAY EVENING RECEPTIONS.

The most resplendent social assemblies which the world has ever seen have been those in which philosophy, politics, and literature mingled with fortune, rank, beauty, grace, and wit. Nor was this commingling of dazzling human forces identical only with the Parisian *salon*. "Blue-stocking" in our day is synonymous only with a stiff, stilted, queer literary woman of a dubious age. Yet the first blue-stocking, Elizabeth Montague, was a woman who dazzled with her wit, as well as by her beauty, and who blazed with diamonds at fourscore. A purely blue-stocking party, to-day, would doubtless give us sponge cake, weak tea, and the dreariest of driveling professional talk. Yet the first assemblies which bore the name of blue-stocking were made up of actors, divines, beaux, belles, the pious and the worldly, the learned and the fashionable, the titled and the lowly born. Here, in the drawing-room of Montague House, mingling gayly together, might have been seen volatile Mrs. Thrale, wise Hannah More, and foolish Fanny Burney; the Greek scholar, Elizabeth Carter, with Garrick, Johnson, Reynolds, Young, Beattie, Burke, Lord Kames, Lord Chatham, and Horace Walpole, with many others as personally brilliant if less renowned. One never thinks of calling a man a blue-stocking now; yet it was a man who first wore "cerulean hose" in a fashionable assembly — Dr. Stillingfleet, who was a sloven as well as a scholar. Admiral Boscawen, glancing at his gray-blue stockings, worn at one of Mrs. Montague's assemblies, gave it the name of the Blue-stocking Assembly, to indicate that the full dress, still indispensable to evening parties, might be dispensed with, if a person so chose, at Mrs. Montague's. A Frenchman, catching at the phrase, exclaimed, "*Ah! les bas bleus!*" And the title has clung to the literary woman ever since.

The nearest approach to the first ideal blue-stocking reception ever reached in this country was the Sunday evening receptions of Alice and Phœbe Cary. Here, for over fifteen years, in an unpretending home, gathered not only the most earnest, but many of the most brilliant Americans of our time. There are like assemblies still, wherein men and women rich in all fine gifts and graces meet and mingle; yet I doubt if there be one so catholic, so finely comprehensive, as to make it the rallying spot, the outraying centre of the artistic and literary life of the metropolis. Its central magnet lost, such a circle, once broken and scattered in all its parts, cannot be easily regathered and bound. Society must wait till another soul, equally potent, sweet, unselfish, sympathetic, and centripetal, shall draw together once more its scattered forces in one common bond. For the relief of Puritan friends who are troubled that those receptions occurred on Sabbath evening, I must say that they never hindered anybody from going to church. Horace Greeley, who never missed a Sabbath evening in this house when in the city, used to drink his two cups of sweetened milk and water, say his say, and then suddenly vanish, to go and speak at a temperance meeting, to listen to Dr. Chapin, or to write his Monday morning leader for the "Tribune." Sabbath evening was their reception evening because it was the only one which the sisters had invariably free from labor; and, as a rule, this was equally true of their guests. While her health permitted, Alice attended church regularly every Sunday morning, and till her last sickness Phœbe was a faithful church-goer; but Sabbath evening was their own and their friends'. In their receptions there was no formality, no rule of dress. You could come as simply or as finely arrayed as you chose. Your costly costume would not increase your welcome, nor your shabby attire place you at discount. Indeed, if anything about you ever so remotely suggested poverty or loneliness, it would, at the earliest possible moment, bring Alice to your side. Her dark, gentle, tender eyes would make you feel at home at once. You would forget your clothes and yourself altogether, in a quiet, impersonal, friendly flow of talk which would begin at once between you. If a stranger, she would be sure not to leave you till Phœbe came, or till she had introduced you to some pleasant person, and you would not find yourself again alone during the evening. This was the distinctive characteristic of these Sunday evenings, that they opened welcoming doors to all sympathetic souls, without the slightest reference to the state of their finances or mere worldly condition.

"What queer people you do see at the Carys'! It is as good as a show!" exclaimed a merely fashionable woman.

"I have *no* desire to go to the Carys'," said a supercilious literary dame, "while they admit *such* people."

"Why, they are reputable, are they not?" was the astonished reply.

"For aught I know; but they are so odd, and they have no position — absolutely none."

"Then the more they must need friends, Alice and Phœbe think. They contradict Goldsmith's assertion: 'If you want friends, be sure *not to need them.*'"

Phœbe's attention was called one day to a young man, poor, little known, ungraceful in bearing, and stiff in manner, who had artistic tastes and a desire to know artistic people, and who sometimes came quietly into the little library, on Sunday evening, without any special invitation, but who no less was cordially received.

"—— says she is astonished that you receive him," said a friend. "He is so pushing and presumptuous, and his family is very common."

"You tell ——," said Phœbe, with a flash in her black eyes, "that we like him very much; that he is just as welcome here as she is, and we are always glad to see *her.*"

There are centres of reunion still in New York, where literary, artistic, and cultured people meet; but we doubt if there is another wherein the poor and unknown, of aspiring tastes and refined sensibilities, could be so certain of an entire, unconscious welcome, untinged by even the suggestion of condescension or of patronage; where, in plain garb and with unformed manners, they could come and be at home. Yet the Sunday evening reception was by no means the rendezvous of the queer and ne'er-do-well alone.

During the fifteen years or more in which it flourished, at the little house in Twentieth Street, it numbered among its guests and *habitués* as many remarkable men and women as ever gathered around the abundant board at Streatham, or sat in the library of Strawberry Hill.

There was Horace Greeley, who so rarely missed a Sabbath evening at this house — a man in mind greater than Johnson, and in manners not unlike him ; who will live in the future among the most famous of his contemporaries, as the man who, perhaps, more than any other, left his own distinctive, individual mark upon the times in which he lived. There was Oliver Johnson, rarely absent from that cheery tea-table, the apostle of human freedom, who stood in the van of its feeble guard when it cost much to do that ; strong, earnest, brave, and true, a king of radicals, whose swiftest theories never outran his faith in God, his love for human nature, his self-abnegating devotion to his friends, even when his only reward was selfishness and unworthiness. There was Mary Ann Johnson, his wife, so recently translated, whose memory of simple, dignified, wise, and tender womanhood is a precious and imperishable legacy to all who ever knew and loved her. And Julia Deane, Alice Cary's beloved friend, golden-haired, matchless as a Grecian goddess. I see her now as I saw her first, in the radiance of her undimmed beauty, sitting by Whittier's side, great poet and gentle man, in his plain Friends' garb, yet worshipping, as man and poet must, the loveliness of woman ! What a troop of names, more or less famous, arise as I recall those who at different times have mingled in those receptions ! Bayard Taylor, with his gifted and lovely wife ; the two married poets, Richard and Elizabeth Stoddard ; Prof. R. W. Raymond, Robert Dale Owen, Justin McCarthy, Hon. Henry Wilson, Samuel Bowles, George Ripley, Edwin Whipple, Richard Kimball, Thomas B. Aldrich, Carpenter (the artist), Robert Chambers of Edinburgh, Robert Bonner of New York, a man as generous in nature and pure in character as he has been preëminently successful in acquiring wealth and fame, and who for many years, till their death, was the faithful friend of Alice and Phœbe. Among clergymen there were Rev. Dr. Abel Stevens, Methodist; Rev. Dr. Chapin, Universalist; Rev. Dr. Field, Presbyterian; Rev. Dr. Deems, Methodist. Whatever their theologies, all agreed in their faith in womanhood, as they found it embodied in Alice and Phœbe Cary. Among women much beloved by the sisters, who always had the *entrée* of their home, were Mary L. Booth, Mrs. Wright, Mrs. Mary E. Dodge, Mrs. Croly, Mrs. Victor, Mrs. Rayl, Mrs. Mary Stevens Robinson. I have not space for one tenth of the names I might recall — actors, artists, poets, clergymen, titled people from abroad, women of fashion, women of letters, women of home, the known and the unknown. In each type and class they found friends ; and what better proof could be given of the richness of their humanity, that, without being narrowed by any, their hearts were large enough for all!

Perhaps neither sister could have attracted into one common circle so many minds, various, if not conflicting in their separate sphere of thought and action. Each sister was the counterpart of the other. To the sympathy, appreciation, tact, gentleness, and tenderness of Alice were added the wit and *bonhomie* and sparkling cheer of Phœbe. The combination was perfect for social effect and success.

Rev. Charles F. Deems, Phœbe's pastor at the time of her death, and the cherished and trusted friend of both sisters, at the request of its editor wrote for "Packard's Monthly," February, 1870, an article entitled "Alice and Phœbe Cary: Their Home and Friends," which contains so vivid a sketch of some of their Sunday evening visitors that I quote from it: —

"If they could all be gathered into one room, it would really be a sight to see all the people who have been attracted by these charming women during the years they have occupied this cozy home. Let us fancy that they are so collected.

"There is, *facile princeps* of their friends, Horace Greeley — not so very handsome, perhaps, but owing so much to his toilet! He is sitting in a listening or abstracted attitude, with his great, full head bent, or smiling all over his great baby face as he hears or tells something good; perhaps especially enjoying the famous Quaker sermon which Oliver Johnson, of the 'Independent,' is telling with such *friendly* accentuation, and with such command over his strong features, while all the company are at the point of explosion. That round-headed Professor of Rhetoric in the corner, who reads Shakespeare in a style that would make the immortal William thrill if he could only hear him, is Professor Raymond. That slightly built man with a heavy moustache is Lord Adare, son of a Scotch Earl; and the bonny, bright-eyed woman by his side is his wife — immensely pleased with Phœbe's frequent and rapid sallies of wit. And there are Robert Dale Owen, author of 'Footfalls on the Boundary of Another

World,' and Edwin Whipple, the Boston essayist and lecturer, whose forehead doth so forcibly oppress all the rest of his face; and there, Samuel Bowles, of the 'Springfield Republican,' and author of 'Across the Continent;' and the nobly built and genial traveller, Col. Thomas W. Knox, of the 'Sun,' who has charmed us so in print with his sketches of Russia and Siberia, and who can talk quite as well as he can write; and there, Justin McCarthy, formerly of the London 'Morning Star,' and author of 'My Enemy's Daughter;' and that handsome old gentleman, with the smile of the morning in his face, so courtly that you feel he should be some king's prime minister, and so venerable that he would give dignity to an archbishop's crozier, is Ole Bull, whose cunning hands have wrung ravishing music from the strings of the violin; and just beyond, burly and full of good nature, is Phineas T. Barnum, 'showman,' and more than that, with great brains, which would have made him notable in any department. If the public have had pleasure in seeing his shows, he has had pleasure in studying the public; and his knowledge of human nature makes him a most entertaining talker. If any have thought of him only as a 'humbugger,' let the profound regard he has for these sincere and honest ladies, whose guest he so often is, plead against all that he has confessed against himself in his autobiography. He 'does good by stealth, and blushes to find it fame,' but tells all the bad about himself unblushingly. A whole group of editors might be fancied — only that they have enough of each other 'down town,' and so in society seek some one else, and do not 'group:' for there are Dr. Field, the excellent editor of the 'Evangelist;' and Mr. Elliott and Mr. Perry, of the 'Home Journal;' and Whitelaw Reid, of the 'Tribune;' and Mr. R. W Gilder, of the 'Hours at Home;' and last but not least, Mr. Robert Bonner, of the 'Ledger,' of whom, seeing that I have never had literary and financial dealings with him on my own account, I may say that he has made illustrious the proverb, 'There is that scattereth, and yet increaseth.' The publishers are represented by Robert Chambers, of Edinburgh, who has given so much 'Information for the People' that people need not be informed who he is; and George W. Carleton, the prince of publishers, whose elegant new book house, on Broadway, has already become the resort of literary and tasteful people.

"And then, what ladies have been in that house! How many of the most refined and noble women, whose names are unknown to fame, but whose minds and manners have given to society its aroma and beauty! How many whose names are known all over Christendom! If that of Elizabeth Cady Stanton suggests to a stranger — as, until I knew her, it certainly did to me — anything not beautifully feminine, how he will be disappointed when he sees her. She is quiet, self-poised, 'lady-like' — for she is a lady — plump as a partridge, of warm complexion, has a well formed head, adorned with white hair, put up unstiffly in puffs, and she would anywhere be taken for the mother of a governor or president, if governors and presidents were always gentlemen. I have studied Mrs. Stanton hours at a sitting, when she was presiding over a public meeting in the Cooper Union, when the brazen women who have brought such bad fame to the Woman's Rights movement were trying to secure 'the floor,' and gaunt fanatics of my own sex were contending with them for that 'privilege,' and the mob were hissing or shouting, and the tact with which Mrs. Stanton managed that whole assembly was a marvel. Except Henry Clay, of Kentucky, and Edward Stanly, formerly of North Carolina and now of California, she is the best presiding officer I have ever seen.

"And that nice little person with short curls, so admirably dressed, and self-sufficient, and handsome, not beautiful; her *tout ensemble* a combination of author, artist, actor — strong as a young man and sensitive as a young woman — is Anna Dickinson. And there, with so thoughtful a face, sits Mary L. Booth, industrious and accurate translator of huge volumes of French history and science, and now editor of 'Harper's Bazar.' Her conversation is an intellectual treat. And there is Madame Le Vert, of Mobile, who in English and American society has so long held the place of '*the* most charming woman,' without arousing the envy of any other woman, and who, therefore, must have an exceptional temperament; a lady who never says a very wise, or witty, or weak, or foolish thing, but whom you cannot speak with ten minutes without — weakly and foolishly it may be, but delightfully — feeling yourself to be both wise and witty. 'It is not always May,' even with Madame Le Vert. She has had losses and disappointments, and physical pain, and is no longer young, but she does marvelously draw the summer of her soul through the autumn months of her years. But space would fail if each lady were particularly described, from Kate

Field, the brilliant journalist and lecturer, and 'Jennie June' (Mrs. Croly of 'Demorest's Magazine'), and Mary E. Dodge, of 'Hearth and Home,' who wrote 'Hans Brinker's Silver Skates,' to the sallow, self-denying missionary sister from Cavalla, clad in the costume of ten years ago, now a stranger in her own land.

"Of the spiritual teachers, all are welcome at any time, from the Roman Catholic, John Jerome Hughes, and the eloquent Universalist, Chapin, to the adjective-yet-to-be-discovered Frothingham. The house of the Cary sisters is a Pantheon, a Polytechnic Institute, a room of the Committee on Reconstruction, a gathering place for the ecclesiastical and political Happy Family. Original abolitionists and *ab*-original secessionists meet pleasantly in a circle where everybody thinks, but nobody is tabooed for *what* he thinks.

"A great city is generally a mass of cold, but there are always 'warm places' even in a huge metropolis; and strangers are peculiarly endowed with the instinct for detecting them. It is genuine goodness that does the warming. And this house is never cold!

"Thus is shown that these sisters are authors of more than books. Their influence in their home is beautiful, and conservative, and preservative.

"May they live forever!"

CHAPTER V.

ALICE CARY. — THE WOMAN.

YEARS ago, in an old academy in Massachusetts, its preceptor gave to a young girl a poem to learn for a Wednesday exercise. It began, —

" Of all the beautiful pictures
  That hang on Memory's wall,
Is one of a dim old forest,
  That seemeth best of all."

After the girl had recited the poem to her teacher, he told her that Edgar Poe had said, and that he himself concurred in the opinion, that in rhythm it was one of the most perfect lyrics in the English language. He then proceeded to tell the story of the one who wrote it — of her life in her Western home, of the fact that she and her sister Phœbe had come to New York to seek their fortune, and to make a place for themselves in literature. It fell like a tale of romance on the girl's heart; and from that hour she saved every utterance that she could find of Alice Cary's, and spent much time thinking about her, till in a dim way she came to seem like a much-loved friend.

In 1857 the school-girl, then a woman, whom actual life had already overtaken, sat for the first time in a New York drawing-room, and looked with attentive but by no means dazzled eyes upon a gathering assembly,

It does not follow, because a person has done something remarkable, that he is, therefore, remarkable or even pleasant to look upon. Thus it happened that the young woman had numerous disappointments that evening, as one by one names famous in literature and art were pronounced, and their owners for the first time took on the semblance of flesh and blood before her. Presently came into the room, and sat down beside her, a lady, whose eyes, in their first glance, and whose voice, in its first low tone, won her heart. Soft, sad, tender eyes they were, and the face from which they shone was lovely. Its features were fine, its complexion a colorless olive, lit with the lustrous brown eyes, softened still more by masses of waving dark hair, then untouched of gray, and, save by its own wealth, wholly unadorned. Her dress was as harmonious as her face. It was of pale gray satin, trimmed with folds of ruby velvet; a dress like herself and her life — soft and sad in the background, bordered with brightness. This was Alice Cary. Even then her face was a history, not a prophecy. Even then it bore the record of past suffering, and in the tender eyes there still lingered the shadow of many vanished dreams. Thus the story of the old academy was made real and doubly beautiful to the stranger. The Alice Cary whom she had imagined had never been quite so lovely as the Alice Cary whom she that moment saw. That evening began a friendship between two women on which, till its earthly close, no shadow ever fell.

As I sit here thinking of her, I realize how futile will be any effort of mine to make a memorial worthy of my friend. The woman in herself so far transcended any work of art that she ever wrought, any song (sweet as her songs were) that she ever sung, that even to attempt to put into words what she was seems hopeless. Yet it is an act of justice, no less than of love, that one who knew her in the sanctuary of her life should, at least partly, lift the veil which ever hung between the lovely soul and the world; that the women of this land may see more clearly the sister whom they have lost, who, in what she was herself, was so much more than in what she in mortal weakness was able to do — at once an example and glory to American womanhood. It must ever remain a grief to those who knew her and loved her best, that such a soul as hers should have missed its highest earthly reward; but, if she can still live on as an incentive and a friend to those who remain, she at least is comforted now for all she suffered and all she missed here.

The life of one woman who has conquered her own spirit, who, alone and unassisted, through the mastery of her own will, has wrought out from the hardest and most adverse conditions a pure, sweet, and noble life, placed herself among the world's workers, made her heart and thought felt in ten thousand unknown homes — the life of one such woman is worth more to all living women, proves more for the possibilities of womanhood, for its final and finest advancement, its ultimate recognition and highest success, than ten thousand theories or eloquent orations on the theme. Such a woman was Alice Cary. Mentally and spiritually she was especially endowed with the rarest gifts; but no less, the lowliest of all her sisters may take on new faith and courage from her life. It may not be for you to sing till the whole land listens, but it is in your power, in a narrower sphere, to emulate the traits which brought the best success to her in her wider life.

Many personally impress us with the fact that they have wrought into the forms of art the very best in themselves. Whatever they may have embodied in form, color, or thought, we are sure that it is the most that they have to give, and in giving that, they are by so much themselves impoverished. In their own souls they hold nothing rarer in reserve. The opposite was true of Alice Cary. You could not know her without learning that the woman in herself was far greater and sweeter than anything that she had ever produced. You could not sit by her side, listening to the low, slow outflow of her thought, without longing that she might yet find the condition which would enable her to give it a fuller and finer expression than had ever yet been possible. You could not feel day by day the blended strength, generosity, charity, and tenderness of the living woman, without longing that a soul so complete might yet make an impression on the nation to which it was born, that could never fade away. Her most powerful trait, the one which seemed the basis of her entire character, was her passion for justice, for in its intensity it rose to the height of a passion. Her utmost capacity for hate went out toward every form of oppression. If she ever seemed overwrought, it was for some wrong inflicted on somebody, very rarely on herself. She wanted everything, the meanest little bug at her feet, to have its chance, *all* the chance of its little life. That this so seldom could be, in this distorted world, was the abiding grief of her life. Early she ceased to suffer chiefly for herself; but to her latest breath she suffered for the sorrows of others. Phœbe truly said: "Constituted as she was, it was not possible for her to help taking upon herself not only all the sorrows of her friends, but in some sense the tribulation and anguish that cometh upon every son and daughter of Adam. She was even unto the end planning great projects for the benefit of suffering humanity, and working with her might to be helpful to those near her; and when it seemed impossible that one suffering herself such manifold afflictions could think even of the needs of others."

It was this measureless capacity to know and feel everything that concerns human nature, this pity for all, this longing for justice and mercy to the lowest and the meanest thing that could breathe and suffer — this largeness lifting her above all littleness — this universality of soul, which made her in herself great as she was tender. Such a soul could not fail to feel, with deepest intensity, every sorrow and wrong inflicted upon her own sex. She loved women with a fullness of sympathy and tenderness never surpassed. She felt pity for their infirmities, and pride in their successes, feeling each to be in part her own. Believing that in wifehood, motherhood, and home, woman found her surest and holiest estate, all the more for this belief, her whole being rebelled against the caste in sex, which would prescribe the development of any individual soul, which would lay a single obstacle in the way of a toiling and aspiring human being, which would degrade her place in the human race, because, with all her aspiration, toil, and suffering, she wore the form of woman. Every effort having for its object the help, advancement, and full enfranchisement of woman from every form of injustice, in Church, State, education, or at home, had her completest sympathy and coöperation. Yet she said: "I must work in my own way, and that is a very quiet one. My health, habits, and temperament make it impossible that I should mix in crowds, or act with great organizations. I must say my little say, and do my little do, at home!" These words add interest to the fact that Alice Cary was the first President of the first Woman's Club (now called Sorosis) formed in New York. The entire history of her relation with it is given in a private letter from Mrs. Jenny C. Croly, written since the death of Alice and Phœbe. As a testimonial of affection to them from a woman whom both sisters honored and loved, and as the history of *how* Alice Cary became President of a Woman's Club, which no other person could write, I take the liberty of quoting from this letter.

Mrs. Croly says: "Alice particularly I loved, and thank God for ever having known; she was so large and all-embracing in her kindliness and charity, that her place must remain vacant; few women exist who could fill it.

"Much as those of us who knew the sisters thought we loved them, few realized the gap it would make in our lives when they were gone. Their loyalty, their truth, their steadfastness, their genial hospitality, their warmth of friendship, their devotion to each other,— the beautiful utterances of their quiet, patient, yet in some respects, suffering lives, which found their way to the world, all belonged to them, and seem almost to have died with them.

"It breaks my heart to remember how hard Phœbe tried to be 'brave' after Alice's death, as she thought her sister would wish to have her; how she opened the windows to let in the sunlight, filled her room with flowers, refused to put on mourning, because Alice had requested her not to do so, and tried to interest herself in general schemes and plans for the advancement of women. But it was all of no use. She simply could not live after Alice was gone. 'I do not know what is the matter with me,' she said to me on one occasion; 'I have lain down, and it seems, because Alice is not there, there is no reason why I should get up. For thirty years I have gone straight to her bedside as soon as I arose in the morning, and wherever she is, I am sure she wants me now.' Could one think of these words without tears?

"In addition to the love I felt for them, I am proud of these two women, as women whose isolated lives were so simple and so pure, who gave back tenderness and devotion and loving charity, for the slights which society deals even to gifted, if lonely womanhood. Some mistaken impressions have been obtained in regard to Alice Cary, in consequence of the sudden termination of her alliance with 'Sorosis.' For her connection with the society at all, I alone am responsible. Some sort of organization among women was my hobby, and I had discussed it with her often at her Sunday evening receptions. She had sympathized, but always refused to take any active part on account of her ill health. When the society was actually formed, therefore, I applied first to Mrs. Parton to become its President, a post which she at first accepted, and afterwards refused for a personal reason. Desirous of having a literary club, with the name of a distinguished literary woman, I begged Alice Cary to accept the position. She found it difficult to refuse my urgent entreaties, but did so, until I rose in great agitation, saying, 'Alice Cary, think what faith, reverence, and affection thousands of women have given to you, and you will not even give to them your name.' I left the house hastily, and went back to my office, concealing hot tears of grief and disappointment behind my veil. A moment after I arrived there, to my astonishment she came in, sank down in a chair, breathless with her haste, and said, 'If my name is worth anything to woman, I have come to tell you to take it.' For answer I knelt down at her feet, and kissed her hand over and over again. Dear Alice Cary! only the argument that she was withholding something she could give had any weight with her."

Alice took her seat as President of the Woman's Club, but from ill health and an instinctive disinclination personally to fill any place publicly, she very soon resigned. Nevertheless, though at times she differed from special methods adopted by its members, the Woman's Club (Sorosis), in its original intent, and in its possibilities as a source of mutual culture and help to women, always had her sympathy to her dying day. Her address on taking the chair of the Woman's Club, unique and entirely characteristic, I give as the first and last speech ever made by Alice Cary on a public occasion. Yet this public occasion of hers was a most genial and gracious one. In the sumptuous parlor of Delmonico's, in an easy chair, sat Alice Cary, surrounded by a party of ladies, while she read to them in her low, forceful tones the words of her address. Not an ungraceful or unfeminine thing was this to do, even the most prejudiced must acknowledge. "I believe in it," she said afterwards, "especially for any one who works best in concert with others, and to whom the attrition and stimulus of contact with other minds is necessary. To many women such a weekly convocation will be of the highest advantage, but so far as I personally am concerned, I enjoy better sitting up-stairs, chatting with a friend, while I trim a cap for Aunt Lamson."

But here is the speech: —

Ladies, — As it will not be expected of me to make speeches very often, hereafter, I think I may presume on your indulgence, if I take advantage of this one opportunity. Permit me, then, in the first place, to thank you for the honor you have done me in assigning to me the President's chair. Why I should have been chosen, when there are so many among you greatly more competent to fill the position, I am at a loss to understand; unless, indeed, it be owing to the fact that I am to most of you a stranger, and your imaginations have clothed me with qualities not my due. This you would soon discover for yourselves; I mention it only to bespeak your forbearance, though in this regard, I ventured almost to anticipate your lenity, inasmuch as you all know how untrained to business habits, how ignorant of rules, and how unused to executive management most women are.

If I take my seat, therefore, without confidence, it is not without the hope of attaining, through your generous kindness and encouragement, to better things. "A Woman's Club! Who ever heard of the like! What do women want of a Club? Have you any aims or objects?" These are questions which have been propounded to me day after day, since this project was set afoot — by gentlemen, of course. And I have answered, that, in our humble way, we were striving to imitate their example. You have your exclusive clubs, I have said, and why should not we have ours? What is so promotive of your interests cannot be detrimental to us; and that you find these reunions helpful to yourselves, and beneficial to society, we cannot doubt.

You, gentlemen, profess to be our representatives, to represent us better than we could possibly represent ourselves; therefore, we argue, it cannot be that you are attracted by grand rooms, fine furniture, luxurious dinners and suppers, expensive wines and cigars, the bandying of poor jests, or the excitement of the gaming table. Such dishonoring suspicions as these are not to be entertained for a moment.

Of our own knowledge, I have said, we are not able to determine what special agencies you employ for your advantage and ours, in your deliberative assemblies, for it has not been thought best for our interests that we should even sit at your tables, much less to share your councils; and doubtless, therefore, in our blindness and ignorance, we have made some pitiful mistakes.

In the first place, we have "tipped the tea-pot." This is a hard saying, the head and front of the charges brought against us, and we cannot but acknowledge its justice and its force; we are, in fact, weighed down with shame and humiliation, and impelled, while we are about it, to make full and free confession of all our wild and guilty fantasies. We have, then, to begin at the beginning, proposed the inculcation of deeper and broader ideas among women, proposed to teach them to think for themselves, and get their opinions at first hand, not so much because it is their right, as because it is their duty. We have also proposed to open out new avenues of employment to women, to make them less dependent and less burdensome, to lift them out of unwomanly self-distrust and disqualifying diffidence, into womanly self-respect and self-knowledge; to teach each one to make all work honorable by doing the share that falls to her, or that she may work out to herself agreeably to her own special aptitude, cheerfully and faithfully, not going down to it, but bringing it up to her. We have proposed to enter our protest against all idle gossip, against all demoralizing and wicked waste of time; also against the follies and tyrannies of fashion, against all external impositions and disabilities; in short, against each and every thing that opposes the full development and use of the faculties conferred upon us by our Creator.

We have proposed to lessen the antagonisms existing at present between men and women, by the use of every rightful means in our power; by standing upon our divine warranty, and saying and doing what we are able to say and to do, without asking leave, and without suffering hindrance: not for the exclusive good of our own sex, for we hold that there is no exclusive, and no separate good; what injures my brother injures me, and what injures me injures him, if he could but be made to know it; it injures him, whether or not he is made to know it. Such, I have said, are some of our objects and aims. We do not pretend, as yet, to have carefully digested plans and clearly defined courses. We are as children feeling our way in the dark, for it must be remembered that it is not yet half a century since the free schools, even in the most enlightened portions of our country, were first opened to girls. How, then, should you expect of us the fullness of wisdom which you for whole centuries have been gathering from schools, colleges, and the exclusive knowledge and management of affairs!

We admit our short-comings, but we do feel, gentlemen, that in spite of them, an honest, earnest, and unostentatious effort toward broader culture and nobler life is entitled to a heartier and more sympathetic recognition than we have as yet received from you anywhere; even our representatives here at home, the leaders of the New York press, have failed in that magnanimity which we have been accustomed to attribute to them.

If we could have foreseen the sneers and sarcasms with which we have been met, they of themselves would have constituted all-sufficient reasons for the establishment of this Woman's Club; as it is, they have established a strong impulse towards its continuance and final perpetuity. But, ladies, these sneers and sarcasms are, after all, but so many acknowledgements of our power, and should and will stimulate us to braver assertion, to more persistent effort toward thorough and harmonious organization; and concert and harmony are all that we need to make this enterprise, ultimately, a great power for good. Indeed, with such women as have already enrolled their names on our list, I, for my part, cannot believe failure possible.

Some of us cannot hope to see great results, for our feet are already on the downhill side of life; the shadows are lengthening behind us and gathering before us, and ere long they will meet and close, and the places that have known us, know us no more. But if, when our poor work is done, any of those who come after us shall find in it some hint of usefulness toward nobler lives, and better and more enduring work, we, for ourselves, rest content.

The love, sympathy, and pity which Alice felt for the whole human race, she lavished with concentrated power on those near to her, the members of her own family, and all who had been drawn into the inner circle of her personal life. She had not a relative who did not share her solicitude and care. Of her young nieces, the daughters of Rowena and Susan Cary, she was especially fond. The house on Twentieth Street was often graced and brightened by their presence, and one, "little Alice," grew up almost as an own daughter in her home, giving in return, to both her aunts to their latest hour, a filial devotion and tenderness which the most loving daughter never surpassed.

No child ever called her mother, yet to the end of life the heart of motherhood beat strong within her breast. Her love for children never grew faint. She was especially fond of little girls, and was wont to send for her little friends to come and spend a day with her. This was a high privilege, but any little girl that came was at once put at her ease, and felt perfectly at home. She took the individuality of each child into her heart, and reproduced it in her intercourse with it, and in her songs and stories.

Her little girl visitors were sometimes silent ones. Going into her room one day, there was a row of photographs, all little girls, arranged before her on her desk.

"Whose little girls?" was the eager question.

"*Mine!*" was the answer, breaking into a laugh. "They are all Alice Carys; take your choice. The only trouble they make me is, I can't possibly get time to write to them all, though I do try to, to the babies' mothers." All had been sent by strangers, fathers and mothers, photographs of the children named "Alice Cary."

It is this real love for children, *as* children, which has given to both Alice and Phœbe Cary's books for little folks, such genuine and abiding popularity.

No more touching proof could be given of Alice Cary's passionate sympathy with child nature, than her never-waning love for her own little sister Lucy. Though but three years old when she passed away, the impress of her child-soul was as vivid and powerful in her sister's heart after the lapse of thirty changeful years, as on the day that she died. It was more than sister mourning for sister, it was the woman yearning for the child whose vacant place in her life no other child had ever filled. The following lines, more than Wordsworthian in their bare simplicity, are an unfeigned utterance of her deepest heart.

MY LITTLE ONE.

At busy morn — at quiet noon —
 At evening sad and still,
As wayward as the lawless mist
 That wanders where it will,
 She comes — my little one.

I cannot have a dream so wrought
 Of nothings, nor so wild

With fantasies, but she is there,
  My heavenly-human child —
  My glad, gay little one.

She never spake a single word
  Of wisdom, I agree;
I loved her not for what she was,
  But what she was to me —
  My precious little one.

You might not call her beautiful,
  Nor haply was she so;
I loved her for the loveliness
  That I alone could know —
  My sweet-souled little one.

I say I loved, but that is wrong;
  As if the love could change
Because my dove hath got her wings,
  And taken wider range!
  Forgive, my little one.

I still can see her shining curls
  All tremulously fair,
Like fifty yellow butterflies
  A-fluttering in the air:
  My angel little one.

I see her tender mouth, her eyes,
  Her garment softly bright,
Like some fair cloud about the morn
  With roses all a-light:
  My deathless little one.

She had, in full, the keen sensitiveness of the poetic temperament. A harsh tone, even, would bring tears into her eyes ; a cold look would haunt her for days. It was an absolute grief to her to differ in opinion from any one she loved, although with her intensity of conviction this was sometimes inevitable. It pained her if two friends rose to any heat of temper in argument. If this ever occurred in her own parlor, though it rarely did, she would refer to it with a pained regret for weeks afterwards. This fine sensitiveness of temperament was manifested in her extreme personal modesty, which, to the end of her life, impelled her to shrink from all personal publicity, and to avoid everything which could attract attention to herself. She felt strong in rectitude, in her sense of justice, in her will to do for herself and others ; but, in comparison with her friends, always plain and poor and lowly in person, attainment, and performance. Her standard of excellence, both in character and in work, was too high to admit of self-satisfaction. Her ideals in all things were absolutely perfect. She took no pride in *them*. She only sighed that with all her striving she could not reach them.

No better proof could be given of the lack of self-consciousness in both sisters, than the absence of all personal diaries, letters, and allusions to themselves among their effects. Amid the mass of their papers which remain, not a written line has either sister left referring personally to herself. They held the humblest opinion of their own epistolary powers, probably never wrote a letter in their lives for the mere sake of writing it, while they periodically sent requests to their friends to burn all letters from them in their possession. Thus, amid their large circle of friends, very few letters remain, and nearly all of these are of too personal a character to admit of extracts. Alice never wrote a letter save on business, or to a person whom she loved. These letters were written in snatches of time between her tasks at early morning, or in the evening. She had no leisure to discuss art, or new books, seldom current events. The letter was always a direct message from her heart to her friend. In nothing, save in her self-denial for their sakes, did she manifest her brooding tenderness and care for those she loved, more than in her personal letters.

The following extracts from private letters to one person, give an example of the letter-writing style which she held in such low esteem, and show what were the direct utterances of Alice Cary's heart in private to a friend. As the expression of herself in a form of which so little remains, they are full of interest.

The first is dated September 3, 1866: —

"I have not forgotten you, though you might think so. The truth is, in the first place, my letters are very poor affairs, and in the next, I know it. So you see I do not like to essay my poor powers in that direction, unless for a special reason, and such an one is my love for you. I think of you daily, indeed hourly, and wish you were only back among us. Can't you come for a little while this winter? . . . . Go on! We need all the strong words for the right that can be uttered. We never needed them more, it seems to me. I am afraid you are lonesome. I know how lonesome I used to be in the country and alone. Alone, I mean, so far as the society to which one belongs is concerned. For we all need something outside of ourselves and our immediate family. I don't care how much they may be to us, we require it both for mind and body.

"I am here in my own room, just where you left me. How I wish you could come in. Wouldn't we talk? I see all our old friends, but I do so wish for you.

"I am very busy, never so busy in my life, but whether to good purpose or not, I cannot say. Did you read my story in the July and August numbers of the 'Atlantic,' 'The Great Doctor'?

"My poems are expected out this fall, but not in a shape to please me; the cuts are dreadfully done; they look like frights. So things go, nothing quite as we would have it in this world; let us hope we are nearing a better country. I could *tell* you a thousand things, but how can I write them?

"You have seen that poor Mrs. —— has passed from among us? Her poor little struggle of a life is ended. I trust she has found one more satisfactory. My struggle still goes on. I am writing stories and verses — I can't say poems.

"Write me, my dear, just from your heart."

The next letter bears the date of September 17, 1866: —

"My dear, I've taken time by the forelock, as they say. I am up before the sun.

"We had an interesting company last evening, among them Mr. Greeley, Mr. Beecher, and Robert Dale Owen. I thought of you, and wished you here. I am glad you are at work again; you *must* work, you have every encouragement. A word about my story. I had no design to write a word against the Methodists. I believe them to be just as good as any other people. But I had to put my characters in some Church, and as I lived among Methodists in my youth, I know much about their ways. But I have a good Methodist preacher to set against my poor one, as will appear in due time. I would not do so foolish or mean a thing as to attempt to write down, or to write up, any denomination. There is good in all; but human nature is human nature everywhere.

"Thank you for your kind offer about my poems. I shall certainly remember your goodness. I *do* want the book to get before the public, and not be left to die in its cradle. I can say this much for it, It is *mine.* It is what I have thought, what I have seen, lived, and felt myself, not through books, or through other persons. I have taken the wild woods, corn fields, school-houses, rustic boys and girls, whatever I know best that has helped to make me; and however poor, there is the result.

"I must see you somehow this winter, and your dear friend Mrs. ——, whom I love without having seen.

"There is breakfast! God bless you, and for a little while, good-by."

Another letter is dated October 21, 1866: —

.... "I am afraid you are sick or very sad, or I am sure I should have heard from you. I think of you *so* much, and always with tearful tenderness, for our souls are kindred. I am more than half sick. My cough, since the weather has changed, is very troublesome, so that I cannot sleep nights, which is dreadful, you know.

"Won't you write and tell me all about yourself? Somehow I feel worried about you, as if there were shadows all around you.

"The house was full of pleasant company last night, but I was too sick to share it.

"I have managed with Carleton about my books. He has been very generous to me. I like him, and you will. I am busy trying to do much more than I ought, but I seem to be driven by a demon to that end, and to what purpose! Who cares for my poor little work, when it is all done! What doth it profit under the sun! I am sad to-day, very sad, and I ought to go to you only with sunshine. I have just finished a long, lonely ballad. I wish I could read it to you. More than that, I wish I could walk with you in the sunshine, out among the falling leaves, and say just what comes into my heart to say. But you are *there*, and I am *here*, 'and the harbor bar keeps nearing.'"

The following is from a letter written a year later, January, 1867: —

"Here am I again, in my corner, thinking of you and of many things of which we did not talk much. I felt a little hurt, at first, that I did not see you more, but I do not now. I know that it was just as you say. Never mind, I half think I will come again, I did enjoy the week in —— so much. I want to begin just where I left off. Dear Mrs. ——, she did so much for our comfort and pleasure. How I hope to do something for her *sometime*. And Mr. —— too, how I like him. It always did me good to see his bright face come in; his very voice gave me confidence and — *what* word shall I use? I don't know, I only know it always helped me to see him.

"I've been working on a little book of poems, or a proposed book, rather, all day at my desk. It is now nearly night, and I am tired, but I got on pretty well; that's some comfort.

"I have not been well since my return, and the immense appetite I had in ——, I left there."

The following bears a still later date: —

. . . . "Thank you most kindly for your letter. If I had only received it earlier, I might have gone with my friends to ——, but they had already left, and anyway it would not have been easy to leave, for the house is full of visitors. I would like to be with you these times, but you can't imagine how busy I am, and have to be, to keep things going. I have been pretty well all winter, or I don't know how I should have got along. I have done a great deal of work, such as it is. Tell me what you propose to do, and all about yourself. First of all, I hope you are well; that is the great thing. We have had very pleasant times this winter; I have so much wished you here to help us. I have seen a good deal of Miss Booth for the last few months, and like her much; have seen Ole Bull at home and elsewhere, and like him, as Anna Dickinson would say, 'excessively!' I have seen much also of the McCarthys of London. You know and like them both; so do I. I do believe I have written my whole letter about myself. Well, pay me back in my own coin; that is all I want. Give me some of those thoughts which go through your mind and heart, when you sit alone with your cheek in your hand.

"Mind, I don't mean to say that you have not done anything well. By no means. But *remember, your* best work you yet must do."

Another letter is dated November 24, 1868:—

"Your kind letter came duly. How I thank you for all your affectionate thoughts of me! I have been thinking and thinking I would write, but it's the old story, I can't write anything worth the reading. If we could only see each other! But written words are so poor and empty! at any rate mine seem so, and I have not the gift to make them otherwise.

"You have been sick and sad. I am so sorry for both, if that could help you. I am not well, either. My dear sick sister has been with me for two months with L——. 'Little Alice' is here now. I have had transient visitors all the time,—two calls for charity since I began this letter. So, my dear, you can see how some of my time, and much of my heart goes. You can imagine I have written very little, and as for reading, my mind is as blank as an idol's.

"I hope to come to —— this winter, and that there we may see one another: but can't you *somehow* come to me,—so that we might steal an hour now and then? I think it would do you good, I am sure it would me. I think of you oftener than you would believe. I have not so many friends that I cannot keep them all in my heart all the time. Have you made your new dress? What are you doing? and hoping to do? Do write and tell me, if you can afford to get in return for good letters such chaff as I send.

"It seems to me, if I only had your years, I would hope everything; but think where I am! So near the night, where no man can work, nor woman either.

"Lastly, my dear, let me admonish you to stand more strongly by your own nature. God gave it to you. For that reason alone you should think well of it, and make the most of it. I say this because I think that your tender conscience is a little morbid, as well as tender. You hardly think that you have a right to God's best gifts, to the enjoyment of the free air and sunshine. Your little innocent delights you constantly buy at a great cost. When you have given the loaf, you hardly think you have a right to the crust. One part of your nature is all the time set against the other, and you take the self-sacrificing side. I know through what straits you are dragged. You could not be selfish if you would, and I would not have you so, if I could. But I do think that you should compel yourself to live a higher, more expansive, and expressive life. You are entitled to it. There is a cloud all the time between you and the sun, and even the soulless plants cannot live in the shade. I did not intend to write all this; somehow, it seemed to write itself. If I have said more than I ought, I pray you pardon me.

"The day is lovely. I wish we were in the woods together, hearing the wind in the dead leaves, and getting from the quiet heart of our mother earth some of her tranquil rest. Good-by, my dear. May the Lord send his angels to abide with you."

Many have inquired concerning her belief in "Spiritualism." She was a spiritualist in the highest meaning of the much-abused term, as every spiritually minded person must be in some sense, and would be if no such thing as professional Spiritualism had ever existed. No one can believe in the New Testament, in God himself, and not be in this sense a spiritualist. One cannot have faith in another and better world, and not feel often that its border lies very near to this; so near, indeed, that our lost ones who have gone thither may come back to us, unseen, unheard, to walk as "ministering angels" by our sides. This is the spiritualism of Jesus and his disciples, and of holy men and women in all ages.

All Alice Cary's spiritual faith is uttered in these lines: —

"Laugh, you who never had
Your dead come back; but do not take from me
The harmless comfort of my foolish dream:
That these our mortal eyes,
Which outwardly reflect the earth and skies,
Do introvert upon eternity;
And that the shapes you deem
Imaginations just as clearly fall,
Each from its own divine original,
And through some subtle element of light,
Upon the inward spiritual eye,
As do the things which round about them lie,
Gross and material, on the external sight."

She hated slavery in every form; she was capable of a burning indignation against every type of wrong; yet in her judgment of individuals she was full of charity and sympathy. I once expressed myself bitterly toward a person who had spoken of Alice most unkindly and falsely. "You would not feel so, my dear," she said, "if you knew how unhappy she is. When I think how *very unhappy she must be herself*, to be willing to injure one who never harmed her, I can only pity her."

This intense tenderness, this yearning over everything human, with a pity and love inexpressible, made the very impulse and essence of her being. Surely, in this was she Christlike. Our Saviour wept over Jerusalem. How many tears did she, his disciple, shed for sorrowing humanity, for suffering womanhood. Nor were tears all she gave. The deepest longing of her life was to see human nature lifted from sin to holiness, from misery to happiness; every thought that she uttered, every deed she did, she prayed might help toward this end. To help somebody, no matter how lowly, to comfort the afflicted, to lift up the fallen, to share every blessing of her life with others, to live (even under the stress of pain and struggle) a life pure, large, in itself an inspiration — this, and more, was Alice Cary.

Filled with the spirit, and fulfilling the law of the Master in her daily life, is it not intolerant, little, and even mean, now she has passed away forever, to cast on the abstract creed of such a woman the shadow of question, much less of reproach?

Why should her "Dying Hymn" be less the hymn of a dying saint, if she did believe that the mercy of her Heavenly Father, and the atonement of Jesus Christ, would, in the fullness of eternity, redeem from sin, and gather into everlasting peace, the whole family of man?

Justice tempered by love, the supreme attribute of her own nature, ran into her individual conception of God, and of his dealings with the human race. Grieving over the fact that ten thousands of her fellow creatures are cursed in their very birth, born into the world with the physical and spiritual taint of depraved generations entailed upon them, with neither the power nor opportunity, from the cradle to the grave, to break the chains of poverty and vice and rise to purity: she believed no less that the opportunity would come to every human being, that everything that God had made would have its chance; if not in this existence, then in another. Without this faith, at times human life would have been to her intolerable. It was her soul's consolation to say: —

"Nay, but 'tis not the end:
God were not God, if such a thing could be;
If not in time, then in eternity,
There must be room for penitence to mend
Life's broken chance, else noise of wars
Would unmake heaven."

Phœbe, in settling the question of her religious faith, said: —

"Though singularly liberal and unsectarian in her views, she always preserved a strong attachment to the church of her parents, and, in the main, accepted its doctrines. Caring little for creeds and minor points, she most firmly believed in human brotherhood as taught by Jesus; and in a God whose loving kindness is so deep and so unchangeable, that there can never come a time to even the vilest sinner, in all the ages of eternity, when if he arise and go to Him, his Father will not see him afar off, and have compassion upon him. In this faith, which she has so often sung, she lived and wrought and hoped; and in this faith, which grew stronger, deeper, and more assured with years of sorrow and trial and sickness, she passed from death unto life."

The friends who shared so long the hospitality of her home, as they turn their eyes toward the closed doors of that home, finally bereft, well as they knew her and truly as they loved her, cannot dream of half the plans for their happiness and comfort that went out when that faithful heart ceased to beat. Nor was it of her friends only whom she thought. Long after suffering had separated her forever from the active world, she took just as keen an interest in its great affairs as if still participating in them. Even when the shadows of eternity were stealing over her, nothing that concerns this mortal life seemed to her paltry or unimportant. She wanted all her friends to come into her room and tell her everything about the life from which she was shut out. She took the deepest interest in everything human, from the grandest affair of state to "poor old Mrs. Brown's last cap," which she persisted in making when so feeble that she could scarcely draw her needle through its lace. Yet this interest in human affairs did not shut from her gaze the things "unseen and eternal." She said to me one morning, after a night of suffering, "While you are all asleep, I lie here and think on the deep things of eternity, of the unknown life. I find I must leave it still with God, and trust Him!"

One of the last things she said to me was, "If you could see all the flowers brought into this room by friends *piled up*, it seems to me they would reach to heaven. I am certainly going toward it on flowery beds, if not beds of ease."

And her last words to me, with a radiant smile, were, "When you come back, you will find me so much better I shall come and stay with you a week. So we won t say good-by." Thus in one sense we never parted. Yet my only regret in thinking of her, is that life with its relentless obligations withheld me from her in her very last days. It is one of those unavailing regrets on which death has set his seal, and to which time can bring no reparation.

For her sake let me say what, as a woman, she could be, and was, to another. She found me with habits of thought and of action unformed, and with nearly all the life of womanhood before me. She taught me self help, courage, and faith. She showed me how I might help myself and help others. Wherever I went, I carried with me her love as a treasure and a staff. How many times I leaned upon it and grew strong. It never fell from me. It never failed me. No matter how life might serve me, I believed without a doubt that her friendship would never fail me; and it never did. If I faltered, she would believe in me no less. If I fell, her hand would be the first outstretched to lift me up. All the world might forsake me; yet would not she. I might become an outcast; yet no less would I find in her a shelter and a friend. Yet, saying this, I have not said, and have no power to say, what as a soul I owe to her.

These autumn days sharpen the keen sense of irreparable loss. These are the days that she loved; in whose balsamic airs she basked, and renewed her life with ever fresh delight. These are the days in which she garnished her house for new reunions, in which she drew nearer to nature, nearer to her friends, nearer to her God. October is here, serene as of old; but she is not. Her house is inhabited by strangers. Her song is hushed. Her true heart is still. But life — the vast life whose mystery enthralled her — that remorselessly goes on. I laid a flower on her grave yesterday; so to-day I offer this poor memorial to her name, because I loved her.

CHAPTER VI.

ALICE CARY. — THE WRITER.

As an artist in literature Alice Cary suffered, as so many women in this generation do, for lack of thorough mental discipline and those reserved stores of knowledge which must be gathered and garnered in youth. When the burden and the heat of the day came, when she needed them most, she had neither time nor strength to acquire them. Her early youth was spent chiefly in household drudgery. Her only chance for study was in dear snatches at books between her tasks, and by the kitchen fire through the long winter evenings. Referring to this period of her life, she said: —

"In my memory there are many long, dark years of labor at variance with my inclinations, of bereavement, of constant struggle, and of hope deferred."

Thus, when her life-work and work for life came, she did it under the most hampering disadvantages, and often amid bodily suffering which any ordinary woman would have made a sufficient excuse for absolute dependence upon others. Thus it was with her as with so many of her sisters. So much of woman's work is artistically poor, not from any poverty of gift, but for lack of that practical training of the faculties which is indispensable to the finest workmanship. The power is there, but not the perfect mastery of the power. Alice's natural endowment of mind and soul was of the finest and rarest; yet as an artistic force, she used it timidly, and at times awkwardly. She never, to her dying hour, reached her own standard; never, in any form of art, satisfied herself.

About ten years ago she wrote to a friend in the West: "I am ashamed of my work. The great bulk of what I have written is poor stuff. Some of it, maybe, indicates ability to do better — that is about all. I think I am more simple and direct, less diffuse and encumbered with ornament than in former years, all, probably, because I have lived longer and thought more."

In dealing with two forces, hers was the touch of mastery. As an interpreter of the natural world she was unsurpassed. And when she spoke from her own, never did she fail to strike the key-note to the human heart. Her absorbing love for nature, inanimate and human, her oneness with it, made her what she was, a poet of the people. She knew more of principles than of persons, more of nature than of either. Her mind was introspective. Instinctively she drew the very life of the universe into her soul, and from her soul sent it forth into life again. By her nothing in nature is forgotten or passed by. "The luminous creatures of the air," the cunning workers of the ground, "the dwarfed flower," and the "drowning mote," each shares something of her great human love, which, brooding over the very ground, rises and merges into all things beautiful. One can only wonder at the reverent and observant faculties, the widely embracing heart, which makes so many of God's loves its own. The following is a verse in her truest vein: —

"O for a single hour
To have life's knot of evil and self-blame
All straightened, all undone!
As in the time when fancy had the power
The weariest and forlornest day to bless,
At sight of any little common flower,
That warmed her pallid fingers in the sun,
And had no garment but her loveliness."

After having lived in the city for twenty years, with not even a grassy plat of her own on which to rest her feet, the country sights and sounds, which made nearly thirty years of her life, faded into pictures of the past. In these days "life's tangled knot of evil," the phenomena of human existence, absorbed chiefly her heart and faculties. Much of the result of her questionings and replies we find in her "Thoughts and Theories." Even these are deeply veined with her passionate love of nature, though she speaks of it as a companion of the past. She says: —

"I thank Thee that my childhood's vanished days
Were cast in rural ways,
Where I beheld, with gladness ever new,
That sort of vagrant dew
Which lodges in the beggarly tents of such
Vile weeds as virtuous plants disdain to touch,
And with rough-bearded burs, night after night,
Upgathered by the morning, tender and true,
Into her clear, chaste light.

"Such ways I learned to know
That free will cannot go

Outside of mercy; learned to bless his name
Whose revelations, ever thus renewed
Along the varied year, in field and wood,
His loving care proclaim.

"I thank Thee that the grass and the red rose
Do what they can to tell
How spirit through all forms of matter flows;
For every thistle by the common way,
Wearing its homely beauty; for each spring
That, sweet and homeless, runneth where it will;
For night and day;
For the alternate seasons, — everything
Pertaining to life's marvelous miracle."

But these later poems, with all their spiritual thought and insight, with all their tender retrospection, never equaled in freshness and fullness of melody, in a nameless rush of music, her first lyrics; those lyrics written when the young soul, attuned to every sound in nature, thrilling with the first consciousness of its visible and invisible life, like the reed of Pan, gave it all forth in music at the touch of every breeze. No wonder that so many pilgrims out in the world turned and listened to the first notes of a song so natural and "piercing sweet." To the dusty wayfarer the freedom and freshness and fullness of the winds and waves swept through it. Listen: —

"Do you hear the wild birds calling?
Do you hear them, O my heart?
Do you see the blue air falling
From their rushing wings apart?

"With young mosses they are flocking,
For they hear the laughing breeze
With dewy fingers rocking
Their light cradles in the trees!"

And here is one of her early contributions to the "National Era," written before she was known to fame, and before she was paid money for her writing.

TO THE WINDS.

Talk to my heart, O winds —
Talk to my heart to-night;
My spirit always finds
With you a new delight —
Finds always new delight,
In your silver talk at night.

Give me your soft embrace
As you used to long ago,
In your shadowy trysting-place,
When you seemed to love me so —
When you sweetly kissed me so,
On the green hills, long ago.

Come up from your cool bed,
In the stilly twilight sea,
For the dearest hope lies dead
That was ever dear to me;
Come up from your cool bed,
And we'll talk about the dead.

Tell me, for oft you go,
Winds — lovely winds of night —

About the chambers low,
  With sheets so dainty white,
If they sleep through all the night
In the beds so chill and white?

Talk to me, winds, and say
  If in the grave be rest,
For, O! Life's little day
  Is a weary one at best;
Talk to my heart and say
If Death will give me rest.

In her minor lyrics of this period, those singing of some sad human experience, we find the same intimate presence of natural objects, the same simple, inimitable pictures of country life. I was a young girl when the following stanzas first met my eye. The exquisite sensation which thrilled me when I read them, was among the never-to-be-forgotten experiences of a life-time. It was as if I had never read a poem before, and had but just received a new revelation of song; though the soul from whence it came was to me but a name.

Very pale lies Annie Clayville,
  Still her forehead, shadow-crowned,
And the watchers hear her saying,
  As they softly tread around —
"Go out, reapers! for the hill-tops
  Twinkle with the summer's heat;
Lay out your swinging cradles,
  Golden furrows of ripe wheat!
While the little laughing children,
  Lightly mingling work with play,

From between the long green winrows
  Glean the sweetly-scented hay,
Let your sickles shine like sunbeams
  In the silvery flowing rye;
Ears grow heavy in the corn-fields
  That will claim you by and by.
Go out, reapers, with your sickles,
  Gather home the harvest store!
Little gleaners, laughing gleaners,
  I shall go with you no more!"

Round the red moon of October,
  White and cold, the eve stars climb;
Birds are gone, and flowers are dying—
  'Tis a lonesome, lonesome time!
Yellow leaves along the woodland
  Surge to drift; the elm-bough sways,
Creaking at the homestead window,
  All the weary nights and days;
Dismally the rain is falling,
  Very dismally and cold!
Close within the village grave-yard,
  By a heap of freshest ground,
With a simple, nameless head-stone,
  Lies a low and narrow mound;
And the brow of Annie Clayville
  Is no longer shadow-crowned.
Rest thee, lost one! rest thee calmly,
  Glad to go where pain is o'er;
Where they say not, through the night-time,
  "I am weary!" any more.

In her verses "To an Early Swallow," written within

a year or two of her death, we find lines which revive much of the exquisite imagery which made her earlier lyrics so remarkable. She says: —

My little bird of the air,
If thou dost know, then tell me the sweet reason
Thou comest alway, duly in thy season,
To build and pair.
For still we hear thee twittering round the eaves,
Ere yet the attentive cloud of April lowers,
Up from their darkened heath to call the flowers,
Where, all the rough, hard weather,
They kept together,
Under their low brown roof of withered leaves.

And for a moment still
Thy ever-tuneful bill,
And tell me, and I pray thee tell me true,
If any cruel care thy bosom frets,
The while thou flittest ploughlike through the air —
Thy wings so swift and slim,
Turned downward, darkly dim,
Like furrows on a ground of violets.

Nay, tell me not, my swallow,
But have thy pretty way,
And prosperously follow
The leading of the sunshine all the day.
Thy virtuous example
Maketh my foolish questions answer ample —
It is thy large delights keeps open wide
Thy little mouth; thou hast no pain to hide;
And when thou leavest all the green-topped woods
Pining below, and with melodious floods

Flatterest the heavy clouds, it is, I know,
Because, my bird, thou canst not choose but go
  Higher and ever higher
  Into the purple fire
That lights the morning meadows with heart's-ease,
And sticks the hill-sides full of primroses.

  But tell me, my good bird,
If thou canst tune thy tongue to any word,
Wherewith to answer — pray thee tell me this:
  Where gottest thou thy song,
  Still thrilling all day long,
Silvered to fragments by its very bliss!
  Not, as I guess,
  Of any whistling swain,
With cheek as richly russet as the grain
Sown in his furrows; nor, I further guess,
  Of any shepherdess,
  Whose tender heart did drag
Through the dim hollows of her golden flag
After a faithless love — while far and near,
  The waterfalls, to hear,
Clung by their white arms to the cold, deaf rocks,
  And all the unkempt flocks
  Strayed idly. Nay, I know,
If ever any love-lorn maid did blow
Of such a pitiful pipe, thou didst not get
In such sad wise thy heart to music set.

  So, lower not down to me
From its high home thy ever-busy wing;
I know right well thy song was shaped for thee
  By His unwearying power

Who makes the days about the Easter flower
Like gardens round the chamber of a king.
And whether, when the sobering year hath run
His brief course out, and thou away dost hie
To find thy pleasant summer company;
Or whether, my brown darling of the sun,
When first the South, to welcome up the May,
Hangs wide her saffron gate,
And thou, from the uprising of the day
Till eventide in shadow round thee closes,
Pourest thy joyance over field and wood,
As if thy very blood
Were drawn from out the young hearts of the roses —

'Tis all to celebrate,
And all to praise
The careful kindness of His gracious ways
Who builds the golden weather
So tenderly about thy houseless brood —
Thy unfledged, homeless brood, and thee together.

Ah! these are the sweet reasons,
My little swimmer of the seas of air,
Thou comest, goest, duly in thy season;
And furthermore, that all men everywhere
May learn from thy enjoyment
That that which maketh life most good and fair
Is heavenly employment.

In the very latest of her suffering days, Alice Cary longed with longings unutterable to bring back as a living presence to herself every scene which inspired those early songs. In her portfolio lie her last manuscripts just as she left them, copied, each one, several times, with a care and precision which, in her active and crowded days, she never attempted; copied in the new chirography which she compelled her hand to acquire, a few months before it was laid upon her breast, idle at last, in the rest of death. These late songs breathe none of the faintness of death. Rather they ring with the first lyric fervor; they cry out for, and call back, within the very shadow of the grave, the woman's first delights. Witness these in this "Cradle Song," copied three times by her own hand, and never before published.

CRADLE SONG.

All the air is white with snowing,
  Cold and white — cold and white;
Wide and wild the winds are blowing,
  Blowing, blowing wide and wild.
    Sweet little child, sweet little child,
    Sleep, sleep, sleep little child:
    Earth is dark, but heaven is bright —
    Sleep, sleep till the morning light:
    Some must watch, and some must weep,
    And some, little baby, some may sleep:
    So, good-night, sleep till light;
    Lullaby, lullaby, and good-night!

Folded hands on the baby bosom,
  Cheek and mouth rose-red, rose-sweet;
And like a bee's wing in a blossom,
  Beat, beat, beat and beat,
  So the heart keeps going, going,
  While the winds in the bitter snowing

Meet and cross — cross and meet —
Heaping high, with many an eddy,
Bars of stainless chalcedony
  All in curves about the door,
  Where shall fall no more, no more,
  Longed-for steps, so light, so light.
Little one, sleep till the moon is low,
  Sleep, and rock, and take your rest;
Winter clouds will snow and snow,
  And the winds blow east, and the winds blow west:
Some must come, and some must go,
And the earth be dark, and the heavens be bright:
  Never fear, baby dear,
Wrong things lose themselves in right;
  Never fear, mother is here,
Lullaby, lullaby, and good-night.

O good saint, that thus emboldenest
  Eyes bereaved to see, to-night,
Cheek the rosiest, hair the goldenest,
  Ever gladdened the mother sight.
Blessed art thou to hide the willow,
  Waiting and weeping over the dead,
With the softest, silkenest pillow
  Ever illumined hair o'erspread.
Never had cradle such a cover;
  All my house with light it fills;
Over and under, under and over,
  'Broidered leaves of the daffodils!
All away from the winter weather,
  Baby, wrapt in your 'broideries bright,
Sleep, nor watch any more for father —
  Father will not come home to-night.

Angels now are round about him,
   In the heavenly home on high;
We must learn to do without him —
   Some must live, and some must die.
   Baby, sweetest ever was born,
   Shut little blue eyes, sleep till morn:
   Rock and sleep, and wait for the light,
   Father will not come home to-night.
Winter is wild, but winter closes;
The snow in the nest of the bird will lie,
And the bird must have its little cry;
Yet the saddest day doth swiftly run,
Up o'er the black cloud shines the sun,
And when the reign of the frost is done
The May will come with roses, roses —
Green-leaved grass, and red-leaved roses —
Roses, roses, roses, roses,
Roses red, and lilies white.
Sleep little baby, sleep, sleep;
Some must watch, and some must weep;
Sweetly sleep till the morning light,
Lullaby, lullaby, and good-night.

By its side lies another manuscript, evidently written later. In it the same erect, clear writing is attempted, but the hand wavered and would not obey the will; the lines tremble, and at last grow indistinct. The poem begun was never finished. As the failing hand, the yearning soul left it, word by word, it is here given: —

Give me to see, though only in a dream,
Though only in an unsubstantial dream,

The dear old cradle lined with leaves of moss,
And daily changed from cradle into cross,
What time athwart its dull brown wood, a beam
Slid from the gold deeps of the sunset shore,
Making the blur of twilight white and fair,
Like lilies quivering in the summer air;
And my low pillow like a rose full-blown.

O, give mine eyes to see once more, once more,
My longing eyes to see this one time more,
The shadows trembling with the wings of bats,
And dandelions dragging to the door,
And speckling all the grass about the door,
With the thick spreading of their starry mats.

Give me to see, I pray and can but pray,
O, give me but to see to-day, to-day,
The little brown-walled house where I was born;
The gray old barn, the cattle-shed close by,
The well-sweep, with its angle sharp and high;
The flax field, like a patch of fallen sky;
The millet harvest, colored like the corn,
Like to the ripe ears of the new husked corn.

And give mine eyes to see among the rest
This rustic picture, in among the rest,
For there and only there it doth belong,
I, at fourteen, and in my Sunday best,
Reading with voice unsteady my first song,
The rugged verses of my first rude song.

As a ballad writer she was never equaled by any American man or woman. She loved the ballad, and there is ever in hers a *naive*, arch grace of utterance, inimitable. In the ballad, hers was the very luxury of song. She never waited for a rhyme. Her rhythm rippled and ran with the fervor and fullness of a mountain brook after the springtime rains. Never quite overtaking it, she yet leaped and ran and sang with it in ever new delight. What a wild thrilling rush is there in such lines as these: —

"Haste, good boatman! haste!" she cried,
"And row me over the other side!"
And she stript from her finger the shining ring,
And gave it me for the ferrying.

"Woe's me! my Lady, I may not go,
For the wind is high and th' tide is low,
And rocks like dragons lie in the wave, —
Slip back on your finger the ring you gave!"

"Nay, nay! for the rocks will be melted down,
And the waters, they never will let me drown,
And the wind a pilot will prove to thee,
For my dying lover, he waits for me!"

Then bridle-ribbon and silver spur
She put in my hand, but I answered her:
"The wind is high and the tide is low, —
I must not, dare not, and will not go!"

Her face grew deadly white with pain,
And she took her champing steed by th' mane,
And bent his neck to th' ribbon and spur
That lay in my hand, — but I answered her:

"Though you should proffer me twice and thrice
Of ring and ribbon and steed the price, —
The leave of kissing your lily-like hand!
I never could row you safe to th' land."

"Then God have mercy!" she faintly cried,
"For my lover is dying the other side!
O cruel, O cruellest Gallaway,
Be parted, and make me a path, I pray!"

Of a sudden, the sun shone large and bright
As if he were staying away the night,
And the rain on the river fell as sweet
As the pitying tread of an angel's feet.

And spanning the water from edge to edge
A rainbow stretched like a golden bridge,
And I put the rein in her hand so fair,
And she sat in her saddle th' queen o' th' air.

And over the river, from edge to edge,
She rode on the shifting and shimmering bridge,
And landing safe on the farther side, —
"Love is thy conqueror, Death!" she cried.

The following is, perhaps, a more characteristic illustration of the pensive naturalness of her usual manner. Amid scores, it simply represents her utter ease of rhythm; the blended realism and idealism of her thoughts and feelings: —

And Margaret set her wheel aside,
And breaking off her thread,

Went forth into the harvest-field
  With her pail upon her head, —

Her pail of sweetest cedar-wood,
  With shining yellow bands,
Through clover, lifting its red tops
  Almost unto her hands.

Her ditty flowing on the air,
  For she did not break her song,
And the water dripping o'er th' grass,
  From her pail as she went along, —

Over the grass that said to her,
  Trembling through all its leaves,
"A bright rose for some harvester
  To bind among his sheaves!"

And clouds of gay green grasshoppers
  Flew up the way she went,
And beat their wings against their sides,
  And chirped their discontent.

And the blackbird left the piping of
  His amorous, airy glee,
And put his head beneath his wing, —
  An evil sign to see.

The meadow-herbs, as if they felt
  Some secret wound, in showers
Shook down their bright buds till her way
  Was ankle-deep with flowers.

Her personal acquaintance with all the flowers and herbs of wood and field was as intimate as that she had with people. She never generalizes in writing of them, but sets each one in her verse as she would in a vase, with the most delicate consciousness of its blending lights and shades. A young Southern lady, who from childhood has been a loving student of Alice Cary's poetry, remarked at her funeral, that she believed she could find each flower of our Middle States, and many of those of the South, mentioned with appreciation in some part of Alice Cary's poems.

Yet nothing in her music touches one so nearly as its manifold variations of the hymn of human life — now tender, pathetic, and patient; now grand with resignation and faith, uttered always with a child-like simplicity; telling, most of all, how the human heart can love and suffer, how it can believe and find rest. It was her all-embracing pity, her yearning love for the entire race of Adam, which made her song a personal power, an ever present consolation to thousands of human souls who never measured her by any rule of poetic art. A friend who had loved her long, writing of her after death, said: —

"Having passed one day from her chamber of anguish, musing upon her despondency at being thus laid aside from active employment, we recounted her words at the bedside of another sufferer, who had never seen the afflicted poet. The latter, in reply, drew her common-place book from beneath her pillow, and pointed to poem after poem by Alice Cary, which had been her solace during weary months and years of sickness and pain, and bade us give her greeting of gratitude to that unknown but beloved benefactor. Thus does the All-seeing Father bless our unconscious influence, and often make our seeming helplessness more potent for good than our best hours of purposed effort."

If the scrap-books of the land could to-day be drawn forth from their receptacles, we should find that Alice Cary has a place as a poet in the hearts of the people, which no mere critic in his grandeur has ever allowed. Nor would these scrap-books be solely the property of "gushing" girls, and tearful women. The heart of man responds scarcely less to her music. One of the most eminent and learned of living statesmen remarked, since her death, "It seems as if I had read almost every poem that Alice Cary has ever written: at least my scrap-book is full of them."

There is no sadder inequality than that which exists often between the estimate an author places upon some work that has been wrought from his soul and brain, and the one placed on it by a careless reader, or the average public. It is the very tissue of being, the life-blood of one. To the other, often, it is but mere words; or, at most, an inartistic performance, whose best fate is to be superficially read and quickly forgotten. Nor is it the fault of this public that it is all unknowing of the time and tears, the patience and sorrow and love often inwrought in the book which it so lightly passes over. It has nothing to do with the individual life of the author; yet no less its thoughtless and sometimes unjust judgment makes one of the hard facts of human life. There never was a more touching illustration of this than in Alice Cary's feeling toward her little book of poems called "A Lover's Diary," published by Ticknor and Fields, in 1868, and the average reception of it. To the newspaper noticer it seemed but a tame collection of love-songs, never thrilling and often wearisome. This was the most that it was to many. To her it was her soul's flower laid upon the grave of her darling — the young sister who for so many years was the soul of her soul and the life of her life. It is the portrait of this sister (though casting but a dim shadow of her living loveliness) which graces the front of the book; and the dedication below it, so simple, unfeigned, sorrowful, and loving, is one of the most touching utterances in literature.

Here, and not here!
When following care about my house I tread
Sadly, and all so slowly,
There often seemeth to be round me spread
A blessed light, as if the place were holy;
And then thou art near.

Lost, and not lost!
When silence taketh in the night her place,
And I my soul deliver
All to sweet dreaming of thy sovereign grace,
I see the green hills on beyond the river
Thy feet have crossed.

And so, my friend,
I have and hold thee all the while I wait,
Musing and melancholy;
And so these songs to thee I dedicate,
Whose song shall flow henceforth serene and holy,
Life without end.

For dear, dear one,
Even as a traveller, doomed alone to go

Through some wild wintry valley,
Takes in his poor, rude hand the wayside snow
And shapes it to the likeness of a lily,
So have I done;

The while I wove
Lays that to men's minds haply might recall
Some bower of bliss unsaddened,
Moulding and modulating one and all
Upon thy life, so many lives that gladdened
With light and love.

Elmina Cary, the youngest child of Robert and Elizabeth Cary, seemed to take the place in Alice's heart and care, filled by the little sister Lucy in her youth. Elmina, who was married in early girlhood to Mr. Alexander Swift of Cincinnati, in her health very soon showed symptoms of the family fate. Marked by death at twenty, she lingered eleven years. A portion of this time her home was in New York. The air of Cincinnati was harsh for her, and needing always in her decline the ministry of her sisters, she spent much time with them, and died in their home. She was especially dependent upon Alice, as Phœbe says: "Greatly her junior, and of feeble frame, she was her peculiar care, a sister, child, and darling." She slowly faded from the earth, day by day growing lovelier to the last. She had the face and nature of Alice, touched with the softness of dependence, and the delicate contour of youth. She was of especial loveliness, with a face to inspire a painter: oval, olive-tinted, crowned with masses of dark hair, lit with a pair of dark eyes as steadfast as planets and as shining as stars. All innocence and tenderness, many friends of Alice and Phœbe remember this younger sister as the gentlest genius of their household. She possessed the gift divine of her family — was a poet in temperament and heart, as she must have been in utterance, had she lived. As it was, she wiled away many hours and years of pain in weaving together the ballads and hymns and artless stories of life, which thronged her heart and brain.

Wearing "the rose of womanhood" in perfect loveliness, she faded away from the world, leaving no sign save in the hearts that loved her. There are women striving now to gather into their ripening souls the grace of patience, and that bright serenity which is its finest charm, who feel that it is easier to reach because she lived and because they loved her. And there are men wrestling in the world, their days crowded with its weary affairs, who nevertheless carry this woman's memory like a flower in their hearts, thanking God for it. For no man finds in a woman's soul the revelation of a rarer self, receiving it into his heart as the incentive toward a better life, who ever loses it wholly, or who ever forgets the gentle face that was its visible type.

When, in 1862, she died, Alice wrote: "My darling is dead. My hands are empty; my work seems done." From that hour, till the "Lover's Diary" was published in 1868, Alice, amid her arduous toils, was writing these songs in her praise, and for her sake.

When the book was done, she laid it in the hand of a friend, saying, with tears in her eyes, "It will be something to you, for you knew *her*." Its prevailing fault is its monotony. The sameness of its rhythm, and the constant repetition of one name, is sure to tire a reader after a few consecutive pages, if he knows nothing of its history, and never knew or loved personally its subject. And yet no appreciator of true poetry can turn over its leaves without a constantly recurring sense of surprise at the exquisite beauty of phrase, and tenderness of rhythm running through the minor lyrics. Phœbe says of them: "I do not know how this book may affect others; but to me some of the poems have a most tearful and touching pathos. 'Mona Sick' is perhaps one of the saddest and sweetest." Read as the rhythmic utterance of absolute truth — the heart's real cry over a loved one dying, and that loved one a sister — what a sacred sound these lines take on!

"Low lying in her pallid pain,
A flower that thirsts and dies for rain,
  I see her night and day:
And every heart-beat is a cry,
And every breath I breathe a sigh —
  O, for the May, the May!

. . . .

"All the dreaming is broken through;
Both what is done and undone I rue.
Nothing is steadfast and nothing true,
But your love for me and my love for you,
  My dearest, dear little heart.

"The time is weary, the year is old,
The light o' the lily burns close to the mould;
The grave is cruel, the grave is cold,
But the other side is the city of gold,
  My dearest, dear little heart."

Coldly as this little book was received at its publication, more of its lyrics are afloat on the great newspaper sea to-day than ever before; while several of them have been incorporated in standard books of poetry. There is one, than which Charles Kingsley or Alfred Tennyson never sang a sweeter, which has drifted to Europe and back, and been appropriated in a hundred ways, whose last stanza runs: —

"The fisher droppeth his net in the stream,
And a hundred streams are the same as one;
And the maiden dreameth her love-lit dream;
And what is it all, when all is done?
The net of the fisher the burden breaks,
And always the dreaming the dreamer wakes."

It was in attempting to deal with more material and cruder forces that Alice Cary failed. In the more comprehensive sense, she never learned the world. In her novels, attempting to portray the faults and passions of men and women, we find her rudest work. Her mastery of quaintness, of fancy, of naturalistic beauty penetrated with pathetic longing, tinged with a clear psychological light, revealing the soul of nature and of human life from within, all give to her unaffected utterances an inexpressible charm. But the airy touch, the subtle insight, which translated into music the nature which she knew, stumbled and fell before the conflicting deformity of depraved humanity. The dainty imagination which decked her poetic forms with such exquisite grace could not stand in the stead of actual knowledge; usurping its prerogative, it degenerated into caricature. She held in herself the primal power to portray human life in its most complex relations, and most profound significance. She missed the leisure and the experience which together would have given her the mastery of that power. It wrestled with false, and sometimes unworthy material. The sorrows and wrongs of woman, the injustice of man, the highest possibilities of human nature, she longed to embody them all in the forms of enduring art. A life already nearly consumed, sickness, weariness, and death, said No. Her novels are strong with passages of intense feeling; we feel through them the surges of a wild, unchained power; but as broad, comprehensive portraitures of human life, as the finest exponents of the noble nature from which they emanated, they are often unworthy of her. In interpreting nature, she never failed. Her "Clovernook Stories," her first in prose which reproduced perfectly the life that she knew, are pure idyls of country life and character, and in their fresh, original charm deserve their place amid the classics of English speech. In the utterance of natural emotion, crossed in its very pathos with psychical thought, surely she was never surpassed. I give an illustration from "An Old Maid's Story," in her "Pictures of Country Life."

"When he spoke of the great hereafter, when our souls that had crossed their mates, perhaps, and perhaps left them behind, or gone unconsciously before them, dissatisfied and longing and faltering all the time; and of the deep of joy they would enter into on recognizing fully and freely the other self, which, in this world, had been so poorly and vaguely comprehended, if at all; what delicious tremor, half fear and half fervor, thrilled all my being, and made me feel that the dust of time and the barriers of circumstance, the dreary pain of a life separated from all others, death itself, all were nothing but shadows passing between me and the eternal sunshine of love. I could afford to wait, I could afford to be patient under my burdens, and to go straight forward through all hard fates and fortunes, assured that I should know and be known at last, love and be loved in the fullness of a blessedness, which, even here, mixed with bitterness as it is, is the sweetest of all. What was it to me that my hair was black, and my step firm, while his hair to whom I listened so reverentially was white, and his step slow, if not feeble. What was it that he had more wisdom, and more experience than I, and what was it that he never said, 'You are faintly recognized, and I see a germ close-folded, which in the mysterious processes of God's providence may unfold a great white flower.' We had but crossed each other in the long journey, and I was satisfied, for I felt that in our traversing up the ages, we should meet again."

Another strong quality in much of her prose is its sturdy common sense. In her the poetical temperament never impinged on a keen, unclouded judgment. In dealing with all practical matters she was one of the most practical of women. She betrays this quality in the utter directness with which she meets and answers many questions concerning every-day life and character. The last article in prose which she ever wrote, printed in the "New York Independent," was thus referred to by its editor: —

"Lying upon her sick-bed, she who had never eaten the bread of idleness wrote for us the pungent denunciation of 'Shirks,' that appeared in the paper of February 2d. It was probably her very last article, and after that the weary hand that knew no shirking was still. She intended it to be the first of a series of 'semi-didactic articles' — so she wrote us."

It contained these words: —

"Blessed, indeed, is that roof-tree which has no fungus attachment, and blessed the house that has no dilapidated chair and third-rate bed reserved in some obscure corner for poor Uncle John, or Aunt Nancy! To be sure, there are Uncle Johns and Aunt Nancys who are honestly poor, and legitimately dependent — not guilty, but simply unfortunate. It is not of such, however, that I am discoursing; they will come under another head. It is of that sort that go not out, even through fasting and prayer — your '*truly-begotten shirks.*'

"Talk of divine rights! They are quite beyond that; they do not seek to justify themselves. 'Dick, the rascal, has more than he knows how to spend!' says John. 'He will never miss the little I shall eat and drink.' And so it happens that a lank, dirty, coarse-shirted man, with an ill-flavored budget under his arm, and poverty of blood — for he is poor all through — skulks into John's house some morning; and woe the day, for he never goes out. And after that, 'eternal vigilance is the price' at which his snuffy handkerchief, clay pipe, and queer old hat are kept out of the drawing-room.

"And after the same fashion Aunt Nancy quarters herself upon Susan; bringing with her, perhaps, a broken-boned and flyaway cotton umbrella, a bandbox, and some old-fashioned duds that were the finery of her girlhood. There is some feeling of rebellion, some feeble effort toward riddance, on the part of the householders; but they are rich, and their doom is on them. And by and by things settle into unquiet quiet; and John and Nancy are tolerated, if not accepted — being, whenever their habitual aggressiveness is inordinately aggravated, gotten back with gentle force into their accustomed dens. Thus, facing no responsibility, assuming no position in society, nor even in the household, recognizing no duty, they are dragged along. And when that call comes to which they perforce must answer, Here am I — that event that happeneth unto all, for which there is no evasion and no substitute — they simply disappear. The world was no richer while they stayed, and it is no poorer now that they are gone. No single heart is bereft, even. The worm has eaten all the meat out of the shell, and has perished of the surfeit and of indolence; and why should mourners go about the streets?"

Alice Cary was emphatically a worker, yet she never for a moment believed that mere industry could supply the lack of a mental gift. In an article of great power written for "Packard's Monthly," she replied to Mr. Greeley on this subject, taking issue against him. It contained the following paragraph: —

"I do not believe that a man always passes, in the long run, for what he is worth. It seems to me a hard saying. The vision that the poet or the painter transcribes and leaves a joy and a wonder to all time, may, I believe, have come all the same to some poor, unlettered man, who, lacking the external faculty, so to speak, could not lay it in all its glorious shape and color on the canvas, or catch and hold it in the fastness of immortal verse. No, I cannot give up my comfortable faith, that in other worlds and far-off ages there will appear a shining multitude who shall, through death, have come to themselves, and have found expression denied them on earth: beautiful souls, whose bodies were their prisons — who stammered or stood dumb among their kind, bearing alone the slights and disgraces of fortune, and all the while conscious, in their dread isolation, of being peers of the poets and the kings, and of all the royal men and women of the world."

Alice Cary lived to pass into that serene spiritual atmosphere which outlies the emotions and passions of youth; where, in having outlived its love and sorrow, its loss and longing, no shadow fell between her soul and the Illimitable Love. Her "Thoughts and Theories" and "Hymns," contained in the volume of her poems published by Hurd and Houghton, 1866, were chiefly the utterances of this period of her life. They called forth thousands of expressions of personal thanks and regard from all over the land, and yet they failed of universal recognition in the mere world of literature. They won little or no praise in places from whence she had a right to expect it. She considered them the best expressions of her mature power; and the comparatively cold reception which she thought they received, especially from some of her personal friends, was a cause of grief. Aside from all sympathy of friendship, my opinion is that these poems never received justice. Yet the cause was scarcely with friends or in the public; but was a part of the untoward conditions of her life. She was forced to write too much. Her name was seen in print too often. This is one of the heaviest penalties which genius incurs in earning its living by a pen. Its name comes to have a market value, and is sold and used for that. Mere newspaper work, if tolerably well done, can bear this test for a long time. But it is death to poetry to write it "on time," or to sell it in advance for a name. Necessity forced Alice to do this so often that, while her name never lost its hold upon the masses, it came to be rated lower in the estimation of critics, and in some sense her sweetest lyrics sink to the value of rhymes in the minds of her friends. Many loved Alice as a friend, who ranked her low as a poet; and she knew it. But, heavy as the outer tax upon it was, the deep inner spring of her inspiration never failed; from it chiefly flowed the poems in this book. Yet the excess of her daily labor was so much taken from its chances of success. Some of her warmest personal friends scarcely took the trouble to look within its covers, to see whether it contained rhymes or poems. They drank tea at her table, they waxed eloquent in her parlor, they knew Alice that she was one of the noblest and sweetest of women; after that, what did it matter what she thought, or felt, or did!

They never dreamed that, when the lights were out, and the bright parlor closed, the woman sometimes sat down and wept for the word of encouragement that was not spoken, for the little meed of appreciation that was not proffered, which, could it have come from those whose judgment she valued, would have been new life and inspiration to her amid her ceaseless toil.

No less this book of poems holds in thought and utterance many of the elements of enduring existence. It must live, because it is poetry, embodying in exquisite rhythm and phrase the soul of nature and of human life; live in the heart of the future when we who criticised it, or passed it by, are dead and forgotten.

CHAPTER VII.

ALICE'S LAST SUMMER.

We have many proofs that a life devoted to letters is favorable to longevity in women. With all the anxiety and care of following literature as a profession, with all the toil of obtaining a livelihood by it, they have as a rule lived to venerable years. A passionate yearning for continued human existence was a ruling characteristic of Alice Cary to her last conscious hour. She had inherited a constitutional tendency from her mother, which was unfavorable to robust health or to long life. Yet with different habits of work and of life, established early and persistently pursued, even she might have won the longed-for lease of life, and have added another to the list of venerable names, whom we delight to venerate among women of letters. Truly, some proof of this is to be found in the fact that her brothers, sons of the same mother, who have spent their lives on and near the old homestead farm in active, out-door, farmer life, are to-day strong, healthy, and robust men.

Alice and Phœbe could not have been farmers, but in their twenty years of life in the city they could have followed, nearer than they did, the out-of-doors habits of their old country home. These barefooted rovers in country lanes, who grow up fostered by sunshine, air, and sky, the intimate friends of bees and birds, of horses and cows, of the cunning workers of the ground and the murmuring nations of the summer air; these lovers of common flowers with common names; these rural queens who reigned supreme in their own kingdom, whose richest revenue to the day of their death was drawn from the wealth of nature left so far behind, in the full flower of their womanhood came to the great city, and began a new life, which the vitality of the old enabled them to endure for twenty years, but which drew constantly on their vital springs, without adding one drop to the sources of physical health. To attain the highest success which they sought, they needed both the attrition and opportunities of the city. Had they added to this new life, for a third of every year, their old pastimes and old pursuits, they might have added years to their existence. But no human being, city bred, much less one country born, could have maintained the highest health or have prolonged existence in the hot air, with the sedentary habits, which made the daily life of Alice and Phœbe Cary for many years. The new life encroached upon the old vitality imperceptibly, and not until the very last year of their lives was either of them conscious of the fatal harm it had wrought. They exchanged the country habits and the familiar out-of-door haunts of the old farm for the roar of streets and the confining air of a city house. Moreover, modest as this house was, it took much money to support it in such a place. This was all to be earned by the pen, and for many years it was earned almost exclusively by Alice. With her natural independence, her fear of financial obligation, her hatred of debt, her desire for a com petency, her generous hospitality, it is easy to see how heavy was the yoke of work which she wore. Dear soul! she might have made it lighter, could she have believed it. As it was, even to the last she was never free from its weight. There came a time when her personal life was work, work, work. Then there was the shadow of death always on the house. Elmina, the youngest darling of all, was fading day by day from before their eyes. Her outgoings were infrequent and uncertain. The leisure moments of Alice and Phœbe were spent with her in her room. As she slowly faded, her sisters became more exclusively devoted to her. At last it came to pass that Alice rarely left the house except on some errand of necessity.

After Elmina's death, as the summers came round, she became more and more loth to leave her city home to go any where into the country. Not that her heart had let go of its old love of natural beauty, but because she came to dread journeys and the annoyance and inconvenience of travelling. What had been a necessity at times, during Elmina's life, remained a habit after her death. By this time Alice had herself merged into the invalid of the family. The crisis had come when nature demanded change, recreation, and rest. She turned her back on all. When her friends were away, scattered among the hills and by the sea, Alice, left alone behind her closed blinds, was working harder and more continuously than ever.

The stifling summers waxed and waned, the thermometer would rise and glare at 100°, cars and stages would rattle beneath her windows, but through all the fiery heat, through all the wearing thunder of the streets, the tireless brain held on its fearful tension, and would not let go. Phœbe would spend a month in the country, and return with sea-weeds and mountain mosses and glowing cheeks and eyes, as trophies; but not so would Alice. Not that she never left the city. She did sometimes, for a few days, but it was in a brief, protesting way, that had neither time nor chance to work her help or cure. As the sedentary habits of her life increased, and the circulation of her blood lowered, she had recourse more and more to artificial heat, till at last she and Phœbe lived in a temperature which in itself was enough to make health impossible. In the relaxed condition inevitably produced by this furnace atmosphere, they were sometimes compelled to go into the out-door air, and more than one acute attack of sickness was the result to both sisters.

These years of protracted labor, unbroken by recreation, unblessed by the resuscitating touch of nature's healing hand, brought to Alice, shy and shrinking from birth, greater shrinking, keener suffering, and a more abiding loneliness. She was never selfishly isolated. There was never a moment in her life when tears did not spring to her eyes, and help from her hand at the sight of suffering in any living thing. She would go half-way to meet any true soul. She never failed in faith or devotion to her friends. No less as the years went on, she felt interiorly more and more alone; she shrank more into her own inward life, and more and more from all personal contact with the great unknown world outside of her own existence. She had settled so deeply into one groove of life and labor, there seemed to be no mortal power that could wrest her out of it. She worked much, but it was not work that harmed her; she was sick, but was not sick enough to die. The shadow of death, falling from her mother's life across so many of her sisters, was creeping slowly, surely up to her. No less there was a time when it was in her power to have gone beyond it, out into the sunshine. She needed sunshine; she needed fresher, freer, purer air; she needed change and rest. She needed a will, wiser and more potent than her own, to convince her of the inexorable laws of human life, and then compel her to their obedience. She could never have entirely escaped the inevitable penalty of hereditary law; but that she might have delayed it to the outer line which marks the allotted time of average human life, no one finally believed more utterly than she did. Her disobedience of the laws of life was the result of circumstance, of condition and of temperament, rarely a willful fact; no less she paid the penalty — by her so reluctantly, so protestingly, so pathetically paid — her life.

At last, all that she had she would have given for her life, her human life, but it was too late. I dwell on the fact, for thousands are following her example, and are hurrying on to her fate. We hear so much of people dying of work. Yet work rarely kills man or woman. If it is work at all, it is work done in violation of the primeval laws of life; it is work which a compelling will wrings out from a dying or overtaxed body.

Another summer — her last; the ceaseless, eager worker, how was it with her now? The low, quick rustle of her garments was no longer heard upon the stairs. The graceful form no longer bent over her desk; the face no longer turned from it, with the old thrilling glance of welcome, to the favored comet allowed to pass the guarded door sacred to consecrated toil.

That winter of mortal anguish had done more to wreck Alice Cary, than all the years which she had lived before. The rounded contours were wasted, the abundant locks, just touched with gray, were bleached white, the colorless skin was tightly drawn upon the features; for the first time she looked a wreck of her former self. Yet she was a beautiful wreck; the splendor of her eyes made her that. No agony, no grief, had been able to make their lustre less: till they closed in death, their tender glory never went out. She was almost a helpless prisoner now. She could not take a step save on crutches. She could not stir without help. Yet that which no power of entreaty could move her to do the summer before, she now longed to do at any hazard. The thunder of the streets had become intolerable to her tortured nerves and brain. The very friends who had urged her to leave the city the year before, now believed, in her helpless condition, that her going would be impossible. No less she went, — first to Northampton.

A correspondent of the "New York Tribune" writes thus of her appearance at Round Hill: —

"Alice, during a few weeks past, has been used to sit on the same east porch, when the sunsets have been particularly fine, and then the cane-seat rocking-chair of the dark eyed poetess has become a sort of throne. A respectful little group has always been gathered about it, and whenever it used to be whispered about of an evening, that Alice Cary had come out, somehow the tide of promenaders used to set more and more in that direction, but always in a quiet and reticent manner, just to get a glimpse of her, you know, while accidentally passing her chair. I believe that she dropped among the Round Hill people early one day in August, and was so quiet that she was regarded as a sort of myth by most of the frequenters of the place, never going into the dining-room nor into the great parlor, bigger than a barn; but the people said she was there, and that she invested the house with an unusual interest. Her city home, however snugly appointed, cannot, I am sure, compensate one like her for the loss of country air, country sights, and country sounds." This writer apparently realized not her helpless state. At that time she could not rise in her chair to take her crutches without assistance. Yet as she sat there with the scarlet shawl thrown over her white robe, contrasting so vividly with pallid face and brilliant eyes, she made a lovely picture, to which many allusions have been made in public print since she passed away. The following is from Laura Redden ("Howard Glyndon"), a woman who, under life-long affliction, embodies in her own character the beautiful patience and peace which she felt so intuitively and perfectly in our friend.

"I knew her in every way, except through her own personality. I knew her through others; through her writings; through the interpretation of my own heart; and I remember very well, that once, when broken in health and saddened in spirit, I felt an undefinable impulse to go to her, and knew that it would do me good to do so. But I stopped, and asked myself, 'Will it do *her* any good? What can I give in return for what I take?' And I dismissed the impulse as selfish. I had, in spirit, gone up to the very door that stood between us, and after hesitating, as I stood beside it, I went away. But while I stood there, I thought of the meek, sweet sufferer on the other side. 'She has so much more to crush her than I have, but she does not let herself be crushed,' I said. Then I felt ashamed and went away, resolving to murmur less, and to struggle more for strength and patience. I really believe that standing on the other side of the door did me almost as much good as going in would have done.

"Later, when I came to Northampton, I found that she was under the same roof with me. But when some one said, 'Would you like to see her?' and it seemed as if the door stood ajar, I drew back, without knowing why, and said, 'No, not now.'

"Once, when I sat reading under the trees, she came out leaning upon her two friends, one on each side. They spread a gay shawl on the grass for her, and she sat there under the shining light which came through the trees, and enjoyed the delicious calm of a cool, summer, Sabbath afternoon. How pale and worn and weak she looked, but how bright and unselfish through it all! I watched her, unseen, and I prayed very earnestly that God would bless the pure country air and the country quiet to her. She thought then that they made her better; but there were greener pastures and purer breezes in store for her, and she was not to stay long away from them.

"I remember another evening that she came out on the east porch, and sat long in the dusk of the twilight. I sat so close that my garments brushed hers — but in the dark — quiet, unseen, and unknown; and I was glad to have it so. Somehow there was an undefin able charm in holding this relation to a person in whom I had so large an interest. It was so much better to feel that I knew her than it would have been to realize that she knew me. It seemed as if formal words would have taken away all this charm. Whenever my hand was upon the handle of the door, I drew it away again and said, 'Wait!'

"When I heard the next morning that she was gone, I was sorry — not sorry that I had not spoken to her, but only sorry that she was gone. The place had lost half its beauty for me."

Alice, who had promised a dear friend to visit her in her home in Northern Vermont, went thither from Northampton. Faithful hands served her, strong, gentle arms bore her on, in this last struggle for life. "How I was ever to get out of the cars, I did not know; the thought of it filled me with dread and terror," she said, "but there was —— to lift me out and carry me to the carriage. I never felt a jar, and when I sat down in the bay-window, and saw the view before it, and felt the loving kindness which enveloped me, it seemed as if I had reached heaven."

These words are written in that room in which she sat by the window where she afterwards wrote her "Invalid's Plea." From this bay-window in which she sat, she looked through a vista of maples out upon a broad expanse of meadow-lawn, whose velvet turf is of the most vivid malachite green, softened on its farther edge by a grove wherein the shades of spruce and pine, elm and maple, contrast and blend. Beyond these woods Lake Memphremagog sets its glittering shield between the hills. On its farther side green mountains arise till they hold the white clouds on their heads. Below, Jay Peak stands over four thousand feet above the sea, while above, Owl's Head soars over three thousand, covered with forest to its summit. It is a picture fit for Paradise. Yet it is but one glimpse amid many of the inexpressible beauty of this lake and mountain country of the North. She, sitting here, looked out upon this consummate scene; looked with her tender, steadfast eyes across these emerald meadows, to the lake shining upon her through the opening hills, to the mountains smiling down on her from the distant heaven, their keen amethyst notching the deep, deep blue of a cloudless sky. The splendor of this northern world fell upon her like a new, divine revelation. The tonic in its atmosphere touched her feeble pulses; the peace brooding in its stillness penetrated her aching brain with the promise of a new life. Without, the world was full of tranquillity; within, it was full of affection and the words of loving kindness. Then she wondered (and her wonder was sad with a hopeless regret) why summer after summer she had lingered in her city home, till the crash and roar of the streets, coming through her open windows, had filled body and brain with torture.

"How blind I was!" she exclaimed. "I said that I could not take the time from my work; and now life has neither time nor work left for me. How much more, how much better I could have worked, had I rested. If I am spared, how differently I will do. I will come here every summer, and *live.*"

Alas! before another summer, the winter snow had

wrapped her forever from the earthly sight of this un utterable beauty.

Hers from the beginning was the fatal mistake of so many brain-workers — that all time given to refreshment and rest is so much taken from the results of labor; forgetting, or not realizing, that the finer the instrument, the more fatal the effects of undue strain, the more imperative the necessity of avoiding overwear and the perpetual jar of discordant conditions; forgetting, also, that the rarest flowering of the brain has its root in silence and beauty and rest.

Here in this window, whither she, wasted and suffering, had been borne by gentle arms, our dear friend wrote her "Invalid's Plea," one of the most touching of her many touching lyrics: —

"O Summer! my beautiful, beautiful Summer,
I look in thy face and I long so to live;
But ah! hast thou room for an idle new-comer,
With all things to take and with nothing to give?
With all things to take of thy dear loving kindness —
The wine of thy sunshine, the dew of thy air;
And with nothing to give but the deafness and blindness
Begot in the depths of an utter despair?
The little green grasshopper, weak as we deem her,
Chirps day in and out for the sweet right to live;
And canst thou, O Summer! make room for a dreamer,
With all things to take and with nothing to give —
Room only to wrap her hot cheeks in thy shadows,
And all on thy daisy-fringed pillow to lie,
And dream of the gates of the glorious meadows,
Where never a rose of the roses shall die?"

CHAPTER VIII.

ALICE'S DEATH AND BURIAL.

WHEN a dear one, dying willingly, lets go of life, the loosened hands by so much reconcile us to their going. It was not so with Alice. Through physical suffering almost beyond precedent, through days and nights and years of hopeless illness, she yet clung to this life. Not through any lack of faith in the other and higher; but because it seemed to her that she had not yet exhausted the possibilities, the fullness, and sweetness of this. She thought that there was a fruition in life, in its labor, its love, which she had never realized; and even in dying she longed for it.

The autumn before her death, in a poem entitled, "The Flight of the Birds," she uttered this prayer:—

"Therefore I pray, and can but pray,
Lord, keep and bring them back when May
Shall come, with shining train,
Thick 'broiderèd with leaves of wheat,
And butterflies, and field-pinks sweet,
And yellow bees, and rain.

"Yea, bring them back across the seas
In clouds of golden witnesses—
The grand, the grave, the gay;

And, if thy holy will it be,
Keep me alive, once more to see
The glad and glorious day."

It could not be. "The golden witnesses" could only chant their spring music above her couch of final rest. Yet within one month of death, she was busier than ever with plans of happiness for others. "O! if God only *could* let me live ten years longer," she said; "it seems as if I wouldn't ask for any more time. I would live such a different life. I would never shut myself up in myself again. *Then* I would do something for my friends!"

Phœbe, writing of her last days, says:—

"Though loving and prizing whatever is good and lovely here, and keeping firm and tender hold of the things that are seen, yet she always reached one hand to grasp the unseen and eternal. She believed that God is not far from any one of us, and that the sweet communion of friends who are only separated by the shadowy curtain of death, might still remain unbroken.

"During her last year of illness she delighted much in the visits of her friends; entered with keenest zest into their hopes and plans, and liked to hear of all that was going on in the world from which she was now shut. She talked much of a better country with those who came to talk to her upon the land to which her steps drew near; and so catholic and free from prejudice was her spirit, that many of those friends whom she loved best, and with whom she held the most sacred communion, differed widely from herself in their religious faith.

"She loved to listen to the reading of poetry and of

pleasant stories, but not latterly to anything of an exciting or painful nature; and often wanted to hear the most tender and comforting chapters of the Gospels, especially those which tell of the Saviour's love for women. At the beginning of each month she had been accustomed for some time to furnishing a poem to one of our city papers. On the first of that month of which she never saw the ending, she was unable to write or even to dictate. A whole week had gone by, when, speaking suddenly one day with something of the old energy, she asked to be placed in her chair, and to have her portfolio, saying, "That article must be ready to-day." She was helped from the bed as she desired, and, though unable to sit up without being carefully supported, she completed the task to which she had set herself. The last stanza she wrote reads thus:—

"'As the poor panting hart to the water-brook runs,
As the water-brook runs to the sea,
So earth's fainting daughters and famishing sons,
O Fountain of Love, run to Thee!'

"The writing is trembling and uncertain, and the pen literally fell from her hand; for the long shadows of eternity were stealing over her, and she was very near the place where it is too dark for mortal eyes to see, and where there is no work, nor device, nor knowledge."

She had written earlier what she herself called "A Dying Hymn," and it was a consolation to her to repeat it to herself in her moments of deepest agony.

Earth, with its dark and dreadful ills,
Recedes, and fades away;

Lift up your heads, ye heavenly hills:
  Ye gates of death, give way!

My soul is full of whispered song;
  My blindness is my sight;
The shadows that I feared so long
  Are all alive with light.

The while my pulses faintly beat,
  My faith doth so abound,
I feel grow firm beneath my feet
  The green, immortal ground.

That faith to me a courage gives,
  Low as the grave to go:
I know that my Redeemer lives —
  That I shall live I know.

The palace walls I almost see
  Where dwells my Lord and King;
O grave! where is thy victory?
  O death! where is thy sting?

As her strength failed, she grew more and more fond of the hymns of her childhood, and frequently asked her friends to sing such hymns as, "Jesus, Lover of my soul," "Show pity, Lord, O Lord, forgive," "A charge to keep I have;" and she loved to have them sung to old tunes.

Her frequent quotation from Holy Scripture, when in intense pain, was, "Though He slay me, yet will I trust in Him."

On Tuesday, February 7, she wrote her last poem,

the last line of which is, "The rainbow comes but with the cloud." Even after that, she attempted in her bed to make a cap for an aged woman who greatly loved her, and whose sobs in the Church of the Stranger, when her death was announced, moved the whole audience to tears. But her fingers failed, and the needle stands in the unfinished cap; for her own crown was ready, and she could not stay away from her coronation. She fell in a deep sleep, out of which she once exclaimed, "I want to go away." She passed away as she had always desired — waking into the better land out of a slumber in this. "For so He giveth his beloved sleep."

The last published words that Phœbe ever wrote of her sister were these: "Life was to Alice Cary no holiday, and though her skies had gracious hours of sunshine, they had also many dark and heavy clouds; and going back in memory now, I cannot recall a time when, looking upon her face, even during the deepest slumber that she ever knew, I could not see there the sad characters of weariness and pain; until I beheld her at last resting from her labors in that sweet, untroubled sleep which God giveth his beloved."

When, February 13, 1870, the telegraphic dispatch swept through the land saying, "Alice Cary died yesterday. She will be buried to-morrow, from the Church of the Stranger," the announcement was followed by a simultaneous outburst of sorrow. Almost every journal throughout the country published a biographical sketch, accompanied with expressions of personal loss. In hundreds of these notices, still preserved, the remarkable feature is that no matter how remote the journal in which each was published, it is more an expression of individual sorrow at the departure of a beloved friend, than of mere regret at the death of an author. Thus, quoting at random, we find whole columns of her life beginning with sentences like these: "With a sense of bereavement that we cannot express, we record the death of our dear friend, Alice Cary."

"The bare mention of the death of Alice Cary will be sadly sufficient to cause a feeling of sorrow in many a household in every part of the country."

"A woman who could stand up for her rights without arousing the animosities of others, who was a philanthropist without either cant, affectation, or bitterness, who wrote many true poems, but lived one sweeter and truer than she ever wrote; such was our universally beloved Alice Cary. May He that giveth his beloved peace, give us, who knew her beautiful life, the grace to imitate it."

"She had created for herself many friends whom she never saw, and many who had never seen her until they beheld her lying in her last sleep in the house of prayer. Among these was one gentleman well known in scientific circles, — a man supposed to have little of poetic juice in the dry composition of his nature. He surprised a friend who sat near him, by his exhibition of feeling while the address was delivered; and at the close, in explanation of his great emotion, he said: 'I have read every line that woman ever published. I have never spoken to her; but I tell you she was the largest-hearted woman that ever lived!'"

A letter from New York to the "Boston Post," dated February 15, 1870, contains the following allusions to her funeral.

"Dear Alice Cary, sweet singer of the heart, is gone. New York was shrouded in snow when her gentle face was shut away from human sight forever. In the plain little Church of the Stranger, with her true friend, Dr. Deems, officiating, and many other true friends gathered around in mourning silence, with streets all muffled into sympathetic stillness by the heavy drifting snow, and deep, strong sorrow rising from hearts to eyes, the sad funeral rites were performed. Rarely has a more touching scene been witnessed than that which separated Alice Cary from the world that loved her. Many of those present were moved to tears, though only one was bound to her by kinship. That one was her sister Phœbe, her constant companion from childhood, and more than her sister — her second self — through thirty years of literary trial. The little church was filled with literary friends who had grown warmly attached to both during their twenty years' residence in New York. All the members of Sorosis were present to pay a final tribute to her who had been their first President. Many prominent journalists and authors were also there, forgetful, for the time, of all but the solemn sadness around them. Near the rosewood coffin that contained the body of the sweet poet, sat Horace Greeley, Bayard Taylor, Richard B. Kimball, Oliver Johnson, P. T. Barnum, Frank B. Carpenter, A. J. Johnson, and Dr. W. W. Hall, who, for near and special friendship during her life, were chosen to be nearest to her to the grave. When the sad rites of the Church were concluded, the body was borne forth and taken to Greenwood Cemetery, the snow still falling heavily, and covering all things with a pure white shroud. It seemed as though nature were in sympathy with human sorrow, till the grave was closed, for then the snow almost ceased, though the sky remained dark, and the silence continued. And thus the mortal part of Alice Cary was laid at rest forever."

Horace Greeley, speaking in private of her obsequies, said that such a funeral never before gathered in New York in honor of any woman, or man either; that he never saw before in any one assembly of the kind, so many distinguished men and women, so many known and so many unknown.

One of the greatest scholars of his time, sitting there, shed a silent tear for the sister-woman who, alone, unassisted, in life and death had honored human nature; while a few seats off wept aloud the women, poor and old, who had lived upon her tender bounty.

The next morning's issue of the "Tribune" gave the following report of the funeral:

ALICE CARY'S FUNERAL.

The funeral of Miss Alice Cary took place at the Church of the Stranger, on Mercer Street, at one o'clock yesterday afternoon; and, despite the severe snow-storm which must have prevented many from coming, was attended by a very large number of the friends and admirers of the deceased poet. The service opened with an organ voluntary from the "Messiah," followed by the anthem, "Vital Spark of Heavenly Flame." Dr. Deems, the pastor of the church, read a selection from the 15th chapter of St. Paul's Epistle to the Corinthians, and then said: —

"I have not thought of a single word to say to you to-day, and I do not know that it is necessary to say one word more than is set down in the Church service. Most of us knew and loved Alice Cary, and to those who did not know her, my words would fail in describing the sweetness and gentleness of her disposition and temper. It seems, indeed, that instead of standing here, I, too, should be sitting there among the mourners."

The speaker then described the patience with which she had borne her last sickness, and told how he had been by her side when the pain was so intense, that the prints of her finger-nails would be left in the palm of his hand as he was holding hers. But she never made a complaint.

"She was a parishioner," said he, "who came very close to my heart in her suffering and sorrow. I saw how good and true she was, and the interest she had in all the work I had in hand; and I feel as if an assistant had died out of my family. The people of my congregation who did not know her, ought to be glad that I did. How many traits of tenderness have come before you here, how many observations have I been able to make to you, because I had been with her! To-day I can only make my lament over her as you do, in the simplicity of affection. Men loved Alice Cary, and women loved her. When a man loves a woman, it is of nature: when a woman loves a woman, it is of grace — of the grace that woman makes by her loveliness; and it is one of the finest things that can be said of Alice Cary, that she had such troops of friends of her own sex. On the public side of her life she had honor, on the private side, honor and ten derest affection.

"And now she has gone from our mortal sight, but not from the eyes of our souls. She is gone from her pain, as she desired to die, in sleep, and after a deep slumber she has passed into the morning of immortality. The last time I saw her, I took down her works and alighted on this passage, so full of consonance with the anthems just sung by the choir, and almost like a prophecy of the manner in which she passed away: —

"'My soul is full of whispered song,
My blindness is my sight;
The shadows that I feared so long
Are all alive with light.'

"There was one thing in Alice Cary of which we had better remind ourselves now, because many of us are working-people, and people who work very much with our brains; and I see a number of young people who are come, out of tenderness to her memory, to the church to-day, and there may be among them literary people just commencing their career, and they say, 'Would I could write so beautifully and so easily as she did!' It was not easily done. She did nothing easily; but in all this that we read she was an earnest worker; she was faithful, painstaking, careful of improving herself, up to the last moment of her life. Yesterday I looked into the drawer, and the last piece of MS. she wrote turned up, and I said to Phœbe, 'That is copied;' and she said, 'No, that is Alice's writing.' It was so exceedingly plain, it looked like print in large type, though she wrote a very wretched hand. But her sister told me that when she came to be so weak that she couldn't write much any longer, she began to practice like a little girl, to learn to form all her letters anew. She worked to the very last, not only with the brains, but the fingers.

"When Phœbe wrote me last Sunday that she was alone, and that Alice was gone, I couldn't help telling my people, and there was a sob heard that went through the congregation. It was from an old lady, a friend of hers, who often told me about her, and spoke of her nobility of soul. Alice Cary once thought of making a cap for her, and she said, 'I will make a cap for Mrs. Brown,' but her fingers ached so, and her arm became so tired, she had to drop it; and the needle is sticking in that unfinished cap now, just as she left it. She would have finished it, but they had finished her own crown in glory, and she couldn't stay away from her coronation. And we will keep that cap with care; and I think Jesus will remind her of it, and say, 'Child, inasmuch as you did it to one of the least ones, you did it unto me.' Should I speak for hours, I could only tell you how I loved her. She came to me in the winter of my fortunes, when I had very few friends, and I loved her, and will revere her memory forever — forever. And now I will not shed a tear for Alice Cary; I am glad she is gone. I felt at once like saying, 'Thanks be to God,' when I heard that the pain was over; and it was so delightful to go to stand over her, and see her face without a single frown, and to think, 'She is gone to her Father and my Father;' and into his hands I commit her."

After the Episcopal Burial Service had been read, the choir sang a hymn composed by Miss Phœbe Cary, called, "What Sweetly Solemn Thoughts." Then the friends of Alice Cary were requested to look upon her for the last time. The body was taken to Greenwood Cemetery for interment. The pall-bearers were Horace Greeley, Bayard Taylor, P. T. Barnum, Oliver Johnson, Dr. W. F. Holcombe, A. J. Johnson, F. B. Carpenter, and Richard B. Kimball. Among the persons present were Wm. Ross Wallace, the Rev. O. B. Frothingham, the Rev. C. F. Lee, the Rev. Dr. Cookman, James Parton, Fanny Fern, Mrs. Professor Botta, Theodore Tilton, Dr. Hallock, Mrs. Croly, Mrs. Wilbour, John Savage, George Ripley, and many others.

The casket was plain, having merely a silver plate, on which was inscribed: "Alice Cary. A. D. 1820; A. D. 1871."

At a special meeting of Sorosis, yesterday morning, the following preamble and resolutions were read and adopted: —

"In Miss Cary's inaugural address to Sorosis, occurs a passage made memorable by the late sad event. After enlarging upon her own hopes and wishes concerning the growth and position which women should yet attain, and the manner in which they should yet vindicate themselves against all unjust charges, she said: 'Some of us cannot hope to see great results, for our feet are already on the down-hill side of life. The shadows are lengthening behind us and gathering before us, and ere long they will meet and close, and the places that have known us shall know us no more. But if, when our poor work is done, any of those who come after us shall find in it some hint of usefulness toward nobler lives, and better and more enduring work, we for ourselves rest content.'

"Sooner, perhaps, than she then thought, the way

began to narrow, and her feet to falter on the road which leads to immortal life; and,

"*Whereas,* This change, so feelingly alluded to by Miss Cary, has finally overtaken her in the midst of her labors; therefore,

"*Resolved,* That in her removal this Society not only mourns the loss of its first President and most gifted member, but sympathizes with all womanhood in the loss of an earnest helper and most devoted friend.

"*Resolved,* That her exceeding kindness, her enlarged charity, her absolute unselfishness, her wonderful patience, her cordial recognition of every good word and work, endeared her inexpressibly to her friends; while her genius commanded the warmest admiration of all those capable of appreciating sweetest expression married to noblest thought.

"*Resolved,* That her loyalty to woman, and her unceasing industry, shall incite us to renewed earnestness of effort, each in our own appointed place, to hasten the time when women shall receive recognition not only as honest and reliable workers, but as a class faithful and true to each other.

"*Resolved,* That in presenting our heartfelt sympathy to the bereaved and lonely sister, we add the loving hope, that even as the shadows have been swept from the bright, upward pathway of the departed spirit, they may also be dispelled from her sorrowing heart, by an abiding faith in that Love which ordereth all things well."

Rev. Henry M. Field, long a kind friend to both sisters, in a sketch of Alice in the "New York Evangelist," thus referred both to Mr. Greeley and the funeral of Alice: —

"No wonder Mr. Greeley felt so deeply the death of one who had been to him as a sister, that he followed so tenderly at her bier, and in spite of the terrible snow-storm that was raging, insisted on following her remains to Greenwood, determined not to leave them till they were laid in their last resting-place. She was buried on Tuesday, amid one of the most violent storms of the winter. It seems sad to leave one we love in such desolation. But the storms cannot disturb her repose. There let her sleep, sweet, gentle spirit, child of nature and of song. The spring will come, and the grass grow green on her grave, and the flowers bloom, emblems of the resurrection unto life everlasting."

LINES TO ONE GONE.

A tribute to the memory of Alice Cary, delivered at the fifth anniversary of Sorosis, March 31, 1873. *Repeated by request, March* 1894,

The cowslips and the violets
And daisies pink and pied
Peep out from 'neath the hawthorn hedge
A border either side,
The lanes are green with dewy grass
And brightly gemmed with flowers;
The Spring is new, but we, alas!
We dream of other hours.
She comes no more.

The soft warm days she loved are here
And birds on every tree
Are chanting loud and chanting clear
In happy minstrelsy.
And all the world has waked to bliss
Beneath the Spring-tide sun;
The south wind's gently wooing kiss
The morning's smile has won,
She comes no more.

How can the Spring be warm and sweet
When she, its soul, is gone?
I wonder how the birds repeat
Their selfsame tuneful song.
I wonder at the willful ways
Of flowers, and birds, and trees,
When she who always sang their praise,
On reverent bended knees,
Comes now no more.

Perhaps the birds, more wise than I,
Still feel or see her near;
Perhaps unto this flower's blue eye
She living doth appear.
And I alone am sorrowing
Because I cannot guess
That she their joy is borrowing,
And in the Spring's green dress
Comes now once more.

My heart alone is sore and sad,
It feels no joyous thrill
At all the sights that made her glad,
And wild birds' warbling trill.
The Spring that seemed to bloom for her
Now blooms when she is gone;
Her absence does not even stir
The wind to make a moan.
She comes no more.

I pray you all sweet living things,
To make your pleasure mine,
Tell me the news the wild bird brings
And whispers to the,pine;
And tell me where our loved one stays
Amid the enchanted air,
And let me understand your lays
Which joyously declare
She comes once more.

And all sweet flowers, pink, white and blue,
That seem but dreams of her,
Tell me, O flowers, and tell me true,
And trees of balm and fir,
And all wild things that bloom or sing,
That laugh and love and live,
I charge you some remembrance bring
Some token to me give—
She comes once more.

And I will then join in your praise
And gladly, gladly sing;
And own that these are happier days
And this the merriest Spring
That ever warmed the land or sea
Or opened starry flowers
If you will bring her back to me
And prove that with these hours
She comes once more.

—*Ella Dietz Clymer.*

ELLA DIETZ CLYMER IN 1873.

H. W. Smith.

Phebe Cary.

CHAPTER IX.

PHŒBE CARY. — THE WRITER.

No singer was ever more thoroughly identified with her own songs than Phœbe Cary. With but few exceptions, they distilled the deepest and sweetest music of her soul. They uttered, besides, the cheerful philosophy which life had taught her, and the sunny faith which lifted her out of the dark region of doubt and fear, to rest forever in the loving kindness of her Heavenly Father. There were few things that she ever wrote for which she cared more personally than for her "Woman's Conclusions." The thought and the regret came to her sometimes, as they do to most of us, that in the utmost sense her life was incomplete — unfulfilled. Often and long she pondered on this phase of existence; and her "Woman's Conclusions," copied below, were in reality her final conclusions concerning that problem of human fate which has baffled so many.

A WOMAN'S CONCLUSIONS.

I said, if I might go back again
  To the very hour and place of my birth;
Might have my life whatever I chose,
  And live it in any part of the earth;

Put perfect sunshine into my sky,
  Banish the shadow of sorrow and doubt;
Have all my happiness multiplied,
  And all my suffering stricken out;

If I could have known, in the years now gone,
  The best that a woman comes to know;
Could have had whatever will make her blest,
  Or whatever she thinks will make her so;

Have found the highest and purest bliss
  That the bridal-wreath and ring inclose;
And gained the one out of all the world,
  That my heart as well as my reason chose;

And if this had been, and I stood to-night
  By my children, lying asleep in their beds,
And could count in my prayers, for a rosary,
  The shining row of their golden heads;

Yea! I said, if a miracle such as this
  Could be wrought for me, at my bidding, still
I would choose to have my past as it is,
  And to let my future come as it will!

I would not make the path I have trod
  More pleasant or even, more straight or wide;
Nor change my course the breadth of a hair,
  This way or that way, to either side.

My past is mine, and I take it all;
  Its weakness — its folly, if you please;
Nay, even my sins, if you come to that,
  May have been my helps, not hindrances!

If I saved my body from the flames
  Because that once I had burned my hand:
Or kept myself from a greater sin
  By doing a less — you will understand;

It was better I suffered a little pain,
  Better I sinned for a little time,
If the smarting warned me back from death,
  And the sting of sin withheld from crime.

Who knows its strength, by trial, will know
  What strength must be set against a sin;
And how temptation is overcome
  He has learned, who has felt its power within!

And who knows how a life at the last may show?
  Why, look at the moon from where we stand!
Opaque, uneven, you say; yet it shines,
  A luminous sphere, complete and grand.

So let my past stand, just as it stands,
  And let me now, as I may, grow old
I am what I am, and my life for me
  Is the best — or it had not been, I hold.

The guarded castle, the lady in her bower, the tumbling sea, the shipwrecked mariner, were as real to Alice as to herself when she yielded to the luxury of ballad singing. But in Phœbe the imaginative faculty was less prevailing; it rose to flood-tide only at intervals. The dual nature which she inherited from her father and mother were not interfused, as in Alice, but distinct and keenly defined. Through one nature,

Phœbe Cary was the most literal of human beings Never did there live such a disenchanter. Hold up to her, in her literal, every-day mood, your most precious dream, and in an instant, by a single rapier of a sentence, she would thrust it through, and strip it of the last vestige of glamour, and you would see nothing before you but a cold, staring fact, ridiculous or dismal. It was this tenacious grip on reality, this keen sense of the ludicrous in the relation between words and things, which made her the most spontaneous of punsters, and a very queen of parodists. Her parodies are unsurpassed. An example of this literal faculty by which she could instantaneously transmute a spiritual emotion into a material fact, is found in a verse from her parody on Longfellow's beautiful lyric: —

> "I see the lights of the village
> Gleam through the rain and mist,
> And a feeling of sadness comes o'er me,
> That my soul cannot resist;
> A feeling of sadness and longing
> That is not akin to pain,
> And resembles sorrow only
> As the mist resembles rain."

Phœbe preserves all the sadness and tenderness of the original, while she transfers it without effort from the psychological yearning of the soul, into the region of physical necessity, from heart-longing to stomach-longing, in the travesty: —

> "I see the lights of the baker
> Gleam through the rain and mist,
> And a feeling of something comes o'er me,
> That my steps cannot resist;

A feeling of something like longing,
And slightly akin to pain,
That resembles hunger more than
The mist resembles rain."

"Maud Muller" is one of the most sentimental as well as one of the most exquisite of modern ballads, yet what it prompts in Phœbe is not a tear for the faded woman sitting under the chimney log, nor a sigh for the judge who wholly deserves his fate, nor even an alas! for the "might have been." It prompts in her, as the most natural antithesis in the world,—

KATE KETCHEM.

Kate Ketchem on a winter's night
Went to a party dressed in white.

Her chignon in a net of gold
Was about as large as they ever sold.

Gayly she went, because her "pap"
Was supposed to be a rich old chap.

But when by chance her glances fell
On a friend who had lately married well,

Her spirits sunk, and a vague unrest
And a nameless longing filled her breast—

A wish she wouldn't have had made known,
To have an establishment of her own.

Tom Fudge came slowly through the throng,
With chestnut hair, worn pretty long.

He saw Kate Ketchem in the crowd,
And knowing her slightly, stopped and bowed;

Then asked her to give him a single flower,
Saying he'd think it a priceless dower.

Out from those with which she was decked,
She took the poorest she could select,

And blushed as she gave it, looking down
To call attention to her gown.

"Thanks," said Fudge, and he thought how dear
Flowers must be at that time of year.

Then several charming remarks he made,
Asked if she sang, or danced, or played;

And being exhausted, inquired whether
She thought it was going to be pleasant weather.

And Kate displayed her "jewelry,"
And dropped her lashes becomingly;

And listened, with no attempt to disguise
The admiration in her eyes.

At last, like one who has nothing to say,
He turned around and walked away.

Kate Ketchem smiled, and said, "You bet
I'll catch that Fudge and his money yet.

"He's rich enough to keep me in clothes,
And I think I could manage him as I chose.

"He could aid my father as well as not,
And buy my brother a splendid yacht.

"My mother for money should never fret,
And all it cried for, the baby should get.

"And after that, with what he could spare,
I'd make a show at a charity fair."

Tom Fudge looked back as he crossed the sill,
And saw Kate Ketchem standing still.

"A girl more suited to my mind
It isn't an easy thing to find;

"And everything that she has to wear
Proves her rich as she is fair.

"Would she were mine, and I to-day
Had the old man's cash my debts to pay!

"No creditors with a long account,
No tradesmen wanting 'that little amount;'

"But all my scores paid up when due
By a father-in-law as rich as a Jew!"

But he thought of her brother not worth a straw
And her mother, that would be his, in law;

So, undecided, he walked along,
And Kate was left alone in the throng.

But a lawyer smiled, whom he sought by stealth,
To ascertain old Ketchem's wealth ;

And as for Kate, she schemed and planned
Till one of the dancers claimed her hand.

He married her for her father's cash ;
She married him to cut a dash.

But as to paying his debts, do you know,
The father couldn't see it so ;

And at hints for help, Kate's hazel eyes
Looked out in their innocent surprise.

And when Tom thought of the way he had wed,
He longed for a single life instead,

And closed his eyes in a sulky mood,
Regretting the days of his bachelorhood ;

And said, in a sort of reckless vein,
"I'd like to see her catch me again,

"If I were free, as on that night
When I saw Kate Ketchem dressed in white!"

She wedded him to be rich and gay ;
But husband and children didn't pay.

He wasn't the prize she hoped to draw,
And wouldn't live with his mother-in-law.

And oft when she had to coax and pout,
In order to get him to take her out,

She thought how very attentive and bright
He seemed at the party that winter's night;

Of his laugh, as soft as a breeze of the south
('Twas now on the other side of his mouth);

How he praised her dress and gems in his talk,
As he took a careful account of stock.

Sometimes she hated the very walls —
Hated her friends, her dinners, and calls;

Till her weak affection, to hatred turned,
Like a dying tallow-candle burned.

And for him who sat there, her peace to mar,
Smoking his everlasting cigar —

He wasn't the man she thought she saw,
And grief was duty, and hate was law.

So she took up her burden with a groan,
Saying only, "I might have known!"

Alas for Kate! and alas for Fudge!
Though I do not owe them any grudge;

And alas for any who find to their shame
That two can play at their little game!

For of all hard things to bear and grin,
The hardest is knowing you're taken in.

Ah, well, as a general thing, we fret
About the one we didn't get;

But I think we needn't make a fuss,
If the one we don't want didn't get us.

Her dual nature is strikingly illustrated in many of her poems. Purely naturalistic in their conception, as they rise they are touched and glorified with the supernatural. It does not blend with the essence of her song, while that of Alice is all suffused with it. The form and flavor of the latter's verse is often mystical. Her sympathies are deeply human, her love of nature a passion; yet it is the psychical sense which impresses her most deeply in all natural and human phenomena. Phœbe has little of this exquisite pantheism. It is not the soul in nature which she instinctively feels first; it is its association with human experiences. The field, the wood, the old garden, the swallows under the eaves, the cherry-tree on the roof—she never wearies of going back to them; all are precious to her for their personal remembrances. It is while she broods over the past, while the tenderest memories of her life come thronging back into her heart, that the muse of Phœbe Cary rises to its finest and sweetest strains. With a less subtle fancy than Alice, a less suffusive and delicate imagination in embodying human passion, she has a dramatic force often, which her sister seldom manifests. The lyric rush in Alice comes with the winds and waves; it sings of nature's moods, interprets nature's voices; in her utterance of human experience it is the tender, the plaintive, the pathetic, which prevail. The dramatic instinct in Phœbe kindles in depicting human passion, and rises with exultant lyrical ring as if it were so strong within her that it would be uttered. Thus some of her ballads are powerful in conception, and wonderfully dramatic in expression. The finest example of this we have in her "Prairie Lamp," a poem full of tragic energy. What a rhvthmic swell we feel through these lines: —

"'And hark! there is something strange about,
For my dull old blood is stirred;
That wasn't the feet of the storm without,
Nor the voice of the storm I heard!

. . . .

"''Tis my boy! he is coming home, he is near,
Or I could not hear him pass;
For his step is as light as the step of the deer
On the velvet prairie grass.'

. . . .

"She rose — she stood erect, serene;
She swiftly crossed the floor,
And the hand of the wind, or a hand unseen,
Threw open wide the door.

"Through the portal rushed the cruel blast,
With a wail on its awful swell;
As she cried, 'My boy, you have come at last,'
And prone o'er the threshold fell.

"And the stranger heard no other sound,
And saw no form appear;
But whoever came at midnight found
Her lamp was burning clear!"

"The Lady Jaqueline," one of the very finest of her ballads, expresses a quality characteristic of herself. It is full of personal fire, and yet in utterance it has the quaintness and sonorousness of an old ballad master.

"False and fickle, or fair and sweet,
I care not for the rest,
The lover that knelt last night at my feet
Was the bravest and the best;
Let them perish all, for their power has waned,
And their glory waxèd dim;
They were well enough when they lived and reigned,
But never was one like him!
And never one from the past would I bring
Again, and call him mine;
The King is dead, long live the King!
Said the Lady Jaqueline."

Nothing could be more dramatic than this gradation from exultation in the new, to a yet tender remembrance of the old.

"And yet it almost makes me weep,
Aye! weep, and cry, alas!
When I think of one who lies asleep
Down under the quiet grass.
For he loved me well, and I loved again,
And low in homage bent,

And prayed for his long and prosperous reign,
 In our realm of sweet content.
But not to the dead may the living cling,
 Nor kneel at an empty shrine;
The King is dead, long live the King!
 Said the Lady Jaqueline.

. . . .

"Yea, all my lovers and kings that were
 Are dead, and hid away
In the past, as in a sepulchre,
 Shut up till the judgment day.
False or fickle, or weak or wed,
 They are all alike to me;
And mine eyes no more can be misled,
 They have looked on royalty!
Then bring me wine, and garlands bring
 For my king of the right divine;
The King is dead, long live the King!
 Said the Lady Jaqueline."

Equally powerful is she in the expression of personal experience. Her friend Dr. Deems said that it always took his breath away to read her

DEAD LOVE.

We are face to face, and between us here
 Is the love we thought could never die;
Why has it only lived a year?
 Who has murdered it — you or I?

No matter who — the deed was done
 By one or both, and there it lies;

The smile from the lip forever gone,
  And darkness over the beautiful eyes.

Our love is dead, and our hope is wrecked;
  So what does it profit to talk and rave,
Whether it perished by my neglect,
  Or whether your cruelty dug its grave!

Why should you say that I am to blame,
  Or why should I charge the sin on you?
Our work is before us all the same,
  And the guilt of it lies between us two.

We have praised our love for its beauty and grace;
  Now we stand here, and hardly dare
To turn the face-cloth back from the face,
  And see the thing that is hidden there.

Yet look! ah, that heart has beat its last,
  And the beautiful life of our life is o'er,
And when we have buried and left the past,
  We two, together, can walk no more.

You might stretch yourself on the dead, and weep,
  And pray as the Prophet prayed, in pain;
But not like him could you break the sleep,
  And bring the soul to the clay again.

Its head in my bosom I can lay,
  And shower my woe there, kiss on kiss,
But there never was resurrection-day
  In the world for a love so dead as this!

And, since we cannot lessen the sin
  By mourning over the deed we did,
Let us draw the winding-sheet up to the chin,
  Aye, up till the death-blind eyes are hid!

No American poet has ever shown more passion, pathos, and tenderness combined, than we find embodied in many of the minor love poems of Phœbe Cary. Not only the "Dead Love," but the little poem which follows, is an example of these qualities.

ALAS!

Since, if you stood by my side to-day,
  Only our hands could meet,
What matter if half the weary world
  Lies out between our feet?

That I am here by the lonesome sea,
  You by the pleasant Rhine?
Our hearts were just as far apart,
  If I held your hand in mine!

Therefore, with never a backward glance,
  I leave the past behind;
And standing here by the sea alone,
  I give it to the wind.

I give it all to the cruel wind,
  And I have no word to say;
Yet, alas! to be as we have been,
  And to be as we are to-day!

The literal quality of Phœbe's mind showed itself in her undoubting faith in spiritual communion, as it did in everything else. She would remark, "I think —— just came into the room; I feel her presence as distinctly as I do yours," speaking of one who long before had passed into spirit life. She "knew that the dead came back," she said, "just as she knew that she thought, or saw, or knew anything else." It was simply a fact which she stated literally and unexcitedly as she would any other. "It was not any more wonderful to her," she said, "that she could see and perceive with her soul, than that she was able to discern objects through her eyeballs." Never were any words which she uttered more literally true to her than these: —

> "The veil of flesh that hid
> Is softly drawn aside;
> *More clearly I behold them now,*
> *Than those who never died.*"

Nor must this simple faith of these sisters in communion with spirits be confounded with any mere modern delusion. They inherited this belief from their parents. There had been no moment in their conscious existence, when they did not believe in this New Testament faith, that the dead are ministering spirits sent forth of God, to the heirs of salvation. Never did woman live possessed of a more sturdy common sense than Phœbe Cary. Nevertheless she spoke constantly of sympathy and communion with those whom death had taken, precisely as she spoke of intercourse with the living. To her, life held no verity more blessed than this which finds expression in her

BORDER-LAND.

I know you are always by my side,
  And I know you love me, Winifred, dear;
For I never called on you since you died,
  But you answered tenderly, I am here!

So come from the misty shadows, where
  You came last night and the night before;
Put back the veil of your golden hair,
  And let me look in your face once more.

Ah! it is you; with that brow of truth,
  Ever too pure for the least disguise;
With the same dear smile on the loving mouth,
  And the same sweet light in the tender eyes.

You are my own, my darling still;
  So do not vanish or turn aside;
Wait till my eyes have had their fill,
  Wait till my heart is pacified!

You have left the light of your higher place;
  And ever thoughtful, and kind, and good,
You come with your old familiar face,
  And not with the look of your angel-hood.

Still the touch of your hand is soft and light,
  And your voice is gentle, and kind, and low;
And the very roses you wear to-night
  You wore in the summers long ago.

O World! you may tell me I dream or rave,
So long as my darling comes to prove
That the feet of the spirit cross the grave,
And the loving live, and the living love!"

Perhaps the utterances of her soul which have most deeply impressed others, and by which she will be longest remembered, are her religious poems. They are among the rarest in the English tongue, as felicitous in utterance as they are devout and helpful in spirit. It is the soul of their melody, more than the melody itself, which makes us glad. It is the faith in the good, visible and invisible; the lark-like hope that soars and sings so high with such spontaneity of delight; the love brooding over the lowliest things, yet yearning out toward God's eternities, resting in his love at last, which make the inspiration of all these hymns.

Hers was a loving and a believing soul. Day by day she walked with God. In no hour was He far from her. As natural as to breathe was it for her to lift her heart to the heart of all-embracing Love, whether she sat in her chamber alone, or went forth to meet Him in the outer world. From her hymns we take in the tonic of a healthy, hearty, happy soul. Like the simples which we draw forth from nature's soil, they are full of savor and healing. How we feel these in her

FIELD PREACHING.

I have been out to-day in field and wood,
Listening to praises sweet, and counsel good,

Such as a little child had understood,
That, in its tender youth,
Discerns the simple eloquence of truth.

The modest blossoms, crowding round my way,
Though they had nothing great or grand to say,
Gave out their fragrance to the wind all day;
Because his loving breath,
With soft persistence, won them back from death.

. . . .

The stately maize, a fair and goodly sight,
With serried spear-points bristling sharp and bright
Shook out his yellow tresses, for delight,
To all their tawny length,
Like Samson, glorying in his lusty strength.

And every little bird upon the tree,
Ruffling his plumage bright, for ecstacy,
Sang in the wild insanity of glee;
And seemed, in the same lays,
Calling his mate, and uttering songs of praise.

The golden grasshopper did chirp and sing;
The plain bee, busy with her housekeeping,
Kept humming cheerfully upon the wing,
As if she understood
That, with contentment, labor was a good.

I saw each creature, in his own best place,
To the Creator lift a smiling face,
Praising continually his wondrous grace;
As if the best of all
Life's countless blessings was to live at all!

So, with a book of sermons, plain and true,
Hid in my heart, where I might turn them through,
I went home softly, through the falling dew,
Still listening, rapt and calm,
To Nature giving out her evening psalm.

While, far along the west, mine eyes discerned,
Where, lit by God, the fires of sunset burned,
The tree-tops, unconsumed, to flame were turned;
And I, in that great hush,
Talked with his angels in each burning bush!

The hymn of Phœbe Cary, by which she is most widely known is her

NEARER HOME.

One sweetly solemn thought
Comes to me o'er and o'er;
I am nearer home to-day
Than I ever have been before;

Nearer my Father's house,
Where the many mansions be;
Nearer the great white throne,
Nearer the crystal sea;

Nearer the bound of life,
Where we lay our burdens down;
Nearer leaving the cross,
Nearer gaining the crown

But lying darkly between,
Winding down through the night,

Is the silent, unknown stream,
 That leads at last to the light.

Closer and closer my steps
 Come to the dread abysm:
Closer Death to my lips
 Presses the awful chrism.

O, if my mortal feet
 Have almost gained the brink;
If it be I am nearer home
 Even to-day than I think;

Father, perfect my trust;
 Let my spirit feel in death
That her feet are firmly set
 On the rock of a living faith!

Yet like Alice with her "Pictures of Memory," she did not set a high intellectual value upon it. Until within a year or two of her death she was not conscious of its universal popularity. Before that time this lovely pilgrim of a hymn had wandered over the world, pausing at many thresholds, filling with "sweetly-solemn thoughts" how many Christian hearts! It had been printed on Sabbath-school cards, embodied in books of sacred song, pasted into scrap-books, read with tearful eyes by patient invalids in twilight sick-chambers, and by brave yet tender souls at their heyday, on whose wistful eyes faint visions of their immortal home must sometimes dawn, even amid the dimness of this clouded world.

Within the last year of her life, Phœbe heard of an

incident connected with this hymn, which made her happier while she lived.

"A gentleman in China, intrusted with packages for a young man from his friends in the United States, learned that he would probably be found in a certain gambling-house. He went thither, but not seeing the young man, sat down and waited, in the hope that he might come in. The place was a bedlam of noises, men getting angry over their cards, and frequently coming to blows. Near him sat two men — one young, the other forty years of age. They were betting and drinking in a terrible way, the older one giving utterance continually to the foulest profanity. Two games had been finished, the young man losing each time. The third game, with fresh bottles of brandy, had just begun, and the young man sat lazily back in his chair while the oldest shuffled his cards. The man was a long time dealing the cards, and the young man, looking carelessly about the room, began to hum a tune. He went on, till at length he began to sing the hymn of Phœbe Cary, above quoted. The words," says the writer of the story, "repeated in such a vile place, at first made me shudder. A Sabbath-school hymn in a gambling den! But while the young man sang, the elder stopped dealing the cards, stared at the singer a moment, and, throwing the cards on the floor, exclaimed, —

"'Harry, where did you learn that tune?'

"'What tune?'

"'Why, that one you've been singing.'

"The young man said he did not know what he had been singing, when the elder repeated the words, with tears in his eyes, and the young man said he had learned them in a Sunday-school in America.

"'Come,' said the elder, getting up; 'come, Harry; here's what I won from you; go and use it for some good purpose. As for me, as God sees me, I have played my last game, and drank my last bottle. I have misled you, Harry, and I am sorry. Give me your hand, my boy, and say that, for old America's sake, if for no other, you will quit this infernal business.'"

The gentleman who tells the story (originally published in "The Boston Daily News") saw these two men leave the gambling-house together, and walk away arm in arm; and he remarks, "It must be a source of great joy to Miss Cary to know that her lines, which have comforted so many Christian hearts, have been the means of awakening in the breast of two tempted and erring men on the other side of the globe, a resolution to lead a better life."

It was a "great joy" to the writer. In a private letter to an aged friend in New York, with the story inclosed, she added: —

"I inclose the hymn and the story for you, not because I am vain of the notice, but because I thought *you* would feel a peculiar interest in them when you know the hymn was written eighteen years ago (1852) in your house. I composed it in the little back third story bedroom, one Sunday morning, after coming from church; and it makes me very happy to think that any word I could say has done a little good in the world."

After the death of Phœbe, the following letter was received at the "New York Tribune" office.

SEQUEL TO THE GAMBLERS' STORY.

To the Editor of the Tribune.

SIR: Having noticed in the columns of the "Tribune" a biographical sketch of Phœbe Cary, which contained an incident from my letters from China, I think that the sequel to the story of "The Gamblers" may interest her many friends.

The old man spoken of in the anecdote has returned to California, and has become *a hard-working Christian* man, while "Harry" has renounced gambling and all its attendant vices. The incident having gone the rounds of the press, the old man saw it, and finding its "credit," wrote to me about it. Thus Phœbe Cary's poem, "One Sweetly Solemn Thought," etc., has saved from ruin at least two who seldom or never entered a house of worship. I am yours,

RUSSELL H. CONWELL.

Traveller Office, Boston, Aug. 9, 1871.

In her latest hymns, although they express all the old love, all the old fullness of faith, we feel through them a vibration of grief, like one tone in a happy voice quivering with tears. Thus she cries in her very last hymn, "Resurgam:"—

"O mine eyes, be not so tearful;
Drooping spirit, rise, be cheerful;
Heavy soul, why art thou fearful?

'Nature's sepulchre is breaking,
And the earth, her gloom forsaking,
Into life and light is waking.

. . . .

"O, the weakness and the madness
Of a heart that holdeth sadness
When all else is light and gladness!

"Though thy treasure death hath taken,
They that sleep are not forsaken,
They shall hear the trump, and waken.

"Shall not He who life supplieth
To the dead seed, where it lieth,
Quicken also man, who dieth?

"Yea, the power of death was ended
When He, who to hell descended,
Rose, and up to heaven ascended.

"Rise, my soul, then, from dejection,
See in nature the reflection
Of the dear Lord's resurrection.

"Let this promise leave thee never:
If the might of death I sever,
Ye shall also live forever!"

In "Dreams and Realities," a poem published in "Harper's Bazar" after Phœbe's death, she exclaims

"If still they kept their earthly place,
The friends I held in my embrace,
And gave to death, alas!
Could I have learned that clear calm faith
That looks beyond the bounds of death,
And almost longs to pass?"

Thus, through the heavy cloud of human loss and longing the lark-like song arose into the very precinct of celestial light, sweet with unfaltering faith and undying love to the very last. The timid soul that fainted in its mortal house grew reassured and calm, rising to the realization of eternal verities. The world is better because this woman lived, and loved, and believed. She wrote, not to blazon her own being upon the world, not to drop upon the weary multitude the weight of an oppressive personality. She drew from the deep wells of an unconscious and overflowing love the bright waters of refreshment and health. Her subtler insight, her finer intuition, her larger trust, her more buoyant hope, are the world's helpers, all. The simplest word of such a soul thrills with an inexpressible life. It helps to make us braver, stronger, more patient, and more glad. We fulfill the lowliest task more perfectly, are more loyal to our duty, more loving to each other and to God, in the turmoil of the world, in the wearing care of the house, in sorrow as well as in joy, if by a single word we are drawn nearer to the all-encircling and everlasting Love. To do this, as a writer, was the mission of Phœbe Cary. Perhaps no lines which she has written express more characteristically or perfectly her devout and childlike faith in a loving Father's ordering of her earthly life, than the poem which closes her "Poems of Faith, Hope, and Love."

RECONCILED.

O years, gone down into the past;
What pleasant memories come to me,

Of your untroubled days of peace,
  And hours almost of ecstasy!

Yet would I have no moon stand still,
  Where life's most pleasant valleys lie;
Nor wheel the planet of the day
  Back on his pathway through the sky.

For though, when youthful pleasures died,
  My youth itself went with them, too;
To-day, aye! even this very hour,
  Is the best time I ever knew.

Not that my Father gives to me
  More blessings than in days gone by;
Dropping in my uplifted hands
  All things for which I blindly cry:

But that his plans and purposes
  Have grown to me less strange and dim;
And where I cannot understand,
  I trust the issues unto Him.

And, spite of many broken dreams,
  This have I truly learned to say,—
The prayers I thought unanswered once,
  Were answered in God's own best way.

And though some dearly cherished hopes
  Perished untimely ere their birth,
Yet have I been beloved and blessed
  Beyond the measure of my worth.

And sometimes in my hours of grief,
  For moments I have come to stand
Where, in the sorrows on me laid
  I felt a loving Father's hand.

And I have learned the weakest ones
  Are kept securest from life's harms;
And that the tender lambs alone
  Are carried in the Shepherd's arms.

And sitting by the wayside blind,
  He is the nearest to the light,
Who crieth out most earnestly,
  "Lord, that I might receive my sight!"

O feet, grown weary as ye walk,
  Where down life's hill my pathway lies,
What care I, while my soul can mount,
  As the young eagle mounts the skies!

O eyes, with weeping faded out,
  What matters it how dim ye be?
My inner vision sweeps, untired,
  The reaches of eternity!

O death, most dreaded power of all,
  When the last moment comes, and thou
Darkenest the windows of my soul,
  Through which I look on nature now;

Yea, when mortality dissolves,
  Shall I not meet thine hour unawed?
My house eternal in the heavens
  Is lighted by the smile of God!

CHAPTER X.

PHŒBE CARY. — THE WOMAN.

THE wittiest woman in America is dead. There are others who say many brilliant things; but I doubt if there is another so spontaneously and pointedly witty, in the sense that Sidney Smith was witty, as Phœbe Cary. The drawback to almost everybody's wit and repartee is that it so often seems premeditated. It is a fearful chill to a laugh to know that it is being watched for, and had been prepared beforehand. But there was an absolute charm in Phœbe's wit; it was spontaneous, so coruscating, so "pat." Then it was full of the delight of a perpetual surprise. She was just as witty at breakfast as she was at dinner, and would say something just as astonishingly bright to one companion, and she a woman, as to a roomful of cultivated men, doing their best to parry her flashing scimitars of speech. Though so liberally endowed with the poetic utterance and insight, she first beheld every object literally, not a ray of glamour about it; she saw its practical and ludicrous relations first, and from this absolutely matter-of-fact perception came the sparkling utterance which saw it, caught it, played with it, and held it up in the same instant. It is pleasant to think of a friend who made you laugh so many happy times, but who never made you weep.

For instantaneously as her arrow of wit came, it sprung from too kind a heart ever to be tipped with a sting. There was always a prevailing vein of good nature in her most satirical or caustic remarks. Indeed, satire and sarcasm rarely sought vent in her glittering speech; it was fun, sheer fun, usually, as kindly innocent in spirit as it was ludicrous and brilliant in utterance. But a flash of wit, like a flash of lightning, can only be remembered, it cannot be reproduced. Its very marvel lies in its spontaneity and evanescence; its power is in being struck from the present. Divorced from that, the keenest representation of it seems cold and dead. We read over the few remaining sentences which attempt to embody the repartees and *bon mots* of the most famous wits of society, such as Beau Nash, Beau Brummel, Madame Du Deffand, and Lady Mary Montagu; we wonder at the poverty of these memorials of their fame. Thus it must be with Phœbe Cary. Her most brilliant sallies were perfectly unpremeditated, and by herself never repeated, or remembered. When she was in her best moods, they came like flashes of heat lightning, like a rush of meteors, so suddenly and constantly you were dazzled while you were delighted, and afterward found it difficult to single out any distinct flash, or separate meteor from the multitude. A niece of Phœbe says that when a school-girl she often thought of writing down in a book the marvelous things which she heard her Aunt Phœbe say every day. Had she carried out her resolution, her book would now be the largest volume of Phœbe Cary's thoughts. As it is, this most wonderful of all her gifts can only be represented bv a few stray sen tences, gleaned here and there from the faithful memories of loving friends; each one invariably adding, "O, if I had only taken down the many wonderfully bright things that I heard her say." She had a necklace made of different articles which her friends had given her; from one there was a marble, from another a curious nut from the East, from another a piece of amber, from another a ball of malachite or crystal, and so on, till the necklace consisted of more than fifty beads, and, when open, stretched to a length of nearly four feet.

She often wore this necklace on Sunday evenings, and while in conversation would frequently occupy her fingers in toying with the beads. "One evening a friend told her that she looked, with her necklace, like an Indian princess; she replied that the only difference was that the Indian had a string of scalps in place of beads. She said that she thought that the best place for her friends was to hang about her neck, and with this belief she had constructed the necklace, and compelled her friends to join it. Some of her friends used to tell her that she ought to have a short-hand reporter as a familiar spirit, to jot down her sharp sayings, and give them out to the world. But she replied that it would not be to her taste to be short-handed down to fame; she preferred the lady with the trump, though she thought the aforesaid lady would be more attractive, and give a better name to her favorites, if she dressed in the costume of the period."

A friend tells how, at a little party, where fun rose to a great height, one quiet person was suddenly attacked by a gay lady with the question, "Why don't you laugh? You sit there just like a post!"

"There! she called you a post; why don't you rail at her?" was Phœbe's instantaneous exclamation.

Another tells how, at a dinner-table where wine flowed freely, some one asked the sisters what wines they kept.

"O!" said Phœbe, "we drink Heidsick; but we keep mum."

Mr. P. T. Barnum mentioned to her that the skeleton man and the fat woman, then on exhibition in the city, were married.

"I suppose they loved through thick and thin," answered Phœbe.

"On one occasion, when Phœbe was at the Museum, looking about at the curiosities," says Mr. Barnum, "I preceded her, and had passed down a couple of steps. She intently watching a big anaconda in a case at the top of the stairs, walked off (not noticing them), and fell. I was just in time to catch her in my arms, and save her from a severe bruising.

"'I am more lucky than that first woman was, who fell through the influence of the serpent,' said Phœbe, as she recovered herself."

Being one day at Wood's Museum, she asked Mr. Barnum to show her the "Infernal Regions," advertised to be represented there. On inquiring, he found that they were out of order, and said, —

"The Infernal Regions have vanished; but never mind, Phœbe, you will see them in time."

"No, in eternity," was the lightning-like reply.

On one occasion a certain well-known actor, then recently deceased, and more conspicuous for his professional skill than for his private virtues, was discussed. "We shall never," remarked some one, "see —— again."

"No," quickly responded Phœbe; "not unless we go to the pit."

Says Oliver Johnson in his last tribute to her, in the "Tribune:"

"Her religious sentiments were deep and strong, her faith in the Eternal Goodness unwavering. Educated in the faith of Universalism, she believed to the last in the final salvation of all God's children. On this subject she spoke to the writer with great distinctness and emphasis only a few weeks before her death; and once she indicated her faith by repeating with approbation the remark of one who said, in reply to the argument in favor of endless misery, 'Well, if God ever sends me into such misery, I know He will give me a constitution to bear it.'"

On entering a shop one day, she asked the clerk to show her a lady's cap. He understood her to say "a baby's cap."

"What is the child's age?" he inquired.

"*Forty!*" exclaimed Phœbe, in a tone which made the young man jump with amazement.

Among her papers there is an envelope that she has left behind, on which, in her own hand, is written one word: "*Fun!*" It is packed with little squibs of rhyme and travesty, evidently written for her own amusement, and thrust here out of sight, as unworthy to be seen by any eyes but her own. But they are so characteristic, and so illustrative of the quality of her mind which we are considering, that I am tempted to give two of them: not that either of the two is as funny as those left in the envelope; but because it trenches upon less pointedly absurd themes. One is,

MORAL LESSONS.

BY AMOS KEATER.

How doth the little busy flea
  Improve each awful jump;
And mark her progress, as she goes,
  By many an itching lump!

How skillfully she does her "sell;"
  How neat she bites our backs,
And labors hard to keep her well
  Beyond the reach of whacks!

I, too, in games of chance and skill,
  By Satan would be led;
For if you're always sitting still,
  You cannot get ahead.

To lively back-biting and sich,
  My great ambition tends;
Thus would I make me fat and rich
  By living off my friends.

The other bears no title:

Go on, my friend, speak freely, pray;
Don't stop till you have said your say;
But, after you are tired to death,
And pause to take a little breath,
I'll name a dish I think is one
To which no justice can be done!

It isn't pastry, old and rich,
Nor onions, garlic, chives, and sich;

Not cheese that moves with lively pace,
It is'nt even *Sweitzer Kase:*
It isn't ham, that's old and strong,
Nor sausage kept a month too long;
It isn't beefsteak, fried in lard,
Nor boiled potatoes when they're hard
(All food unfit for Goth or Celt);
It isn't fit even when they're smelt;
It ain't what Chinamen call nice,
Although they dote on rats and mice;
For, speaking honestly and truly,
I wouldn't give it to a Coolie!
I wouldn't vally even a pup,
If he could stoop to eat it up;
Nor give my enemy a bit,
Although he sot and cried for it.
Recall all pizen food and slop
At stations where the rail-cars stop;
It's more than each and all of these,
By just about sixteen degrees.
It has no nutriment, it's trash!
It's meaner than the meanest hash,
And sourer twenty thousand times,
Than lemons, vinegar, and limes;
It's what I hate the man who eats;
It's poor, cold, cussed, pickled beets!"

I pause in these quotations with a sense of pain. The written line is such a feeble reflection of the living words which flashed from the speaking woman, so tiny a ray of that abounding light, that bounteous life, from earth gone out!

The same powerful sense of justice, the same delicate honor, the sensitive conscience, the tender sympathies, which prevailed in the nature of Alice, were also dominant in Phœbe.

She not only wanted every breathing thing to have its little mortal chance, but, so far as she felt able to assist, it *had* it. She was especially sympathetic to the aged and the young, yet her heart went out to the helpless, the poor, the oppressed everywhere.

One of her most marked traits was a fine sense of honor which pervaded her minutest acts. This was manifested in her personal relations with others, in the utter absence of all curiosity. If ever a woman lived who absolutely "minded her own business, and let that of other people alone," it was Phœbe Cary. If ever mortal lived who thoroughly respected the individual life and rights of others, it was Phœbe Cary. From the prevailing "littlenesses" which Margaret Fuller Ossoli says are the curse of women, she was almost entirely free.

Her conscience ruled her in the words of her mouth, the meditations of her heart, and the minutest acts of her life. To do anything which she knew to be wrong would have been an impossibility to Phœbe Cary. This acute and ever accusing-conscience, combined with a lowly estimate of every power of her own, even her power of being good, filled her with a deep and pervading humility. She was not only modest, she was humble; not in any cringing or ignoble sense, but with an abiding consciousness that it was not possible for her to attain to her own standard of excellence in anything. These qualities, together, produced a blended timidity of nature and feeling, which was manifested even in her religious experience.

Her apprehension of God as the universal and all-loving Father was deep and comprehensive. Her belief in Christ as an all-sufficient Saviour was sure and sufficing. Her faith and hope in them soared and sang in the sunshine of abiding trust. But the moment she thought of herself, she felt all unworthiness. It was her last thought, uttered in her last words, "O God, have mercy on my soul!"

As it is to all self-distrusting persons, personal approbation was dear to her. The personal responses which many of her poems called forth made her genuinely happy, and were to her, often, the most precious recompense of her labor. Nothing could have been more ingenuous or modest than the pleasure which she showed at any spontaneous response from another heart, called out by some poem of her own. She did not set a high value on herself, but if others valued her, she was glad. If she received the assurance that in any way her words had helped another human being, she was happier still. This happiness probably never rose to such fullness from the same cause, as when the incident of the two wanderers in China, and her hymn, "Nearer Home," first met her eyes in a newspaper.

While she frankly said that she was happy in believing that she came of good lineage, no one on earth was more ready to say, —

> "A man's a man, for a' that,"

whatever the shadow might be which rested on his birth or ancestry. Of sycophancy and snobbery she was incapable. She took the most literal measure of every human being whom she gauged at all, and the valuation was precisely what the individual made it, without reference to any antecedent whatever. Shams collapsed in the presence of this truthful soul, and pretense withered away under her cool, measuring gaze. Mere wealth had no patent which could command her respect, and poverty no sorrow that did not possess her sympathy and pity. "I have felt so poor myself," she said; "I have cried in the street because I was poor. I am so much *nearer* to poor people, than to rich ones."

The child of such parents, Phœbe, as well as Alice, could scarcely help growing up to be the advocate of every good word and work. Phœbe's pen, as well as her life, was ever dedicated to temperance, to human rights, to religion, to all true progress. It was impossible that such a woman should not have been devoted to all the best interests of her own sex. She believed religiously in the social, mental, and civil enfranchisement of woman. She hated caste in sex as she hated any other caste rooted in injustice, and the degradation of human nature. She believed it to be the human right of every woman to develop the power that God has given her, and to fulfill her destiny as a human creature, — free as man is free. Yet it was in woman *as* woman that she believed. She herself was one of the most womanly of women. What she longed to see educated to a finer and fuller supremacy in woman, was feminine, not masculine strength. As she believed in man's, she believed no less in woman's kingdom. Her very clearly defined ideas and feelings on this subject can in no way be so perfectly expressed as in her own words, published in the "New York Tribune."

ADVICE GRATIS TO CERTAIN WOMEN.

BY A WOMAN.

O, my strong-minded sisters, aspiring to vote,
And to row with your brothers, all in the same boat,
When you come out to speak to the public your mind,
Leave your tricks, and your airs, and your graces behind!

For instance, when you by the world would be seen
As reporter, or editor (first-class, I mean),
I think — just to come to the point in one line —
What you write will be finer, if 'tis not too fine.

Pray, don't let the thread of your subject be strung
With "golden," and "shimmer," "sweet," "filter," and "flung;"
Nor compel, by your style, all your readers to guess
You've been looking up words Webster marks *obs.*

And another thing: whatever else you may say,
Do keep personalities out of the way;
Don't try every sentence to make people see
What a dear, charming creature the writer must be!

Leave out affectations and pretty appeals;
Don't "drag yourself in by the neck and the heels,"
Your dear little boots, and your gloves; and take heed,
Nor pull your curls over men's eyes while they read.

Don't mistake me; I mean that the public's not home,
You must do as the Romans do, when you're in Rome;

I would have you be womanly, while you are wise;
'Tis the weak and the womanish tricks I despise.

On the other hand: don't write and dress in such styles
As astonish the natives, and frighten the isles;
Do look, on the platform, so folks in the show
Needn't ask, "Which are lions, and which tigers?"
you know!

'Tis a good thing to write, and to rule in the state,
But to be a true, womanly woman is great:
And if ever you come to be that, 'twill be when
You can cease to be babies, nor try to be men!

After months of solicitation from those connected with it, and at the earnest entreaty of Alice, she became at one time the assistant editor of the "Revolution." But the responsibility was always distasteful to her, and after a few months' trial, she relinquished it with a sense of utter relief.

She, like Alice, was unfitted by natural temperament and disposition for all personal publicity. But in private intercourse, at home or abroad, her convictions on all subjects were earnestly and fearlessly expressed.

Although so uncompromising in her convictions, Phœbe very rarely aroused antagonism in her expression of them. If she uttered them at all, it was in a form which commanded merriment, if not belief. The truth which many another might unfold in an hour's declamation, she would sheathe in witty rhyme, in whose lines it would run and sparkle as it never could have done in bald prose.

In the following lines we find her usual manner of

expressing a truth, which so many others offer in a form harsh and repelling. Phœbe, who had just written these lines, brought them in, and read them one day to Alice, who was too ill to sit up. The turn of her words, and the tones of her voice, combined, were irresistible, and in a moment the beating rain outside, and the weary pain within were forgotten in merriment. Thus the truth of the rhyme, which from many another nature would have shot forth in garrulous fault-finding or expostulation, in the dress wherewith Phœbe decked it, amused far more than it exasperated, although the keenness of its edge was in no wise dulled or obscured.

WAS HE HENPECKED?

"I'll tell you what it is, my dear,"
Said Mrs. Dorking, proudly,
"I do not like that chanticleer
Who crows o'er us so loudly.

"And since I must his laws obey,
And have him walk before me,
I'd rather like to have my say
Of who should lord it o'er me."

"*You'd like to vote?*" he answered slow,
"Why, treasure of my treasures,
What can you, or what should you know
Of public men, or measures?

"Of course, you have ability,
Of nothing am I surer;
You're quite as wise, perhaps, as I;
You're better, too, and purer.

"I'd have you just for mine alone,
  Nay, so do I adore you,
I'd put you queen upon a throne,
  And bow myself before you."

"*You'd put me! you?* now that is what
  I do not want, precisely;
I want myself to choose the spot
  That I can fill most wisely."

"My dear, you're talking like a goose —
  Unhenly, and improper" —
But here again her words broke loose,
  In vain he tried to stop her:

"I tell you, though she never spoke
  So you could understand her,
A goose knows when she wears a yoke,
  As quickly as a gander."

"Why, bless my soul! what would you do?
  Write out a diagnosis?
Speak equal rights? join with their crew
  And dine with the Sorosis?

"And shall I live to see it, then —
  My wife a public teacher?
And would you be a crowing hen —
  That dreadful unsexed creature?"

"Why, as to that, I do not know;
  Nor see why you should fear it;
If I can crow, why let me crow,
  If I can't, then you won't hear it!"

"Now, why," he said, "can't such as you
Accept what we assign them?
You have your rights, 'tis very true,
But then, we should define them!

"We would not peck you cruelly,
We would not buy and sell you;
And you, *in turn*, should think, and be,
And do, just what we tell you!

"I do not want you made, my dear,
The subject of rude men's jest;
I like you in your proper sphere,
The circle of a hen's nest!

"I'd keep you in the chicken-yard,
Safe, honored, and respected;
From all that makes us rough and hard,
Your sex should be protected."

"Pray, did it ever make you sick?
Have I gone to the dickens?
Because you let me scratch and pick
Both for myself and chickens?"

"O, that's a different thing, you know,
Such duties are parental;
But for some work to do, you'd grow
Quite weak and sentimental."

"Ah! yes, it's well for you to talk
About a parent's duty!
Who keeps your chickens from the hawk?
Who stays in nights, my beauty?"

"But, madam, you may go each hour,
Lord bless your pretty faces!
We'll give you anything, but power
And honor, trust and places.

"We'd keep it hidden from your sight
How public scenes are carried;
Why, men are coarse, and swear, and fight"—
"I know it, dear; I'm married!"

"Why, now you gabble like a fool;
But what's the use of talking?
'Tis yours to serve, and mine to rule,
I tell you, Mrs. Dorking!"

"O, yes," she said, "you've all the sense,
Your sex are very knowing;
Yet some of you are on the fence,
And only good at crowing."

"Ah! preciousest of precious souls,
Your words with sorrow fill me;
To see you voting at the polls
I really think would kill me.

"To mourn my home's lost sanctity;
To feel you did not love me;
And worse, to see you fly so high,
And have you roost above me!"

"Now, what you fear in equal rights
I think you've told precisely;
That's just about the 'place it lights,'"
Said Mrs. Dorking wisely.

Phœbe was very fond of children. Like Alice, she always had her special pets and darlings among the children of her friends. She was interested in all childhood, but, unlike Alice, she preferred little boys to little girls. All her child lyrics are exceptionably happy, going straight to the understanding and hearts of little folk. She addresses them ever as dear little friends, jolly little comrades, never in a mother-tone; while in Alice, we feel constantly the yearning of the mother-heart. *Her* utterances to children thrill through and through with mother-love, its tenderness, its exultation. It is often difficult to realize that she is not the mother of the child to whom she speaks, and of whose loveliness she sings.

Phœbe had a childlike love of decoration. Not that she was ever satisfied with her looks. She had the same distrust of her personal appearance, that she had of her personal powers. Nevertheless she had a passionate love of ornaments.

Alice delighted in ample robes, rich fabrics, India shawls, and wore very few jewels. But Phœbe would wear two bracelets on one arm, from the sheer delight of looking on them. The Oriental warmth of her temperament was revealed in her delight in gleaming gems. She loved them for their own sakes. There were ardors of her heart which seemed to find their counterpart in the imprisoned, yet inextinguishable fires of precious stones. She would watch and muse over them, moment after moment, as if in a dream. Her senses, pure and strong, were the avenues of keen and swift delights. If her conscience was stern, her heart was warm, and her capacity for joy immeasurable. The flashing of a jewel, the odor of a flower, the face of youth, the subtle effluence of outraying beauty, the touch of a hand, the moulding of a perfect arm, everything which revealed, in sight or sound or form, the more subtle and secret significance of matter, moved a nature powerful in its passionate sensibility.

To her dying hour she was a child in many ways. The Phœbe Cary who faced the world was dignified, self-contained, and self-controlled. But the child-heart avenged itself for what the world had cost it, when it came back to its own sole self. The last great struggle, in which alone it essayed to meet and conquer sorrow, snapped the cord of life. Thus in the slightest things, often, Phœbe could not bear disappointment any better than a child. No matter how bravely she tried, afterwards, in greater or less degree, she always went through the reaction of complete prostration. Often a disappointment like missing a train of cars, having a journey put off, or even a pleasant evening out deferred, would send her to her room in floods of tears. To be sure, she made no ado. The door was shut, and nobody was allowed to hear the wailing, nor were any comments made on it afterwards. Nevertheless, when she appeared again, two or three, at least, always knew that "Phœbe had had her cry, and felt better."

Modest and reticent in herself, yet merry and witty in her conversation with men, her habitual manner to the women whom she loved was most endearing. Without the shallow "gush," and insipid surface effervescence of sentimental adjectives, which in many women take the place, and attempt to hide the lack, of any deep affection, Phœbe was full of loving little ways, dear to remember. She had a fashion of smoothing back your hair from your forehead, as if you were a child; and of coming and standing beside you, with her hand laid upon your shoulder in a caressing touch. This action of hers was especially comforting and assuring. It was not a startling, nervous hand resting on your shoulder. It was deep, dimpled, and abiding. It rested, soothed, and helped you at once. It came with a caress, and left you with a laugh. For by that time, its owner had surely said something which had changed the entire current of your thoughts and feeling, if you had been woe-begone and lonesome when she came.

Emerson says, "All mankind love a lover;" and Phœbe Cary surely did. But rarely in any solemn, heart-tearing way.

"Believe me," she said once, "I never loved any man well enough to lie awake half an hour, to be miserable about him."

"I *do* believe you," said Alice. "It would be hard to believe it, were you to say you ever had."

Till within a few years of her death, it was only a distant adorer that Phœbe desired, a *cavalier servente*, who would escort her to public places occasionally, pay her chivalric homage on Sabbath evenings, and through the week retire to his affairs, leaving her "unbothered" to attend to hers. Her ideal of marriage was most exalted; and she would deliberately have chosen to have lived "solitary to her dying day," rather than to have entered that sacred state, without the assurance that its highest and purest happiness would have been hers.

"I prefer my own life to that of the mass of married people that I see," she would say; "it is a dreary material life that they seem to me to live, no inspiration of the deepest love in it. And yet I believe that true marriage holds the highest and purest possibilities of human happiness." It was a perfectly characteristic reply that she made to the person who asked her if she had ever been disappointed in her affections: —

"No; but a great many of my married friends have."

Equally characteristic was her answer to the erratic officer of our late war, who invited her to drive with him, and improved the opportunity it gave to ask her to marry him. She requested a short time to consider.

"No," said the peremptory hero. "Now, or never."

"Never!" was the response.

We may believe that the "never" did not lose in vim from the fact, known to her, that the same daring adorer had offered his name and fame no less ardently, but a few days before, to her sister Alice. They parted at the Twentieth Street door forever. He died not long after, of wounds received in battle.

Phœbe was as innocently fond of admiration as she was of decoration. She was never vain of it, but always delighted when she received it. She received much. When it culminated in an offer of marriage, as it repeatedly did, Phœbe invariably said, "No, I thank you: I like you heartily; but I don't want to marry anybody." The result was, her lover remained her friend. If he married, his wife became her friend; and the two women exchanged visits on the most cordial terms. There was not an atom of sentimentality, in the form that young Sparkler calls "non sense," in the character of Phœbe Cary.

During the last ten years of her life, the woman's heart asserted itself in behalf of the woman's life. In 1867, an offer of marriage was made her by a gentleman eminent in the world of letters, a man of the most refined nature, extensive culture, and real piety. She felt a deep and true affection for him, as he did for her. The vision of a new life and home shone brightly in upon the shadow which disease and death had hung over her own.

Although unconsciously, Alice had already entered the Valley of Death; and when, with her failing strength, the loss of Phœbe suddenly confronted her, she shrunk back appalled. "I suppose I shall be sustained, if *worst comes to worst!*" she wrote; "but I am very sad now." Phœbe looked into the face of her lover, and every impulse of her heart said, "Yes;" she looked into the face of her sister, and her lips said without faltering, "No." Making the sacrifice, she made it cheerfully, and without ado. I doubt if Alice, to her dying day, realized how much Phœbe relinquished in her own heart, when she sacrificed the prospect of this new life for her sake.

Referring to it once, Phœbe said, "When I saw how Alice felt, I could not leave her. If I had married, I should have gone to my own home; now, she could never live anywhere but in her own house. I could not leave her alone. She has given so much to me, I said, I will give the rest of my life to her. It is right. I would not have it otherwise. Yet when I think of it, I am sure I have never lived out my full nature, have never lived a complete life. My life is an appendage to that of Alice. It is my nature and fate to walk second to her. I have less of everything that is worth having, than she; less power less money, fewer friends.

"Sometimes I feel a yearning to have a life my very own; my own house, and work, and friends; and to feel myself the centre of all. I feel now that it is never to be. O, if you knew how I carry her on my heart! If she goes down town, I am anxious till she comes back. I am so afraid some harm will happen *to her*. Think of it! for more than thirty years our house has never been free from the sound of that cough. One by one, all have had it, and gone, but we two. Now, when I am alone, I have that constant dread on me about Alice. Of course I could not leave her. Yet (with a pathetic smile) I am sure *we* would have been very happy. Don't you think so?" Taking a picture from the inner drawer of her desk, she gazed on it long. "Yes, I am *sure* of it," she said, as she slowly put it back.

Through the teachings of her parents, and the promptings of her own soul, Phœbe Cary believed in the final restoration, from sin to happiness, of the entire human race, through the love of the Father and the atonement of Jesus Christ. Her faith in God, her love for humanity, never wavered. No less, through her very temperament, her dependent soul needed all the support of outward form, as well as of inward grace. Alice could worship and be happy in the solitude of her own room; but Phœbe wanted all the accessions of the Church service. She was deeply devotional. In her unostentatious devoutness, there was a touch of the old Covenanter's spirit. In her utter dependence on the mercy and love of God, there was an absolute humility of heart, touching to see.

Although she believed in the final restoration of the human race to holiness, she believed no less in extreme penalties for sin. She expected punishment for every evil deed she did, not only here but hereafter. This belief, with her own natural timidity and humility, explains every cry that she ever uttered for divine mercy, even to the last.

How much more to her was the Spirit of the Divine Master than the tenets of any creed, we may know from the fact that for many years of her life in New York, she was a member of the Church of the Pilgrims (Congregational), its pastor, Dr. Cheever, her dear friend : while at the time of her death she was a regular attendant at an independent church (the Church of the Stranger), and with its pastor, Rev. Dr. Deems, was the associate editor of "Hymns for All Christians." Faith, hope, and love — love for God, love for her fellow-creatures — were the prevailing elements of her religious faith and experience. In the belief and practice of these she lived and died, a brilliant, devout, humble, loving, and lovable woman.

CHAPTER XI.

PHŒBE'S LAST SUMMER. — DEATH AND BURIAL.

THERE is something inexpressibly sad in the very thought of Phœbe's last summer. One must marvel at the providence of God, which demanded of a soul so dependent upon the ministries of love, so clinging in every fibre of its being, that it should go down into the awful shadow, and confront death alone. Though hard, it would have been easier for Alice to have met such a fate. Yet it was not Alice, it was Phœbe, who died alone. She not only was alone, but sadder still, she knew it. In the very last days she said, "I am dying alone."

The general impression is that with a constitution exceptional in her family, in robust health, she was suddenly smitten, and, without warning, died. This is far from the truth. Even in the summer of 1869, she complained of symptoms which proved to be the forerunners of fatal disease. More than once she exclaimed, "O this heaviness, this lethargy which comes over me, as if I could never move again! I wonder what it is!" But Alice was so confirmedly, and every day becoming so hopelessly the invalid of the household, Phœbe's ailments were ignored by herself, and scarcely known to her friends. In the presence of the mortal agony which had settled on her sister's frame,

Phœbe had neither heart nor desire to speak of the low, dull pain already creeping about her own heart. Her first anxiety was to spare her sister every external cause for solicitude or care.

Nevertheless, there were times when her own mortality was too strong for her, and in the December before the death of Alice, she lay for many days in the little room adjoining, sick almost unto death, with one form of the disease of which, at last, she died. While convalescing from this attack, I found her one day lying on a sofa in Alice's room, while Alice, in an arm-chair, was sitting by her side. It was one of Alice's "best days." Not two months before her death, after days and nights of anguish which no language can portray, she yet had life enough left to be seated in that arm-chair, dressed in white, wrapped in a snowy lamb's-wool shawl, with a dainty cap, brave with pink ribbons, on her head. Moving against the back of the chair, she at last pushed this jaunty cap on one side, when Phœbe looked up from her pillow, and said with a sudden laugh, "Alice, you have no idea what a *rakish* appearance you present. I'll get you the hand-glass that you may see how you wear your cap." And this remark was the first of a series of happy sallies which passed between these two, stricken and smitten, yet tossing to and fro sunny words, as if neither had a sorrow, and as if all life stretched fair and bright before them.

Phœbe probably never knew, in this world, to what awful tension her body and soul were strained, in living through the suffering of Alice, and beholding her die.

She herself said: "It seems to me that a cord

stretches from Alice's heart to mine; nothing can hurt her that does not hurt me." That that cord was severed at death, no one can believe. Beyond the grave Alice drew her still, till she drew her into the skies.

After her sister's death she remarked to a friend, "Alice, when she was here, always absorbed me, and she absorbs me still; I feel her constantly drawing me."

You have read how, after seeing the body of her sister laid beneath the snow in Greenwood, Phœbe came back to the empty home, let the sunshine in, filled the desolate room with flowers, and laid down to sleep on the couch near that of Alice, which she had occupied through all her last sickness; how she rose with the purpose and will to work, to prepare a new edition of all her sister's writings, — not to sit down in objectless grief, but to do all that her sister would, and, she believed, did still desire her to do. There was not a touch of morbidness in her nature. By birthright hers was an open, honest, sunshiny soul. The very effluence of her music sprang from the inspiration of truth, faith, and love. In herself she had everything left to live for. Mentally, she had not yet risen to the fullness of her powers. She was still in the prime of a rich, attractive womanhood; her black hair untouched of gray, her hazel eyes sparkling as ever, her cheeks as dimpled as a baby's, her smile, even with its droop of sadness, more winsome than of old. To her own little store were now added her sister's possessions. Save a few legacies and mementos, everything of which she died possessed, Alice had bestowed upon Phœbe. The house was hers; she its sole mistress, possessed of a life competency. All Alice's friends were hers now in a double sense; for they loved her for herself, and her sister also. She sat enshrined in a tenderer and deeper sympathy than had ever enveloped her before; her fame was growing, offering her every promise of a more brilliant and enduring repute in the world of letters; her position as the leader of a most brilliant and intellectual society was never so assured. Dear soul! life had come to her, why should she not be sunshiny and brave? Nobody had left her, not even her dead; were not Alice and Elmina, and all her lost ones, going in and out with her, supporting her, cheering her? why should she be bowed down and sorrowful? No less that realistic nature, that tenacious heart, cried out for the old, tangible fellowship, for the face to face communion, the touch of the hand, the tender, brooding smile, even for the old moan of pain telling of the human presence. Alice was there — yes, she believed it; yet it was with spiritual insight, not with the old mortal vision, that she beheld her. She was all womanly, made for deep household loves. With all her sweet beliefs, she was alone.

"Alice left me this morning, and I am in the world alone," was the message she sent me, hundreds of miles away, the day that Alice died.

Everything was hers, but what did it avail now? There was no Alice waiting on her couch, no Alice at the table, no Alice to pour out long, sweet songs in her ear; the soul of her soul had passed from her. She tried to see the light, but the light of her life had gone out.

Phœbe's resolution was to go on with her own life work, not as if her sister had not died, but as if in passing away she had left a double work for her to perform. She felt that she had not only her own, but Alice's works to revise and edit, Alice's name to honor and perpetuate. For the first time in her life, the impulse, the energy to do, was to come from herself alone. It could not be. Unconsciously she drooped. There was no Alice to whom to read what she had written. No Alice to live through and for, as she lived through her and for her for so many years. The tension of those years of watching and of ceaseless anxiety broken, the reaction of unutterable weariness and helplessness told how fearful had been their strain. She did not quiescently yield to it. She went out and sought her friends. She called her friends in to her. She did all in her power to shake off the lethargy stealing upon her; not only to believe, but to feel, that she had much left to live for. In vain. She who had so loved to live, who by her physical as well as mental constitution could take delight in simple existence; she who was in sympathy with every hope and fear which animates humanity, came to herself at last, to find that her real interest had all been transferred to the beloved objects who had passed within the veil of the unseen and eternal.

Possessing, as she believed she did, "the old Cary constitution," with a vital hold on life which no other of her sisters had possessed, she made her plans in expectation of long life. And yet, when attacked with what seemed to be slight illness, when her physician spoke hopefully to her of recovery, she replied, "that she knew of no reason why she should *not* recover, except that she neither found, nor could excite, any desire in herself to do so; and this she said with a sort of wonder." Sickness, grief, it was not in her power to bear. They struck at once to the very core of life. She grew gray in a few weeks. She began to look strangely like Alice. Her own sparkling expression was gone; and in the stead, her whole face took on the pathetic, appealing look of her sister. This resemblance increased till she died. "She grew just like Miss Alice," said Maria, her nurse, after her death. "She grew just like her in looks, and in all her ways. Sometimes it seemed as if she *was* Miss Alice."

The week before she was taken sick, returning to New York, I called upon her at once. She was well, and out attending the meeting of a convention. I left a message that, as it would be impossible for me to come again for some time, I should await her promised visit in my own home. Weeks passed, in which a task I was bound in honor to perform by a certain time, withheld me from everything else, even from the reading of newspapers. Yet in the midst of it the thought of Phœbe often came to me, and I felt almost hurt at her non-appearance. Long after its date, a miscarried letter, written by the hand of another, came to me, telling of her sickness. When it reached me, she had already gone to Newport. I answered it, telling her that had I known of her state, I should have left everything and come to her, as I was still ready to do. Carrying the letter down to post without delay, I took up the "Tribune," and the first line on which my eye rested was, "The death of Phœbe Cary."

A short time before, Mrs. Clymer, the niece who had all her life-time been as a daughter to Alice and

Phœbe, stood over the death-bed of her only brother. She closed his eyes for the last time, to lie down on her own bed of suffering, to which she was bound for weeks. Lying there, she learned of the sickness of her aunt Phœbe, but nothing of its degree; the latter withholding it from her. As soon as she was able to sit up, she left Cincinnati for Newport. Reaching New York, and stopping at the house on Twentieth Street for tidings, she was met with the telegram of her aunt's death.

Such were the inexorable circumstances which withheld two who loved her, from her in her last hours; a fact, the very memory of which, to them, must be an unavailing and life-long sorrow. Thus it was with nearly all of her friends; they were out of the city, far from her, and scarcely knew of her sickness until they read the announcement of her death.

She felt it keenly; and in her last loneliness her loving heart would call out, "Where are all my friends?" Yet at no time was she wholly bereft of the ministrations of affection. Hon. Thomas Jenckes, of Providence, Rhode Island, and Mr. Francis Nye, of New York, the friend and executor of both Alice and herself, made every arrangement for her conveyance to Newport. She was accompanied thither by a devoted lady friend, and followed thither by another, who remained with her till after her death. Mr. Oliver Johnson made the journey to Newport expressly to see his old friend in her lonely and suffering state. The lady who was with her to the last, Mrs. Mary Stevens Robinson, daughter of Rev. Dr. Abel Stevens of the Methodist Episcopal Church, who, beside her nurse Maria, is the only person living who can tell truly of

Phœbe Cary's last hours, has, at the request of the writer, kindly sent the following graphic personal recollections of Phœbe, and a record of those sad days at Newport. She says: —

"I first met with Phœbe Cary in the winter of 1853–4. She was still young and striking in her appearance, with keen, merry, black eyes, full of intelligence and spirit, a full, well-proportioned figure, and very characteristic in gesture, aspect, and dress. She was fond of high colors, red, orange, etc., and talked well and rapidly. She was entirely feminine in demeanor, careful, in the main, of the sensibilities of those whom she addressed, though so warm by nature, and so quick in her thought, as to be sometimes thrown off guard on this point, in the ardor of discussion. My father was at this period editor of a magazine, and Alice was one of his contributors. As we lived in the same neighborhood, we exchanged frequent visits with the sisters; we attending their evening receptions, and they our unceremonious social gatherings. At these companies Phœbe's conversation was more with gentlemen than with ladies; partly because she liked them better, and partly because they were sure to be entertained by her; but she maintained invariably a gentle reserve, was never 'carried away' in the ardor or brilliancy of talking. Her wit had no sting, her frankness and sincerity were those of a child, and she was always 'pure womanly.' In remarks upon persons and their performances, she was free and discriminating. Herein it was perhaps less habitual for her to use restraint, than it was with Alice. The latter was carefully, conscientiously just and generous. She was content only to give full credit for whatever was commendable in others, or in what they accomplished.

"Our removal from town, and other interferences, interrupted this acquaintance, until, one spring day some five or six years ago, I chanced to meet Phœbe in a store, on the quest of shopping, like myself. We exchanged warm greetings, talked perhaps for five minutes; but instead of the usual formulas, her words were so fresh and piquant that I recall them even now. I mentioned the fact of my father's being pastor of a Methodist church at Mamaroneck. 'I don't belong among the Methodists,' said Phœbe, in her reply, 'but whenever I feel my heart getting chilly, I go to a meeting of your people, — any kind of a meeting. Their warmth is genuine and irresistible. It is contagious, too, and has crept inside other walls than your own.'

"When I asked her to visit us, she answered in her ready way: 'Well, if you will, I will come to-morrow. Alice is away, and I can leave now, better than when she comes back.'

"Yes, Alice was away. I discovered afterward that this cheery soul, who could sing songs, get books into market, and whose plenitude of spirits was apparently unfailing, whose very gait, at once smooth and rapid, expressed swift and direct force, this hearty, happy woman, pined somewhat when severed from her mate. In the stillness of the house her gayety drooped, and she had no one to think of. The tender curves of her mouth, the arch of her eyelids, something round and child-like in the whole contour, betokened this dependence of affection in her.

"She came to us on the morrow, told numberless

stories and jests, talked with her habitual earnestness, bordering on vehemence when the conversation turned on spiritualism (apologizing afterward, fearing she had 'forgotten herself'), and seemed heartily to enjoy everything connected with her visit. We were all comfortable in her presence, and utterly ignored that slight constraint one often experiences along with the pleasure of having a guest in the house. The second day was rainy, so she could not ride out, as we had planned, to see the scenes of the neighborhood. But she fell to discoursing on the charms of a wet day in a country house, the fresh, growing verdure without, the open fire, the friendly aspect of a library, the converse on men, women, and books, till we ceased to regret the weather, and congratulated ourselves silently through the day, saying, 'What a happy time, what a charming rainy day we are having!'

"In the course of conversation some one remarked her resemblance to Sappho, as she is known to us by the bust, and by descriptions; the olive-brown tint, the stature rather under size, the low brow, etc. Phœbe accepted the comparison smilingly, in silence, but with a natural, modest pleasure. She won the favor of a child, the only one in the family. He wanted a poem, but dared not ask for it. Later, when the request reached her ears, she sent him some simple, characteristic verses upon himself.

"During this visit, as often afterward, I could but note the rapid movement of her mind. She thought quickly, spoke quickly; never chattering nonsense, nor filling spaces of conversation with phrases, but always racy, healthful utterances, full of sense, wit, and vigor. Her natural simplicity never forsook her; something of rural life, of virgin soil, the clear breeziness of Western plains was suggested by her character, as manifested in speech, aspect, and manner.

"After this visit I did not see her again till the day of Alice's funeral. There, her extreme but restrained grief touched my heart; for Death had entered my own door, and borne away my best-beloved. When she turned from her last look at her sister's face, and was supported by friends to her seat, it was plain that this bereavement had taken hold of the roots of her life, and drowned its bases in tears. I sent a note of sympathy, not wishing to intrude upon her sorrow. But some weeks later, hearing that she was much alone, and needed society, I called one evening, and continued my visits weekly and finally daily, up to her last departure from town. In some measure, she recovered her natural flow of spirits. Once, speaking of the Franco-German war, I said that the French more than any other nation were tainted with the virus of Roman corruption, as evident in the latter (Roman) empire, instancing their epicurism, sensuality, cruelty, ostentation, luxury, etc.

"'I see,' said Phœbe, 'you think they are still in the gall of bitterness and bond of iniquity.'

"She liked to talk of love and marriage, though entirely reticent of her own *affaires du cœur*; and she was not without them. On those subjects she spoke with a woman's heart, and conceived the noblest ideals of them.

"'Whenever I write a story, often when only a poem,' she said once, 'it must turn upon love.'

"One evening, the first birthday of Alice after her death, I made one of a tea-party of four at the little hense where so many guests had been so charmingly entertained. An elderly widow, Mrs. C——, who stayed with Phœbe after Alice's death, an old friend, Miss Mary B——, Phœbe, and myself surrounded the table. The snug dining-room, the old-fashioned tea-service, the quaint china, the light biscuit, sweet butter, all the dishes *comme il faut*, everything bespeaking a carefully-ordered domestic life — I am sure you can recall similar evenings full of the same delightful impressions. We had jellied chicken that Phœbe had tried for the first time, for the occasion, and with entire success. We gossiped over our fragrant tea, and smiled at ourselves, a gathering of lone women; and all agreed that the hostess was less like an old maid than any of the others. Cheerful she was, in truth, much like her natural self; yet in the evening, sitting apart with Miss B——, she confessed that the absence of Alice affected her seriously; that when she tried to write, no words would come; that failing here, she turned to household affairs, but could scarcely accomplish anything. Every morning her first thought on waking was, 'Here is another leaden day to get through with; it will be precisely like yesterday, and such will be all days in all time to come!'

"Plainly the watching and anxiety of the previous year had jarred her nerves. They were firmly set by nature, but through her illness their attenuation became extremely painful; they grew sharp and fine as the worn strings of an instrument; it was as if one could see them stretched too long, and too tensely — about to snap, as they did, indeed, at last.

"One Wednesday afternoon I stopped at the door, and hearing that she was lying down, I simply left a bouquet with my love. When next I called, she entered the room with a poem about my flowers, the last verses she ever wrote, about the last paper that she touched with a pen. It seems that on the day of my former call she had given the morning to a memorial article of Alice (for the 'Ladies Repository' of Boston) and being quite worn out when it was done, lay down to rest. My flowers were brought freshly-cut, moistened by some drops of a spring shower, and set on a stand by her lounge. She looked at them a few minutes, rose quickly, 'as if quite rested,' Mrs. C—— said, was gone about twenty minutes in the opposite room, and returned with this pretty resolution of thanks.

"Shortly afterward we attended the anniversary of one of the Woman Suffrage Societies, where we heard Mrs. Livermore, Grace Greenwood, Dr. Eggleston, Mrs. Howe, Lucy Stone, and others. Miss Cary's interest in the movement was strong, and her remarks on the speakers just, and admirably to the point. She was then apparently as well and as cheerful as usual.

"The following Sunday she passed in New Jersey, with her friends, Mrs. Victor and Mrs. Rayl. On her return, Monday, she was seized with a chill, which recurred more or less regularly for upwards of three weeks. They were extremely severe; the suffering and exhaustion, for the time, were like those of death itself. Her appetite grew capricious, and soon failed altogether. We tried to tempt it by following her fancies; but as soon as a new dish or drink was brought, she ceased to care for it. A stomachic cough connected with a derangement of the liver, that was common to the entire family, and imperfect sleep, combined to undermine her strength. She suffered no pain, but an appalling misery, attended with extreme depression of spirits. She lamented often her lonely and forlorn condition, and said her illness was 'quite as much in the mind as in the body.' This however, was an attendant symptom of her malady.

"After seeing her at the time of Alice's funeral, most of her friends were too busy in the affairs of spring, etc., to make visits; and she had been ill for several weeks, before any of them knew of her affliction. I visited her daily, answered her correspondence, read much aloud, laughed, and chatted; did anything I could to alleviate the mortal weariness that had come over her. She confessed to no confidence in any medical aid. Invalids had not been wanting in the family; and no physician or medicine had availed for them. She thought that when they were so ill as to need the regular visits of a physician, they were subjects for death. Occasionally the old vigor would shine forth for a day; but it was sure to be followed by a relapse.

"On one of these better evenings, her friends, Miss Mary L. Booth and Mrs. Wright, called to see her. She lay on her lounge, and talked with much of her former vivacity; recounted an accident that had happened some nights previously. Feeling restless and feverish, she had risen in the dark and made her way to the bath-room, wishing to bathe her head. In the dark she fell, hit her head against a chair with such force as to cut it, fainted, and lay insensible till restored to consciousness by the air from an open window. She then crept back to her couch, and was found quite exhausted in the morning. This serious accident she related with all the lightness it would admit, and actually made sport of some of the details.

"'You have read in sensation stories of heroines weltering in their gore,' she said; 'I understand now exactly what that means, for I lay and weltered in my gore for the best of the night, and it was a very disagreeable proceeding: I never want to welter again.'

"As her strength declined each day instead of mending, she was possessed of a desire to go away, and was persuaded that an entire change would be of benefit. But in her invalid state she was unwilling to impose herself on any of her friends. Finally we persuaded her to accept a very cordial invitation from Mrs. H. O. Houghton of Cambridge, Mass., wife of Mr. Houghton, the publisher. Preparations were made for the journey; but on the day appointed for it, she was too ill to be moved from her room, and the plan was abandoned.

"We then considered several places, deciding at last upon Newport, as offering homelike quarters, with two single ladies, sisters, of a Quaker family with whom I was acquainted. It was arranged for Mr. Jenckes (of Providence) and Mrs. Rayl to escort her thither, while I was to follow a fortnight later. The journey taxed her severely, and prostrated her to such an extent for some days after her arrival, that her life was despaired of. The air, that we hoped would prove medicinal, was thought to be too strong for her shattered frame, though the house stands a mile from the sea. Whether it was too strong or not, I cannot tell; she herself chose it in preference to mountain air; but she sank steadily after reaching Newport, and was too feeble to bear removal. She had been for nearly three months without regular or healthful rest. She ate and drank almost nothing, could not lie down, but sat most of the time in a chair, leaning forward, supported on pillows, or was propped up in the bed. From dawn till eight or nine o'clock she was in the sharpest misery; for the rest she sat with closed eyes in a semi-stupor, from which she would arouse when addressed.

"Reading and conversation were given over. But one day I found Mr. Whittier's poem on Alice, in 'The Atlantic,' 'The Singer,' and read it at her request. When I had half done I paused, thinking she had fallen asleep; but she lifted her eyes, and asked why I did not go on. 'It was all one could wish or ask for,' she said, on hearing it to the close.

"Such nursing as she required was very simple. To fan away the flies, give the medicine at regular hours, change her position frequently, lift her from the chair to the bed and back again, and bathe her swollen feet in salt water; this was nearly all that could be done. Of food and drink she took very little, and that mainly cold milk, beef tea, or iced claret. Some two or three times the doctor's prescriptions were too powerful for her exhausted frame, and caused severe pain, accompanied with delirium. She would then rave at Maria and myself, upbraiding us as the cause of her sufferings; but the frenzy past, she was gentle and sweet, like her usual self. One evening, in a paroxysm of this sort, she begged to be laid on the floor, and after expostulating in vain, we spread a quilt down, and laid her on it. Here she remained for above two hours, I standing over her, and by slow degrees lifting her back to the bed. But these sad aberrations were not frequent nor lasting. They ceased with the harmful medicines.

"Many persons in Newport, learning of her illness, called to leave their condolences; among others, Mr. Higginson, and Mrs. Parton. Her friend Oliver Johnson called twice, and though almost too weak to speak, she saw him both times. The first was on Saturday, when he promised to call again the next day. The tears rolled down his face as he beheld her altered aspect; her reception of him was most affectionate. On Sunday evening she seemed quite improved; told the doctor she believed she had begun to get well, and wanted to be all dressed for Mr. Johnson's call: but for that preparation she was not equal. I had not been out for some time, therefore went to church in the morning, leaving her with Maria. On my return I found her still comfortable, though extremely restless, wishing to be moved every five or ten minutes. 'Don't mind if you pull me limb from limb,' she said quite placidly. 'Pull me about,' was her constant request. I repeated much of the sermon, and she commented on it in her naturally rapid manner. All this day she was more or less talkative. She saw Mr. Johnson, who left with her a nosegay of sweet-peas of rare varieties. Their odor was that of sweet apples, and this I spoke of. 'Who said anything of sweet apples?' she asked, lifting her eyes. When I made the comparison again, she buried her face repeatedly in the flowers, crushing them in her strong desire to extract their fragrance. She thought she would like a sweet apple, but, when it was brought, could only smell of it. That afternoon, sitting on the edge of the bed, she kissed and caressed Maria, talked of how they would go home, went over pleasantly every detail of the anticipated journey as a child would talk of it, and seemed altogether so tranquil and comfortable that any one unaware of her low state might have hoped for convalescence. But we could entertain no such hope.

"The restlessness increased all the next day, though in other respects she remained comfortable. Several times I lifted her alone from the chair to the bed, though how, I can hardly tell now. It was something I could do better than the others, for they invariably hurt her; but generally Maria helped me. In the evening her restlessness increased, so that she could not lie still a moment. I was quite worn out, and for the first time, went early to a little room on the floor above, leaving a written report for the doctor, who generally called at eleven. I noticed when I went up-stairs that the moon was shining, and that all was perfectly still; not so much as a leaf was stirring. I lay quiet, but awake; heard the doctor enter, and go into her room.

"Suddenly a gust of wind wailed through the house, and blew my door shut. A moment after I heard Phœbe's voice in a faint, but piercing cry, and some one came up for me. I was two or three minutes in putting on a wrapper, etc., in the room adjoining hers, but all was still in there. When I entered, her eyes were closed, and the repose of death was settling on her brow. The death throe had seized her, but it lasted for a moment only, and for this I gave thanks even at that hour, for she had such fear of pain; and though she suffered much, yet of actual pain she had but little from the beginning to this last hour. This was mercifully ordered, in view of her peculiar inability to bear acute suffering. After death, her face, almost immediately, wore a tranquil smile,—a smile as through tears, of sunlight shining through rain; and though I saw it no more after the last offices of the hour were rendered, I was told that till the coffin-lid closed finally upon it, this repose remained stamped there. Thus passed away one of the dearest souls that God ever set on the earth."

Maria's story of that hour which she spent alone with Phœbe, Phœbe's last hour in this world, is most touching. "She could not lie down, but she was so restless," said Maria; "she kept saying to me, 'Maria, put my hair back. There! — that is just as ——'s hand used to feel on my forehead — so gentle. And to think that you and I are in the world alone — that after all, I've nobody but *you*, Maria! Everybody else gone so far away. Where *are* my friends? Well, when we go back we won't live alone any longer, will we? We won't live alone as we did last spring. We'll open the house and fill it, won't we, Maria.' . . . . 'But if you go back, and I don't know, don't let me look ugly to my friends; go out and buy me a white dress. All my life I've wanted to wear a white dress, and I never could, because I was so dark. I think I could wear one *then*. Put it on me yourself, Maria, and cover me all over with flowers, so I shall not look gloomy and dreadful to anybody who looks on me for the last time.'"

Thus she talked, one moment as if they were going back to life and the old home on Twentieth Street, with uttered yearnings for friends, and an outreaching toward a mortal future full of sunshine and human companionship; the next, speaking as if her death were certain, the feminine instinct of decoration, the longing to look pleasant to those she loved, strong even in dissolution.

The loving heart was mightier than all. She would suddenly stop her low, rapid utterances, and stretching out her arms throw them around Maria's neck, covering her face with caresses and kisses, ending always with the words: "You and I are all alone, Maria. *After all, I've nobody but you!*" bestowing upon her in that moment some of her most precious personal treasures.

Without an instant's warning the death throe came. She knew it. Throwing up her arms in instinctive fright, this loving, believing, but timid soul, who had never stood alone in all her mortal life, as she felt herself drifting out into the unknown, the eternal, starting on the awful passage from whence there is no return cried, in a low, piercing voice, "O God, have mercy on my soul!" and died.

She had her wish. The white robe that she had so longed all her life to wear, fell in fleecy folds about her in death. She slept amid flowers, fresh and fragrant. The tender heart whose depth of affection had never been fully seen or felt within its outward shield of resplendent wit, now shone through and transfigured every feature. Every lineament was smiling, childlike, loving. She had her wish. No look on the living face of Phœbe Cary was ever so sweet as the last.

Phœbe Cary died at Newport, Rhode Island, Monday, July 31, 1871. Her body was brought to the empty house on Twentieth Street, New York, and from thence was taken for funeral services to All Souls Church, corner of Fourth Avenue and Twentieth Street, whose congregation, coming and going, Phœbe had so often watched from her chamber window, with emotions of affection. Her funeral was attended by her four nieces, by the few of her many friends at that time left in the heated city, and by a goodly company of strangers to whom her name was dear. The services were intrusted to the Rev. A. G. Laurie, a Scottish Universalist clergyman, and Rev. Bernard Peters, both old and dear friends of the Cary family, the former having known Phœbe from childhood. The "New York Tribune," speaking of the solemnities, said: —

"The body was placed in the centre aisle, near the chancel, the organ playing a dirge. When the attendants had arranged the final details, and the last strains of music were dying away, a cloud that had obscured the sun passed from before it, and the whole church was illumined by soft, golden tints, seemingly indicative of the glory which awaited the peaceful spirit that had so recently passed away."

At the conclusion of Mr. Laurie's affectionate and tearful address, he read Phœbe's hymn, "Nearer Home," which was sung by the choir, who also sang the following hymn, written by the officiating clergyman: —

O stricken heart, what spell shall move thee,
  What charm shall lift that grief away,
Which, like a leaden mist above thee,
  Shuts out the shining of the day?

Is out of sight the friend unto thee
  'Fore every friend that sat the first?
Let not her silence thus undo thee;
  The blank of Death is not its worst.

And never shade of wrong lay on her;
  She loved her kith, her kind, her God,
And from her mind returned the Donor
  Rich harvest for the seed He sowed.

She died in stress of love and duty,
  On others spent her work and will;
Unself— O, Christ, thy chiefest beauty
  Was hers, and she is with Thee still.

Then, smitten heart, renew thy gladness:
  Rejoice that thou canst not forget;
In every pulse, with solemn sadness,
  Unseen, but present, feel her yet."

Horace Greeley and others went as far as they could with this dear friend on her long journey. When they saw all that was mortal of this last sister of her race laid in Greenwood, and turned back to her empty house, they realized with unspoken sorrow that its last light had gone out, and that the home in Twentieth Street was left desolate forever.

INNER SIGHT.

I think true love is never blind,
  But rather gives an added light,
An inner vision, quick to find
  The beauties hid from common sight.

No soul can ever truly see
  Another's highest, noblest part,
Save through the sweet philosophy,
  And living wisdom of the heart.

Your unanointed eyes shall fall
  On him who fills my soul with light;
You do not see my friend at all,
  You see what hides him from your sight.

I see the feet that fain would climb,
  You but the steps that turn astray;
I see the soul unharmed, sublime,
  You but the garment and the clay.

You see a nature weak, unstead,
  Dwarfed ever by the earthly clod;
I see the manhood perfected,
  May reach the stature of a God.

Blinded I stood, as now you stand,
  Till on mine eyes with touches sweet,
Love, the deliverer, laid his hand,
  And, lo! I worship at his feet.

—*Phœbe Cary.*

CHAPTER XII.

THE SISTERS COMPARED. — THEIR LAST RESTING-PLACE.

It is impossible to estimate either sister without any reference to the other, — as impossible as to tell what a husband and wife, modifed in habit and character by many years of wedded life, would have been had they never lived together.

Alice Cary was remarkable for the fullness and tenderness of her emotional nature, and for the depth and fidelity of her affections; through these she was all softness and gentleness. But mentally she was a strong woman — strong in will, energy, industry, and patience; through these she faced fate with a masculine strength of courage and endurance. It was not easy, but her will was strong enough to compel her life to do noble service.

Phœbe, mentally and emotionally, was in every attribute essentially feminine. The terror of her mortal life was responsibility. It seemed absolutely necessary to her existence to know that somebody stood between her and all the inexorable demands and exigencies of this world. "I believe a consciousness of responsibility could kill Phœbe, even if she were in perfect health," said Alice. "She does not wish to feel responsibility for anything, not even for the saving of her own soul; for that reason alone she would be a Roman

Catholic if she could, and lay the whole burden of her salvation on the Church. Unfortunately for her comfort, the literalness of her mind makes that impossible."

Alice Cary was preëminently, and in the highest and finest sense, an attractive woman. She was beloved of women. Young girls were drawn toward her in a sort of idolatry, and she was universally beloved of men. No man could come within the sphere of her presence without feeling all that was most tender, chivalric, and true in his manhood, instinctively going forth toward the woman by his side. It was the fine potent power of her femininity, her gentleness, and sincerity, her tenderness and purity, which inspired all that was most tender and reverent in him. This feeling of sacred affection for Alice Cary was felt by all men who were her friends, no matter how various or conflicting their tastes might be in other things. When the loveliness of her face was not that of youth, there were artists who used to go to her house Sabbath evening after Sabbath evening, "just to look upon her face." Said one, "It grows more beautiful every year."

Alice was tall and graceful, with a suggestion of majesty in her simple mien. Her dark eyes were of a wonderful softness and beauty, with a fathomless depth of tenderness in their expression, which men and even women love. Yet there were not wanting lines of firmness and energy about the feminine mouth, and there was an impression of silent power pervading her very gentleness. Phœbe had all the soft contours, the complexion, hair, and eyes, of a Spanish woman. And with her sparkle and repartee she had besides a

Spaniard's languors. She was slightly below ordinary height; full, without being heavy in outline. The prevailing expression of Alice's countenance was one of sadness, pervaded with extreme sweetness; but Phœbe's black eyes sparkled as she talked, and even when her face was in repose there was upon it the trace of a smile. Alice dressed with rich simplicity, and in the most resplendent drawing-room would have been noticed as one of the most elegant women in it. Phœbe, in her more animated moments, would have been marked for her dark, brilliant beauty, and would have reminded you of an Oriental princess in the warm brightness of her colors, and the distinctive character of her ornaments.

The mental contrasts of the sisters were as marked as their physical. Alike in tastes and aspiration, they were unlike in temperament, in their habit of thought and of action. Each, in her own way, out of her own life, sacrificed much to the other, — how much only God and their own souls knew. Out of this mutual sacrifice was welded a bond stronger and closer than many sisters know; through their life-long association, their sympathy, their very sisterhood, it drew them nearer and nearer together to the end. It produced at last an identification of existence such as we see where the natures of husband and wife have become perfectly assimilated because their life and fate are one.

Notwithstanding the unity of their pursuits, the identity of their interests, their utter devotion to each other, outside of this dual life each sister lived distinctly and separately her own existence. Each respected absolutely the personal peculiarities of the other, and never consciously intruded upon them.

Each thought and wrought in as absolute solitude as if she alone were in the house. The results of the labor they shared together; but not the labor. Each respected so much the idiosyncrasies of the other's mind, that neither ever thought of criticising the other's work. If one offered a suggestion, it was because the other requested her to do so.

Both had ways that at times were not altogether satisfactory to the other. Each accepted them as a part of the cross that she must bear for her sister, and she did not complain, nor did it cause any bitterness. For example, Alice's tireless energy and unswerving will at times wearied Phœbe, though she found in both the staff and support of her life, while Phœbe's inertia was a much more perpetual trial to Alice. She recognized the fact that she could not make the active law of her own being that of Phœbe's, and acquiesced, but not always with inward resignation,

According to Phœbe's own testimony, Alice used mind and body unsparingly whenever she could compel them to obey her will. With all a woman's softness, she met the responsibilities of life as a man meets them. She never stopped to inquire whether she felt like doing a task, no matter how disagreeable it might be. If it was to be done she did it, and without words and without delay.

It was Phœbe, the protected and sheltered one, who consulted her moods. Perhaps this was scarcely a fault; she obeyed the law of her being and the law of her life in this. Had she compelled her powers to produce a given amount of work, as Alice did, without doubt it would proportionately have depreciated in quality. Absolute necessity did not force her to such toil, therefore she instinctively avoided it. Beside, a most touching humility always held her back from testing her powers to the utmost.

The same self-depreciation was strong in Alice; but her aspiration, her will to do her best, with the impelling demands of life, were so much stronger, that neither brain nor hand were ever for a moment idle. She placed the highest estimate on Phœbe's brilliant wit, clear vision, and apt and shrewd suggestiveness, as well as on her poetical genius. The former, especially, she thought a mine unworked, and for years urged and encouraged Phœbe to test the growing opportunities of correspondence of critical and editorial writing which journalism opened to women. But Phœbe was not to be persuaded even by the necessities of the occasion, or the eloquence of her sister. She continued to coruscate in the little parlor, to fill the air with the flashes of a most exquisite wit, but she never turned it to any material account. When a song came singing through her brain, she would leave her sewing, or her novel, and go and write it down. Yet for a period of eight years she wrote comparatively nothing. In referring to this period she often said: "I thought that I should never write again. I had nothing to say, and felt an unutterable heaviness. If I did write anything it did not seem to me worth copying, much less reading." The causes of this mental barrenness were probably purely physical and temperamental. It is doubtful if in any effective degree it was in her power to help it.

No less those were years in which the burden of life weighed sorely and heavily on Alice. Often she felt herself stagger under the weights of life. She felt her strength failing. No less she knew that she must carry them alone, that there was no one on earth to help her. Phœbe outlived that period of mental inactivity. The war seemed to arouse and quicken all her nature. For the last five years of her life her genius was almost as productive as that of Alice. Her very best poems, with a few exceptions, were written within that period. To the delight of her friends and the joy of her sister, her powers seemed continually to increase, her song to grow sweeter and fuller to the end. Had she lived ten years longer, without a doubt she would have risen to a height never attained by her before. Believing her sister always with her, it would have been as if the song of Alice was added to her own.

Through nearly all their lives Phœbe had materially, intellectually, and spiritually depended upon Alice. Though Phœbe had the more robust health, it was Alice who had the more resolute spirit. Over all the long and toilsome road from poverty to competence, it was Phœbe who leaned on Alice. It was Alice who bore the burden and heat of the day, and who smoothed the paths for her sister's feet. Not that she was idle, and did nothing; but she paused, and doubted, and waited by the way. Tears dimmed the lovely eyes of the elder, how often; pain and weariness would have stayed her steps, but her high heart said, "Nay." Necessity said, "You must not!" She went on, she led her sister on, till they came to a height where both stood side by side. Then, the painful journey done, in the evening shadow it was Alice who leaned on Phœbe, and leaning thus, she died.

But Phœbe lived through and for Alice so long, when she looked and saw her no more, the very impulse and power to live were gone. She sank and died, because she could not live on, in a world where her sister was not.

Turning to the right, after entering Greenwood, a short walk brings you to an embowered slope, crowned by a grassy lot, on whose lowly gate is inscribed the one word: "Cary."

Within, side by side, are three mounds, of equal length, unmarked save by one low head-stone, whose velvet turf holds a few withering flowers, the only token of the loving remembrance of the living for the sleepers who rest below. Elmina, Phœbe, and Alice! names precious to womanhood, names worthy of the tenderest love of the highest manhood. Far from their kindred, here these sisters three sleep at last together. Here the pilgrim feet are stayed. Here the eager brains and tireless hands at last are idle. Here the passionate, tender, yearning hearts are forever still. On one side you hear the murmur and moan of the great metropolis, the turmoil and anguish of human life never stilled. On the other, Ocean chants a perpetual requiem. As you listen, you are sure that it holds that in its call which is eternal; sure that there is that in you which can never end; sure that the love, and devotion, and divine intelligence of the women whom you mourn, still survive; that they whom you loved in all the infirmity of their human state, await you now, redeemed, and glorified, and immortal.

The autumn leaves fall on their graves in tender showers. The spring leaves, the summer flowers, bud and bloom around them in beauty ever renewed. The air is penetrated with sunshine and with song. The place is full of the brightness that Phœbe loved, full of the soothing shade and peace so dear to Elmina, and to Alice.

Farewell, beloved trinity!

The words which Whittier wrote for Alice, this hour belong alike to each one:

"God giveth quietness at last!
The common way that all have passed
She went, with mortal yearnings fond,
To fuller life and love beyond.

"Fold the rapt soul in your embrace,
My dear ones! Give the singer place.
To you, to her — I know not where —
I lift the silence of a prayer.

"For only thus our own we find;
The gone before, the left behind,
All mortal voices die between;
The unheard reaches the unseen.

"Again the blackbirds sing: the streams
Wake, laughing, from their winter dreams,
And tremble in the April showers
The tassels of the maple flowers.

"But not for her has spring renewed
The sweet surprises of the wood;
And bird and flowers are lost to her
Who was their best interpreter!

What to shut eyes has God revealed?
What hear the ears that death had sealed?
What undreamed beauty, passing show,
Requites the loss of all we know?

"O silent land, to which we move,
Enough if there alone be love;
And mortal need can ne'er outgrow
What it is waiting to bestow!

"O white soul! from that far-off shore
Float some sweet song the waters o'er;
Our faith confirm, our fears dispel,
With the old voice we loved so well!"

In the days of her early youth Phœbe wrote:—

"Let your warm hands chill not, slipping
From my fingers' icy tips;
Be there not the touch of kisses
On my uncaressing lips;
Let no kindness see the blindness
Of my eyes' last, long eclipse.
Never think of me as lying
By the dismal mould o'erspread:
But about the soft white pillow
Folded underneath my head,
And of summer flowers weaving
Their rich broidery o'er my bed.
Think of the immortal spirit
Living up above the sky,
And of how my face is wearing
Light of immortality;
Looking earthward, is o'erleaning
The white bastion of the sky."

LATER POEMS BY ALICE CARY

PRETTY IS THAT PRETTY DOES.

BY ALICE CARY.

The spider wears a plain brown dress,
  And she is a steady spinner;
To see her, quiet as a mouse
Going about her silver house,
  You would never, never, never guess
The way she gets her dinner!

She looks as if no thought of ill
  In all her life had stirred her,
But while she moves with careful tread,
And while she spins her silken thread,
  She is planning, planning, planning still
The way to do some murder!

My child, who reads this simple lay
  With eyes down-dropt and tender,
Remember the old proverb says
That pretty is, which pretty does,
  And that worth does not go nor stay
For poverty nor splendor.

'Tis not the house, and not the dress
  That makes the saint or sinner.
To see the spider sit and spin
Shut with her webs of silver in,
  You would never, never, never, guess
The way she gets her dinner!

BALLADS AND LOVE SONGS

THE MIGHT OF LOVE.

"THERE is work, good man, for you to-day!"
 So the wife of Jamie cried,
"For a ship at Garl'ston, on Solway,
 Is beached, and her coal's to be got away
 At the ebbing time of tide."

"And, lassie, would you have me start,
 And make for Solway sands?
You know that I, for my poor part,
To help me, have nor horse nor cart—
 I have only just my hands!"

"But, Jamie, be not, till ye try,
 Of honest chances baulked;
For, mind ye, man, I'll prophesy
That while the old ship's high and dry
 Her master'll have her caulked."

And far and near the men were pressed,
 As the wife saw in her dreams.
"Aye," Jamie said, "she knew the best,'
As he went under with the rest
 To caulk the open seams.

And while the outward-flowing tide
Moaned like a dirge of woe,
The ship's mate from the beach-belt cried:
"Her hull is heeling toward the side
Where the men are at work below!"

And the cartmen, wild and open-eyed,
Made for the Solway sands —
Men heaving men like coals aside,
For now it was the master cried:
"Run for your lives, all hands!"

Like dead leaves in the sudden swell
Of the storm, upon that shout,
Brown hands went fluttering up and fell,
As, grazed by the sinking planks, pell mell,
The men came hurtling out!

Thank God, thank God, the peril's past!
"No! no!" with blanching lip,
The master cries. "One man, the last,
Is caught, drawn in, and grappled fast
Betwixt the sands and the ship!"

"Back, back, all hands! Get what you can —
Or pick, or oar, or stave."
This way and that they breathless ran,
And came and fell to, every man,
To dig him out of his grave!

"Too slow! too slow! The weight will kill!
Up, make your hawsers fast!"
Then every man took hold with a will —

A long pull and a strong pull — still
With never a stir o' th' mast!

"Out with the cargo!" Then they go
At it with might and main.
"Back to the sands! too slow, too slow!
He's dying, dying! yet, heave ho!
Heave ho! there, once again!"

And now on the beach at Garl'ston stood
A woman whose pale brow wore
Its love like a queenly crown; and the blood
Ran curdled and cold as she watched the flood
That was racing in to the shore.

On, on it trampled, stride by stride.
It was death to stand and wait;
And all that were free threw picks aside,
And came up dripping out o' th' tide,
And left the doomed to his fate.

But lo! the great sea trembling stands;
Then, crawling under the ship,
As if for the sake of the two white hands
Reaching over the wild, wet sands,
Slackened that terrible grip.

"Come to me, Jamie! God grants the way,"
She cries, "for lovers to meet."
And the sea, so cruel, grew kind, they say,
And, wrapping him tenderly round with spray,
Laid him dead at her feet.

"THE GRACE WIFE OF KEITH."

No whit is gained, do you say to me,
In a hundred years, nor in two nor three,
 In wise things, nor in holy —
No whit since Bacon trod his ways,
And William Shakespeare wrote his plays!
 Aye, aye, the world moves slowly.

But here is a lesson, man, to heed;
I have marked the pages, open and read;
 We are yet enough unloving,
Given to evil and prone to fall,
But the record will show you, after all,
 That still the world keeps moving.

All in the times of the good King James —
I have marked the deeds and their doers' names,
 And over my pencil drawing —
One Geillis Duncan standeth the first
For helping of "anie kinde sick" accursed,
 And doomed, without trial, to "*thrawing.*"

Read of her torturers given their scope
Of wrenching and binding her head with a rope,
 Of taunting her word and her honor,
And of searching her body sae pure and fair
From the lady-white feet to the gouden hair
 For the wizard's mark upon her!

Of how through fair coaxings and agonies' dread
She came to acknowledge whatever they said,

And, lastly, her shaken wits losing,
To prattle from nonsense and blasphemies wild
To the silly entreaties and tears of a child,
And then to the fatal accusing.

First naming Euphemia Macalzean,
A lord's young daughter, and fair as a queen;
Then Agnes, whose wisdom surpassed her;
"Grace Wyff of Keith," so her sentence lies,
"Adjudged at Holyrood under the eyes
Of the King, her royal master."

O, think of this Grace wife, fine and tall,
With a witch's bridle tied to the wall!
Her peril and pain enhancing
With owning the lie that on Hallowmas Eve
She with a witch crew sailed in a sieve
To Berwick Church, for a dancing!

Think of her owning, through brainsick fright,
How Geillis a Jew's-harp played that night,
And of Majesty sending speedy
Across the border and far away
For that same Geillis to dance and play,
Of infernal news made greedy!

Think of her true tongue made to tell
How she had raised a dog from a well
To conjure a Lady's daughters;
And how she had gript him neck and skin,
And, growling, thrust him down and in
To his hiding under the waters!

How Rob the Rower, so stout and brave,
Helped her rifle a dead man's grave,
And how, with enchantments arming,
Husbands false she had put in chains,
And gone to the beds of women in pains
And brought them through by charming!

Think of her owning that out at sea
The Devil had marked her on the knee,
And think of the prelates round her
Twitching backward their old gray hairs
And bowing themselves to their awful prayers
Before they took her and bound her!

The world moves! Witch-fires, say what you will,
Are lighted no more on the Castle Hill
By the breath of a crazy story;
Nor are men riven at horses' tails,
Or done to death through pincered nails,
In the name of God and his glory.

The world moves on! Say what you can,
No more may a maiden's love for a man,
Into scorn and hatred turning,
Wrap him in rosin stiff and stark,
And roll him along like a log in its bark
To the place of fiery burning.

And such like things were done in the days
When one Will Shakespeare wrote his plays;
And when Bacon thought, for a wonder;
And when Luther had hurled, at the spirit's call,
Inkstand, Bible, himself, and all
At the head of the Papal thunder.

JOHNNY RIGHT.

JOHNNY RIGHT, his hand was brown,
  And so was his honest, open face,
For the sunshine kissed him up and down,
  But Johnny counted all for grace;
And when he looked in the glass at night
He said that brown was as good as white!

A little farm our Johnny owned,
  Some pasture-fields, both green and good,
A bit of pleasant garden ground,
  A meadow, and a strip of wood.
"Enough for any man," said John,
"To earn his livelihood upon!"

Two oxen, speckled red and white,
  And a cow that gave him a pail of milk,
He combed and curried morn and night
  Until their coats were as soft as silk.
"Cattle on all the hills," said he,
"Could give no more of joy to me."

He never thought the world was wrong
  Because rough weather chanced a day;
"The night is always hedged along
  With daybreak roses," he would say;
He did not ask for manna, but said,
"Give me but strength — I will get the bread!"

Kindly he took for good and all
  Whatever fortune chanced to bring,

And he never wished that Spring were Fall,
  And he never wished that Fall were Spring;
But set the plough with a joy akin
To the joy of putting the sickle in.

He never stopped to sigh "Oho!"
  Because of the ground he needs must till,
For he knew right well that a man must sow
  Before he can reap, and he sowed with a will;
And still as he went to his rye-straw bed,
"Work brings the sweetest of rest," he said.

Johnny's house was little and low,
  And his fare was hard; and that was why
He used to say, with his cheeks aglow,
  That he must keep his heart up high:
Aye, keep it high, and keep it light!
He used to say — wise Johnny Right!

He never fancied one was two;
  But according to his strength he planned,
And oft to his Meggy would say he knew
  That gold was gold, and sand was sand;
And that each was good and best in its place,
For he counted everything for grace.

Now Meggy Right was Meggy Wrong,
  For things with her went all awry;
She always found the day too long
  Or the day too short, and would mope and sigh;
For, somehow, the time and place that were,
Were never the time and place for her!

"O Johnny, Johnny!" she used to say,
  If she saw a cloud in the sky at morn,
"There will be a hurricane to-day;"
  Or, "The rain will come and drench the corn!
 And Johnny would answer, with a smile,
"Wait, dear Meggy, wait for a while!"

And often before an ear was lost,
  Or a single hope of the harvest gone,
She would cry, "Suppose there should fall a frost,
  What should we do then, John, O John!"
And Johnny would answer, rubbing his thumbs,
"Wait, dear Meggy, wait till it comes!"

But when she saw the first gray hair,
  Her hands together she wrung and wrung,
And cried, in her wicked and weak despair,
  "Ah, for the day when we both were young!"
And Johnny answered, kissing her brow,
'Then was then, Meg — now is now!"

And when he spectacles put on,
  And read at ease the paper through,
She whimpered, "O, hard-hearted John,
  It isn't the way you used to do!"
And Johnny, wiser than wiser men,
Said, "Now is now, Meg — then was then!"

So night and day, with this and that,
  She gave a bitter to all the bliss,
Now for Johnny to give her a hat,
  And now for Johnny to give her a kiss,
Till, patience failing, he cried, "Peg, Peg!
You're enough to turn a man's head, Meg!"

O, then she fell into despair —
  No coaxing could her temper mend;
For her part now she didn't care
  How soon her sad life had an end.
And Johnny, sneering, made reply,
"Well, Meg, don't die before you die!

Then foolish Meg began to scold,
  And call her Johnny ugly names;
She wished the little farm was sold,
  And that she had no household claims,
So that she might go and starve or beg,
And Johnny answered, "O Meg, Meg!"

Ah, yes, she did — she didn't care!
  That were a living to prefer;
What had she left to save despair?
  A man that didn't care for her!
Indeed, in truth she'd rather go!
"Don't, Meg," says Johnny, "don't say so!

She left his stockings all undarned,
  She set his supper for him cold;
And every day she said she yearned
  To have the hateful homestead sold.
She couldn't live, and wouldn't try!
John only answered with a sigh.

Passing the tavern one cold night,
  Says Johnny, "I've a mind to stop,
It looks so cheery and so bright
  Within, and take a little drop,
And then I'll go straight home to Meg."
There was the serpent in the egg.

He stopped, alas, alas for John.
  That careless step foredoomed his fall.
Next year the little farm was gone, —
  Corn-fields and cattle, house and all;
And Meggy learned too late, too late,
Her own self had evoked her fate.

THE LOVER'S INTERDICT.

Stop, traveller, just a moment at my gate,
  And I will give you news so very sweet
  That you will thank me. Where the branches meet
Across your road, and droop, as with the weight
  Of shadows laid upon them, pause, I pray,
  And turn aside a little from your way.

You see the drooping branches overspread
  With shadows, as I told you — look you now
  To the high elm-tree with the dead white bough
Loose swinging out of joint, and there, with head
  Tricked out with scarlet, pouring his wild lay,
  You see a blackbird: turn your step that way.

Holding along the honeysuckle hedge,
  Make for the meadows lying down so low;
  Ah! now I need not say that you must go
No further than that little silver wedge
  Of daisy-land, pushed inward by the flood
  Betwixt the hills — you could not, if you would.

For you will see there, as the sun goes down,
  And freckles all the daisy leaves with gold,
  A little maiden, in their evening fold
Penning two lambs — her soft, fawn-colored gown
  Tucked over hems of violet, by a hand
  Dainty as any lady's in the land.

Such gracious light she will about her bring,
  That, when the Day, being wedded to the shade,
  Wears the moon's circle, blushing, as the maid
Blushes to wear the unused marriage-ring,
  And all the quickened clouds do fall astir
  With daffodils, your thoughts will stay with her.

No ornaments but her two sapphire eyes,
  And the twin roses in her cheeks that grow,
  The nice-set pearls, that make so fine a show
When that she either softly smiles or sighs,
  And the long tresses, colored like a bee —
  Brown, with a sunlight shimmer. You will see,

When you have ceased to watch the airy spring
  Of her white feet, a fallen beech hard by,
  The yellow earth about the gnarled roots dry,
And if you hide there, you will hear her sing
  That song Kit Marlowe made so long ago —
  "Come live with me, and be my love," you know.

Dear soul, you would not be at heaven's high gate
  Among the larks, that constellated hour,
  Nor locked alone in some green-hearted bower
Among the nightingales, being in your fate,
  By fortune's sweet selection, graced above
  All grace, to hear that — Come, and be my love!

But when the singer singeth down the sweets
  To that most maiden-like and lovely bed —
  All out of soft persuasive roses spread —
You must not touch the fair and flowery sheets
  Even in your thought! and from your perfect bliss
  I furthermore must interdict you this:

When all the wayward mists, because of her,
  Lie in their white wings, moveless, on the air,
  You must not let the loose net of her hair
Drag your heart to her! nor from hushed breath stir
  Out of your sacred hiding. As you guess
  She is my love — this woodland shepherdess.

The cap, the clasps, the kirtle fringed along
  With myrtles, as the hand of dear old Kit
  Did of his cunning pleasure broider it,
To ornament that dulcet piece of song
  Immortaled with refrains of — Live with me!
  These to your fancy, one and all are free.

But, favored traveller, ere you quit my gate,
  Promise to hold it, in your mind to be
  Enamored only of the melody,
Else will I pray that all yon woody weight
  Of branch and shadow, as you pass along,
  Crush you among the echoes of the song.

THE SETTLER'S CHRISTMAS EVE.

In a patch of clearing, scarcely more
  Than his brawny double hands,
With woods behind and woods before,
  The Settler's cabin stands;
A little, low, and lonesome shed,
With a roof of clapboards overhead.

Aye, low, so low the wind-warped eave
  Hangs close against the door;
You might almost stretch a bishop's sleeve
  From the rafter to the floor;
And the window is not too large, a whit,
For a lady's veil to curtain it.

The roof-tree's bent and knotty knees
  By the Settler's axe are braced,
And the door-yard fence is three felled trees
  With their bare arms interlaced;
And a grape-vine, shaggy and rough and red,
Swings from the well-sweep's high, sharp head.

And among the stubs, all charred and black,
  Away to the distant huts,
Winds in and out the wagon-track,
  Cut full of zigzag ruts:
And down and down to the sluggish pond,
And through and up to the swamps beyond.

And do you ask beneath such thatch
  What heart or hope may be?

Just pull the string of the wooden latch,
  And see what you shall see:
A hearth-stone broad and warm and wide,
With master and mistress either side.

And 'twixt them, in the radiant glow,
  Prattling of Christmas joys,
With faces in a shining row,
  Six children, girls and boys;
And in the cradle a head half-hid
By the shaggy wolf-skin coverlid.

For the baby sleeps in the shaded light
  As gently as a lamb,
And two little stockings, scarlet bright,
  Are hanging 'gainst the jamb;
And the yellow cat lies all of a curl
In the lap of a two-years' blue-eyed girl.

On the dresser, saved for weeks and weeks,
  A hamper of apples stands,
And some are red as the children's cheeks,
  And some are brown as their hands;
For cakes and apples must stead, you see,
The rich man's costlier Christmas-tree.

A clock that looks like a skeleton,
  From the corner ticks out bold;
And that never was such a clock to run
  You would hardly need be told,
If you were to see the glances proud
Drawn toward it when it strikes so loud.

The Settler's rifle, bright and brown,
Hangs high on the rafter-hooks.
And swinging a hand's breadth lower down
Is a modest shelf of books;
Bible and Hymn-book, thumbed all through,
"Baxter's Call," and a novel or two.

"Peter Wilkins," "The Bloody Hand,"
"The Sailor's Bride and Bark,"
"Jerusalem and the Holy Land,"
"The Travels of Lewis and Clarke;"
Some tracts: among them, "The Milk-maid's Fall,
"Pleasure Punished," and "Death at a Ball."

A branch of sumach, shining bright,
And a stag-horn, deck the wall,
With a string of birds'-eggs, blue and white,
Beneath. But after all,
You will say the six little heads in a row
By the hearth-stone make the prettiest show.

The boldest urchin dares not stir;
But each heart, be sure, rebels
As the father taps on the newspaper
With his brass-bowed spectacles;
And knitting-needle with needle clicks
As the mother waits for the politics.

He has rubbed the glass and rubbed the bow,
And now is a fearful pause:
'Come, Molly!" he says, "come Sue, come Joe,
And I'll tell you of Santa Claus!"
How the faces shine with glad surprise,
As if the souls looked out of the eyes.

In a trice the dozen ruddy legs
  Are bare; and speckled and brown
And blue and gray, from the wall-side peg
  The stockings dangle down;
And the baby with wondering eyes, looks out
To see what the clatter is all about.

And what will Santa Claus bring?" they tease,
  "And, say, is he tall and fair?"
While the younger climb the good man's knees,
  And the elder scale his chair;
And the mother jogs the cradle, and tries
The charm of the dear old lullabies.

So happily the hours fly past,
  'Tis pity to have them o'er;
But the rusty weights of the clock, at last
  Are dragging near the floor;
And the knitting kneedles, one and all,
Are stuck in the round, red knitting-ball.

Now, all of a sudden the father twirls
  The empty apple-plate;
"Old Santa Claus don't like his girls
  And boys to be up so late!"
He says, "And I'll warrant our star-faced cow,
He's waiting astride o' the chimney now."

Down the back of his chair they slide,
  They slide down arm and knee:
"If Santa Claus is indeed outside,
  He sha'n't be kept for me!"
Cry one and all; and away they go,
Hurrying, flurrying, six in a row.

In the mother's eyes are happy tears
  As she sees them flutter away;
"My man," she says, "it is sixteen years
  Since our blessed wedding-day;
And I wouldn't think it but just a year
If it wasn't for all these children here."

And then they talk of what they will do
  As the years shall come and go;
Of schooling for little Molly and Sue,
  And of land for John and Joe;
And Dick is so wise, and Dolly so fair,
"They," says the mother, "will have luck to spare!

"Aye, aye, good wife, that's clear, that's clear!"
  Then, with eyes on the cradle bent,
"And what if he in the wolf-skin here
  Turned out to be President?
Just think! O, wouldn't it be fine, —
Such fortune for your boy and mine!"

She stopped — her heart with hope elate —
  And kissed the golden head:
Then, with the brawny hand of her mate
  Folded in hers, she said:
"Walls as narrow, and a roof as low,
Have sheltered a President, you know."

And then they said they would work and wait,
  The good, sweet-hearted pair —
You must have pulled the latch-string straight,
  Had you in truth been there,
Feeling that you were not by leave
At the Sett'er's hearth that Christmas Eve.

THE OLD STORY.

THE waiting-women wait at her feet,
  And the day is fading into the night,
And close at her pillow, and round and sweet,
  The red rose burns like a lamp a-light,
And under and over the gray mists fold;
  And down and down from the mossy eaves,
  And down from the sycamore's long wild leaves
The slow rain droppeth so cold, so cold.

Ah! never had sleeper a sleep so fair;
  And the waiting-women that weep around,
Have taken the combs from her golden hair,
  And it slideth over her face to the ground.
They have hidden the light from her lovely eyes;
  And down from the eaves where the mosses grow
  The rain is dripping so slow, so slow,
And the night wind cries and cries and cries.

From her hand they have taken the shining ring,
  They have brought the linen her shroud to make:
O, the lark she was never so loath to sing,
  And the morn she was never so loath to awake!
And at their sewing they hear the rain, —
  Drip-drop, drip-drop over the eaves,
  And drip-drop over the sycamore leaves,
As if there would never be sunshine again.

The mourning train to the grave have gone,
  And the waiting women are here and are there,
With birds at the windows, and gleams of the sun,
  Making the chamber of death to be fair.

And under and over the mist uplaps,
And ruby and amethyst burn through the gray,
And driest bushes grow green with spray,
And the dimpled water its glad hands claps.

The leaves of the sycamore dance and wave,
And the mourners put off the mourning shows;
And over the pathway down to the grave
The long grass blows and blows and blows.
And every drip-drop rounds to a flower,
And love in the heart of the young man springs,
And the hands of the maidens shine with rings,
As if all life were a festival hour.

BALDER'S WIFE.

HER casement like a watchful eye
From the face of the wall looks down,
Lashed round with ivy vines so dry,
And with ivy leaves so brown.
Her golden head in her lily hand
Like a star in the spray o' th' sea,
And wearily rocking to and fro,
She sings so sweet and she sings so low
To the little babe on her knee.
But let her sing what tune she may,
Never so light and never so gay,
It slips and slides and dies away
To the moan of the willow water.

Like some bright honey-hearted rose
        That the wild wind rudely mocks,
She blooms from the dawn to the day's sweet close
        Hemmed in with a world of rocks.
The livelong night she doth not stir,
        But keeps at her casement lorn,
And the skirts of the darkness shine with her
        As they shine with the light o' the morn
And all who pass may hear her lay,
        But let it be what tune it may,
It slips and slides and dies away
        To the moan of the willow water.

And there, within that one-eyed tower,
        Lashed round with the ivy brown,
She droops like some unpitied flower
        That the rain-fall washes down :
The damp o' th' dew in her golden hair,
        Her cheek like the spray o' th' sea,
And wearily rocking to and fro
She sings so sweet and she sings so low
        To the little babe on her knee.
But let her sing what tune she may,
        Never so glad and never so gay,
It slips and slides and dies away
        To the moan of the willow water.

Look for goodness, look for gladness;
You will meet them all the while;
If you bring a smiling visage
To the glass, you meet a smile.
—*Alice Cary.*

POEMS OF THOUGHT.

UNDER THE SHADOW.

My sorrowing friend, arise and go
  About thy house with patient care;
The hand that bows thy head so low
  Will bear the ills thou canst not bear.

Arise, and all thy tasks fulfill,
  And as thy day thy strength shall be;
Were there no power beyond the ill,
  The ill could not have come to thee.

Though cloud and storm encompass thee,
  Be not afflicted nor afraid;
Thou knowest the shadow could not be
  Were there no sun beyond the shade.

For thy beloved, dead and gone,
  Let sweet, not bitter, tears be shed;
Nor "open thy dark saying on
  The harp," as though thy faith were dead.

Couldst thou even have them reappear
  In bodies plain to mortal sense,
How were the miracle more clear
  To bring them than to take them hence?

Then let thy soul cry in thee thus
  No more, nor let thine eyes thus weep;
Nothing can be withdrawn from us
  That we have any need to keep.

Arise, and seek some height to gain
  From life's dark lesson day by day,
Nor just rehearse its peace and pain —
  A wearied actor at the play.

Nor grieve that will so much transcends
  Thy feeble powers, but in content
Do what thou canst, and leave the ends
  And issues with the Omnipotent.

Dust as thou art, and born to woe,
  Seeing darkly, and as through a glass,
He made thee thus to be, for lo!
  He made the grass, and flower of grass.

The tempest's cry, the thunder's moan,
  The waste of waters, wild and dim,
The still small voice thou hear'st alone —
  All, all alike interpret Him.

Arise, my friend, and go about
  Thy darkened house with cheerful feet;
Yield not one jot to fear nor doubt,
  But, baffled, broken, still repeat:

"'Tis mine to work, and not to win;
  The soul must wait to have her wings;
Even time is but a landmark in
  The great eternity of things.

"Is it so much that thou below,
O heart, shouldst fail of thy desire,
When death, as we believe and know,
Is but a call to come up higher?"

GOD IS LOVE.

AH, there are mighty things under the sun,
Great deeds have been acted, great words have been said,
Not just uplifting some fortunate one,
But lifting up all men the more by a head.

Aye, the more by the head, and the shoulders too!
Ten thousand may sin, and a thousand may fall,
And it may have been me, and it yet may be you,
But the angel in one proves the angel in all.

And whatever is mighty, whatever is high,
Lifting men, lifting woman their natures above,
And close to the kinship they hold to the sky
Why, this I affirm, that its essence is Love.

The poorest, the meanest has right to his share—
For the life of his heart, for the strength of his hand,
'Tis the sinew of work, 'tis the spirit of prayer—
And here, and God help me, I take up my stand.

No pain but it hushes to peace in its arms,
No pale cheek it cannot with kisses make bright,

Its wonder of splendors has made the world's storms
To shine as with rainbows, since first there was light.

Go, bring me whatever the poets have praised,
The mantles of queens, the red roses of May,
I'll match them, I care not how grandly emblazed,
With the love of the beggar who sits by the way.

When I think of the gifts that have honored Love's shrine —
Heart, hope, soul, and body, all mortal can give —
For the sake of a passion superbly divine,
I am glad, nay, and more, I am proud that I live!

Fair women have made them espousals with death,
And through the white flames as through lilies have trod,
And men have with cloven tongues preached for their faith,
And held up their hands, stiff with thumb-screws, to God.

I have seen a great people its vantage defer
To the love that had moved it as love only can,
A whole nation stooping with conscience astir
To a chattel with crop ears, and calling it man.

Compared, O my beautiful Country, to thee,
In this tenderest touch of the manacled hand,
The tops of the pyramids sink to the sea,
And the thrones of the earth slide together like sand.

Immortal with beauty and vital with youth,
Thou standest, O Love, as thou always hast stood
From the wastes of the ages, proclaiming this truth,
All peoples and nations are made of one blood.

Ennobled by scoffing and honored by shame,
The chiefest of great ones, the crown and the head,
Attested by miracles done in thy name
For the blind, for the lame, for the sick and the dead.

Because He in all things was tempted like me,
Through the sweet human hope, by the cross that He bore,
For the love which so much to the Marys could be,
Christ Jesus the man, not the God, I adore.

LIFE'S MYSTERIES.

Round and round the wheel doth run,
And now doth rise, and now doth fall;
How many lives we live in one,
And how much less than one, in all!

The past as present as to-day —
How strange, how wonderful! it seems
A player playing in a play,
A dreamer dreaming that he dreams!

But when the mind through devious glooms
Drifts onward to the dark amain,

Her wand stern Conscience reassumes,
  And holds us to ourselves again.

Vague reminiscences come back
  Of things we seem, in part, to have known,
And Fancy pieces what they lack
  With shreds and colors all her own

Fancy, whose wing so high can soar,
  Whose vision hath so broad a glance,
We feel sometimes as if no more
  Amenable to change and chance.

And yet, one tiny thread being broke —
  One idol taken from our hands,
The eternal hills roll up like smoke,
  The earth's foundations shake like sands!

Ah! how the colder pulse still starts
  To think of that one hour sublime,
We hugged heaven down into our hearts,
  And clutched eternity in time!

When love's dear eyes first looked in ours,
  When love's dear brows were strange to frowns,
When all the stars were burning flowers
  That we might pluck and wear for crowns.

We cannot choose but cry and cry —
  O, that its joys we might repeat!
When just its mutability
  Made all the sweetness of it sweet.

Close to the precipice's brink
 We press, look down, and, while we quail
From the bad thought we dare not think,
 Lift curiously the awful vail.

We do the thing we would not do —
 Our wills being set against our wills,
And suffer o'er and o'er anew
 The penalty our peace that kills.

Great God, we know not what we know
 Or what we are, or are to be!
We only trust we cannot go
 Through sin's disgrace outside of Thee.

And trust that though we are driven in
 And forced upon thy name to call
At last, by very strength of sin,
 Thou wilt have mercy on us all!

POEMS OF NATURE AND HOME.

A DREAM OF HOME.

SUNSET! A hush is on the air,
Their gray old heads the mountains bare,
As if the winds were saying prayer.

The woodland, with its broad green wing,
Shuts close the insect whispering,
And lo! the sea gets up to sing.

The day's last splendor fades and dies,
And shadows one by one arise,
To light the candles of the skies.

O wild flowers, wet with tearful dew,
O woods, with starlight shining through,
My heart is back to-night with you!

I know each beech and maple tree,
Each climbing brier and shrub I see, —
Like friends they stand to welcome me.

Musing I go along the streams,
Sweetly believing in my dreams;
For fancy like a prophet seems.

Footsteps beside me tread the sod
As in the twilights gone they trod;
And I unlearn my doubts, thank God!

Unlearn my doubts, forget my fears,
And that bad carelessness that sears
And makes me older than my years.

I hear a dear, familiar tone,
A loving hand is in my own,
And earth seems made for me alone.

If I my fortunes could have planned,
I would not have let go that hand;
But they must fall who learn to stand.

And how to blend life's varied hues,
What ill to find, what good to lose,
My Father knoweth best to choose.

EVENING PASTIMES.

Sitting by my fire alone,
When the winds are rough and cold,
And I feel myself grow old
Thinking of the summers flown.

I have many a harmless art
To beguile the tedious time:
Sometimes reading some old rhyme
I already know by heart;

Sometimes singing over words
Which in youth's dear day gone by
Sounded sweet, so sweet that I
Had no praises for the birds.

Then, from off its secret shelf
I from dust and moth remove
The old garment of my love,
In the which I wrap myself.

And a little while am vain;
But its rose hue will not bear
The sad light of faded hair;
So I fold it up again,

More in patience than regret
Not a leaf the forest through
But is sung and whispered to.
I shall wear that garment yet.

FADED LEAVES.

The hills are bright with maples yet;
But down the level land
The beech leaves rustle in the wind
As dry and brown as sand.

The clouds in bars of rusty red
Along the hill-tops glow,
And in the still, sharp air, the frost
Is like a dream of snow.

The berries of the brier-rose
  Have lost their rounded pride:
The bitter-sweet chrysanthemums
  Are drooping heavy-eyed.

The cricket grows more friendly now,
  The dormouse sly and wise,
Hiding away in the disgrace
  Of nature, from men's eyes.

The pigeons in black wavering lines
  Are swinging toward the sun;
And all the wide and withered fields
  Proclaim the summer done.

His store of nuts and acorns now
  The squirrel hastes to gain,
And sets his house in order for
  The winter's dreary reign.

'Tis time to light the evening fire,
  To read good books, to sing
The low and lovely songs that breathe
  Of the eternal Spring.

THE LIGHT OF DAYS GONE BY.

Some comfort when all else is night,
  About his fortune plays,
Who sets his dark to-days in the light
  Of the sunnier yesterdays.

In memory of joy that's been
  Something of joy is, still;
Where no dew is, we may dabble in
  A dream of the dew at will.

All with the dusty city's throng
  Walled round, I mused to-day
Of flowery sheets lying white along
  The pleasant grass of the way.

Under the hedge by the brawling brook
  I heard the woodpecker's tap,
And the drunken trills of the blackbirds shook
  The sassafras leaves in my lap.

I thought of the rainy morning air
  Dropping down through the pine,
Of furrows fresh from the shining share,
  And smelling sweeter than wine.

Of the soft, thick moss, and how it grew
  With silver beads impearled,
In the well that we used to think ran through
  To the other side of the world.

I thought of the old barn set about
  With its stacks of sweet, dry hay;
Of the swallows flying in and out
  Through the gables, steep and gray;

Thought of the golden hum of the bees,
  Of the cocks with their heads so high,
Making it morn in the tops of the trees
  Before it was morn in the sky.

And of the home, of the dear old home,
  With its brown and rose-bound wall,
Where we fancied death could never come —
  I thought of it more than of all.

Each childish play-ground memory claims,
  Telling me here, and thus,
We called to the echoes by their names,
  Till we made them answer us.

Thank God, when other power decays,
  And other pleasures die,
We still may set our dark to-days
  In the light of days gone by.

A SEA SONG.

Come, make for me a little song —
  'Twas so a spirit said to me —
And make it just four verses long,
  And make it sweet as it can be,
  And make it all about the sea.

Sing me about the wild waste shore,
  Where, long and long ago, with me
You watched the silver sails that bore
  The great, strong ships across the sea —
  The blue, the bright, the boundless sea.

Sing me about the plans we planned:
  How one of those good ships should be

My way to find some flowery land
  Away beyond the misty sea,
  Where, always you should live with me.

Sing, lastly, how our hearts were caught
  Up into heaven, because that we
Knew not the flowery land we sought
  Lay all beyond that other sea —
  That soundless, sailless, solemn sea.

SERMONS IN STONES.

  FLOWER of the deep red zone,
Rain the fine light about thee, near and far,
Hold the wide earth, so as the evening star
  Holdeth all heaven, alone,
And with thy wondrous glory make men see
His greater glory who did fashion thee!

  Sing, little goldfinch, sing!
Make the rough billows lift their curly ears
And listen, fill the violets' eyes with tears,
  Make the green leaves to swing
As in a dance, when thou dost hie along,
Showing the sweetness whence thou get'st thy song.

  O daisies of the hills,
When winds do pipe to charm ye, be not slow.
Crowd up, crowd up, and make your shoulders show
  White o'er the daffodils!

Yea, shadow forth through your excelling grace
With whom ye have held counsel face to face.

Fill fuller our desire,
Gay grasses; trick your lowly stems with green,
And wear your splendors even as a queen
Weareth her soft attire.
Unfold the cunning mystery of design
That combs out all your skirts to ribbons fine.

And O my heart, my heart,
Be careful to go strewing in and out
Thy way with good deeds, lest it come about
That when thou shalt depart,
No low lamenting tongue be found to say,
The world is poorer since thou went'st away!

Thou shouldst not idly beat,
While beauty draweth good men's thoughts to prayer
Even as the bird's wing draweth out the air,
But make so fair and sweet
Thy house of clay, some dusk shall spread about,
When death unlocks the door and lets thee out.

MY PICTURE.

Ah, how the eye on the picture stops
Where the lights of memory shine!
My friend, to thee I will leave the sea,
If only this be mine,
For the thought of the breeze in the tops of the trees
Stirs my blood like wine!

I will leave the sea and leave the ships,
And the light-house, taper and tall,
The bar so low, whence the fishers go,
And the fishers' wives and all,
If thou wilt agree to leave to me
This picture for my wall.

I leave thee all the palaces,
With their turrets in the sky—
The hunting-grounds, the hawks and hounds—
They please nor ear nor eye;
But the sturdy strokes on the sides o' the oaks
Make my pulses fly.

The old cathedral, filling all
The street with its shadow brown,
The organ grand, and the choiring band,
And the priest with his shaven crown;
'Tis the wail of the hymn in the wild-wood dim,
That bends and bows me down.

The shepherd piping to his flock
In the merry month of the May,
The lady fair with the golden hair,
And the knight so gallant and gay—
For the wood so drear that is pictured here,
I give them all away.

I give the cities and give the sea,
The ships and the bar so low,
And fishers and wives whose dreary lives
Speak from the canvas so;
And for all of these I must have the trees—
The trees on the hills of snow!

And shall we be agreed, my friend?
Shall it stand as I have said?
For the sake of the shade wherein I played,
And for the sake of my dead,
That lie so low on the hills of snow,
Shall it be as I have said?

MORNING IN THE MOUNTAINS.

Morn on the mountains! streaks of roseate light
Up the high east athwart the shadows run;
The last low star fades softly out of sight,
And the gray mists go forth to meet the sun.

And now from every sheltering shrub and vine,
And thicket wild with many a tangled spray,
And from the birch and elm and rough-browed pine,
The birds begin to serenade the day.

And now the cock his sleepy harem thrills
With clarion calls, and down the flowery dells;
And from their mossy hollows in the hills
The sheep have started all their tinkling bells.

Lo, the great sun! and nature everywhere
Is all alive, and sweet as she can be;
A thousand happy sounds are in the air,
A thousand by the rivers and the sea.

The dipping oar, the boatman's cheerful horn,
The well-sweep, creaking in its rise and fall;

And pleasantly along the springing corn,
The music of the ploughshare, best of all, —

The insect's little hum, the whir and beat
Of myriad wings, the mower's song so blithe,
The patter of the schoolboy's naked feet,
The joyous ringing of the whetted scythe, —

The low of kine, the falling meadow bar,
The teamster's whistle gay, the droning round
Of the wet mill-wheel, and the tuneful jar
Of hollow milk-pans, swell the general sound.

And by the sea, and in each vale and glen
Are happy sights, as well as sounds to hear,
The world of things, and the great world of men,
All, all is busy, busy far and near.

The ant is hard at work, and everywhere
The bee is balanced on her wings so brown;
And the black spider on her slender stair
Is running down and up, and up and down.

The pine-wood smoke in bright, fantastic curls,
Above the low-roofed homestead sweeps away,
And o'er the groups of merry boys and girls
That pick the berries bright, or rake the hay.

Morn on the mountains! the enkindling skies,
The flowery fields, the meadows, and the sea,
All are so fair, the heart within me cries,
How good, how wondrous good our God must be

THE THISTLE FLOWER.

My homely flower that blooms along
The dry and dusty ways,
I have a mind to make a song,
And make it in thy praise;
For thou art favored of my heart,
Humble and outcast as thou art.

Though never with the plants of grace
In garden borders set,
Full often have I seen thy face
With tender tear-drops wet,
And seen thy gray and ragged sleeves
All wringing with them, morns and eves.

Albeit thou livest in a bush
Of such unsightly form,
Thou hast not any need to blush —
Thou hast thine own sweet charm;
And for that charm I love thee so,
And not for any outward show.

The iron-weed, so straight and fine,
Above thy head may rise,
And all in glossy purple shine;
But to my partial eyes
It cannot harm thee — thou hast still
A place no finer flower can fill.

The fennel, she is courted at
The porch-side and the door —

Thou hast no lovers, and for that
  I love thee all the more;
Only the wind and rain to be
Thy friends, and keep thee company.

So, being left to take thine ease
  Behind thy thorny wall,
Thy little head with vanities
  Has not been turned at all,
And all field beauties give me grace
To praise thee to thy very face.

So, thou shalt evermore belong
  To me from this sweet hour,
And I will take thee for my song,
  And take thee for my flower,
And by the great, and proud, and high
Unenvied, we will live and die.

MY DARLINGS.

My Rose, so red and round,
My Daisy, darling of the summer weather,
You must go down now, and keep house together,
Low underground!

O little silver line
Of meadow water, ere the cloud rise darkling,
Slip out of sight, and with your comely sparkling
Make their hearth shine.

Leaves of the garden bowers,
The frost is coming soon, — your prime is over;
So gently fall, and make a soft, warm cover
To house my flowers.

Lithe willow, too, forego
The crown that makes you queen of woodland graces,
Nor leave the winds to shear the lady tresses
From your drooped brow.

Oak, held by strength apart
From all the trees, stop now your stems from growing,
And send the sap, while yet 'tis bravely flowing,
Back to your heart.

And ere the autumn sleet
Freeze into ice, or sift to bitter snowing,
Make compact with your peers for overstrowing
My darlings sweet.

So when their sleepy eyes
Shall be unlocked by May with rainy kisses,
They to the sweet renewal of old blisses
Refreshed may rise.

Lord, in that evil day
When my own wicked thoughts like thieves waylay me,
Or when pricked conscience rises up to slay me,
Shield me, I pray.

Aye, when the storm shall drive,
Spread thy two blessed hands like leaves above me,

And with thy great love, though none else should love
me,
Save me alive!

Heal with thy peace my strife;
And as the poet with his golden versing
Lights his low house, give me, thy praise rehearsing,
To light my life.

Shed down thy grace in showers,
And if some roots of good, at thy appearing,
Be found in me, transplant them for the rearing
Of heavenly flowers.

THE FIELD SWEET-BRIER.

I LOVE the flowers that come about with spring,
And whether they be scarlet, white, or blue,
It mattereth to me not anything;
For when I see them full of sun and dew,
My heart doth get so full with its delight,
I know not blue from red, nor red from white.

Sometimes I choose the lily, without stain;
The royal rose sometimes the best I call;
Then the low daisy, dancing with the rain,
Doth seem to me the finest flower of all;
And yet if only one could bloom for me —
I know right well what flower that one would be!

Yea, so I think my native wilding brier,
  With just her thin four leaves, and stem so rough,
Could, with her sweetness, give me my desire,
  Aye, all my life long give me sweets enough;
For though she be not vaunted to excel,
She in all modest grace aboundeth well.

And I would have no whit the less content,
  Because she hath not won the poet's voice,
To pluck her little stars for ornament,
  And that no man were poorer for my choice,
Since she perforce must shine above the rest
In comely looks, because I love her best!

When fancy taketh wing, and wills to go
  Where all selected glories blush and bloom,
I search and find the flower that used to grow
  Close by the door-stone of the dear old home —
The flower whose knitted roots we did divide
For sad transplanting, when the mother died.

All of the early and the latter May,
  And through the windless heats of middle June,
Our green-armed brier held for us day by day,
  The morning coolness till the afternoon;
And every bird that took his grateful share,
Sang with a heavenlier tongue than otherwhere.

And when from out the west the low sun shone,
  It used to make our pulses leap and thrill
To see her lift her shadow from the stone,
  And push it in among us o'er the sill —
O'erstrow with flowers, and then push softly in,
As if she were our very kith and kin.

So, seeing still at evening's golden close
  This shadow with our childish shadows blend,
We came to love our simple four-leaved rose,
  As if she were a sister or a friend.
And if my eyes all flowers but one must lose,
Our wild sweet-brier would be the one to choose.

THE LITTLE HOUSE ON THE HILL.

O MEMORY, be sweet to me —
  Take, take all else at will,
So thou but leave me safe and sound,
Without a token my heart to wound,
  The little house on the hill!

Take all of best from east to west,
  So thou but leave me still
The chamber, where in the starry light
I used to lie awake at night
  And list to the whip-poor-will.

Take violet-bed, and rose-tree red,
  And the purple flags by the mill,
The meadow gay, and the garden-ground,
But leave, O leave me safe and sound
  The little house on the hill!

The daisy-lane, and the dove's low plane,
  And the cuckoo's tender bill,
Take one and all, but leave the dreams
That turned the rafters to golden beams,
  In the little house on the hill!

The gables brown, they have tumbled down,
  And dry is the brook by the mill;
The sheets I used with care to keep
Have wrapt my dead for the last long sleep,
  In the valley, low and still.

But, Memory, be sweet to me,
  And build the walls, at will,
Of the chamber where I used to mark,
So softly rippling over the dark,
  The song of the whip-poor-will!

Ah, Memory, be sweet to me!
  All other fountains chill;
But leave that song so weird and wild,
Dear as its life to the heart of the child,
  In the little house on the hill!

THE OLD HOUSE.

My little birds, with backs as brown
  As sand, and throats as white as frost,
I've searched the summer up and down,
  And think the other birds have lost
The tunes you sang, so sweet, so low,
About the old house, long ago.

My little flowers, that with your bloom
  So hid the grass you grew upon,
A child's foot scarce had any room
  Between you, — are you dead and gone?

I've searched through fields and gardens rare,
Nor found your likeness anywhere.

My little hearts, that beat so high
  With love to God, and trust in men,
O, come to me, and say if I
  But dream, or was I dreaming then,
What time we sat within the glow
Of the old house hearth, long ago?

My little hearts, so fond, so true,
  I searched the world all far and wide,
And never found the like of you:
  God grant we meet the other side
The darkness 'twixt us now that stands,
In that new house not made with hands!

"HOE YOUR OWN ROW."

I think there are some maxims
  Under the sun,
Scarce worth preservation;
  But here, boys, is one
So sound and so simple
  'Tis worth while to know;
And all in the single line,
  Hoe your own row!

A good many workers
  I've known in my time—
Some builders of houses,
  Some builders of rhyme;
And they that were prospered,
  Were prospered, I know,
By the intent and meaning of
  Hoe your own row!

I've known, too, a good many
  Idlers, who said,
I've a right to my living,
  The world owes me bread
A *right!* lazy lubber!
  A thousand times No!
'Tis his, and his only
  Who hoes his own row

Alice Cary.

FOR THE LOST.

LOST LILIES.

SHOW you her picture? Here it lies!
  Hands of lilies, and lily-like brow;
Mouth that is bright as a rose, and eyes
  That are just the soul's sweetest overflow.

Darling shoulders, softly pale,
  Borne by the undulating play
Of the life below, up out of their veil,
  Like lilies out o' the waves o' the May.

Throat as white as the throat of a swan,
  And all as proudly graceful held;
Fair, bare bosom "clothed upon
  With chastity," like the lady of eld.

Tender lids, that drooping down,
  Chide your glances over bold;
Fair, with a golden gleam in the brown,
  And brown again in the gleamy gold.

These on your eyes like a splendor fall,
  And you marvel not at my love, I see;
But it was not one, and it was not all,
  That made her the angel she was to me.

So snut the picture and put it away,
  Your fancy is only thus misled;
What can the dull, cold semblance say,
  When the spirit and life of the life is fled?

Seven long years, and seven again,
  And three to the seven — a weary space —
The weary fingers of the rain
  Have drawn the daisies over her face.

Seven and seven years, and three,
  The leaves have faded to death in the frost,
Since the shadow that made for me
  The world a shadow my pathway crossed.

And now and then some meteor gleam
  Has broken the gloom of my life apart,
Or the only thread of some raveled dream
  Has slid like sunshine in my heart.

But never a planet, steady and still,
  And never a rainbow, brave and fine,
And never the flowery head of a hill
  Has made the cloud of my life to shine.

Yet God is love! and this I trust,
  Though summer is over and sweetness done,
That all my lilies are safe, in the dust,
  As they were in the glow of the great, glad sun.

Yea, God is love, and love is might!
  Mighty as surely to keep as to make;
And the sleepers, sleeping in death's dark night,
  In the resurrection of life shall wake.

A WONDER.

Still alway groweth in me the great wonder,
When all the fields are blushing like the dawn,
And only one poor little flower ploughed under,
That I can see no flowers, that one being gone:
No flower of all, because of one being gone.

Aye, ever in me groweth the great wonder,
When all the hills are shining, white and red,
And only one poor little flower ploughed under,
That it were all as one if all were dead:
Aye, all as one if all the flowers were dead.

I cannot feel the beauty of the roses;
Their soft leaves seem to me but layers of dust;
Out of my opening hand each blessing closes:
Nothing is left me but my hope and trust,
Nothing but heavenly hope and heavenly trust.

I get no sweetness of the sweetest places;
My house, my friends no longer comfort me;
Strange somehow grow the old familiar faces;
For I can nothing have, not having thee:
All my possessions I possessed through thee.

Having, I have them not — strange contradiction!
Heaven needs must cast its shadow on our earth;
Yea, drown us in the waters of affliction
Breast high, to make us know our treasure's worth,
To make us know how much our love is worth.

And while I mourn, the anguish of my story
  Breaks, as the wave breaks on the hindering bar:
Thou art but hidden in the deeps of glory,
  Even as the sunshine hides the lessening star,
  And with true love I love thee from afar.

I know our Father must be good, not evil,
  And murmur not, for faith's sake, at my ill;
Nor at the mystery of the working cavil,
  That somehow bindeth all things in his will,
  And, though He slay me, makes me trust Him still.

MOST BELOVED.

My heart thou makest void, and full;
  Thou giv'st, thou tak'st away my care;
O most beloved! most beautiful!
  I miss, and find thee everywhere!

In the sweet water, as it flows;
  The winds, that kiss me as they pass;
The starry shadow of the rose,
  Sitting beside her on the grass;

The daffodilly, trying to bless
  With better light the beauteous air;
The lily, wearing the white dress
  Of sanctuary, to be more fair;

The lithe-armed, dainty-fingered brier,
  That in the woods, so dim and dear,

Lights up betimes her tender fire
  To soothe the homesick pioneer;

The moth, his brown sails balancing
  Along the stubble, crisp and dry;
The ground-flower, with a blood-red ring
  On either hand; the pewet's cry;

The friendly robin's gracious note;
  The hills, with curious weeds o'errun;
The althea, in her crimson coat
  Tricked out to please the wearied sun;

The dandelion, whose golden share
  Is set before the rustic's plough;
The hum of insects in the air;
  The blooming bush; the withered bough;

The coming on of eve; the springs
  Of daybreak, soft and silver bright;
The frost, that with rough, rugged wings
  Blows down the cankered buds; the white,

Long drifts of winter snow; the heat
  Of August falling still and wide;
Broad cornfields; one chance stalk of wheat,
  Standing with bright head hung aside:

All things, my darling, all things seem
  In some strange way to speak of thee;
Nothing is half so much a dream,
  Nothing so much reality.

MY DARLINGS.

WHEN steps are hurrying homeward,
  And night the world o'erspreads,
And I see at the open windows
  The shining of little heads,
I think of you, my darlings,
  In your low and lonesome beds.

And when the latch is lifted,
  And I hear the voices glad,
I feel my arms more empty,
  My heart more widely sad;
For we measure dearth of blessings
  By the blessings we have had.

But sometimes in sweet visions
  My faith to sight expands,
And with my babes in his bosom,
  My Lord before me stands,
And I feel on my head, bowed lowly
  The touches of little hands.

Then pain is lost in patience,
  And tears no longer flow:
They are only dead to the sorrow
  And sin of life, I know;
For if they were not immortal
  My love would make them so.

IN DESPAIR.

I KNOW not what the world may be, —
For since I have nor hopes nor fears,
All things seem strange and far to me,
As though I had sailed on some sad sea,
For years and years, and years and years!

Sailed through blind mists, you understand,
And leagues of bleak and bitter foam;
Seeing belts of rock and bars of sand,
But never a strip of flowery land,
And never the light of hearth or home.

All day and night, all night and day,
I sit in my darkened house alone;
Come thou, whose laughter sounds so gay,
Come hither, for charity come! and say
What flowers are faded, and what are blow

Does the great, glad sun, as he used to, rise?
Or is it always a weary night?
A shadow has fallen across my eyes,
Come hither and tell me about the skies, —
Are there drops of rain? are there drops of light?

Keep not, dear heart, so far away,
With thy laughter light and laughter low,
But come to my darkened house, I pray,
And tell me what of the fields to-day, —
Or lilies, or snow? or lilies, or snow?

Do the hulls of the ripe nuts hang apart?
  Do the leaves of the locust drop in the well?
Or is it the time for the buds to start?
O gay little heart, O little gay heart,
  Come hither and tell, come hither and tell!

The day of my hope is cold and dead,
  The sun is down and the light is gone;
Come hither thou of the roses red,
Of the gay, glad heart, and the golden head,
  And tell of the dawn, of the dew and the dawn.

WAIT.

Go not far in the land of light!
  A little while by the golden gate,
Lest that I lose you out of sight,
  Wait, my darling, wait.

Forever now from your happy eyes
  Life's scenic picture has passed away;
You have entered into realities,
  And I am yet at the play!

Yet at the play of time — through all,
  Thinking of you, and your high estate;
A little while, and the curtain will fall —
  Wait, my darling, wait!

Mine is a dreary part to do —
  A mask of mirth on a mourning brow;

The chance approval, the flower or two,
  Are nothing — nothing now!

The last sad act is drawing on;
  A little while by the golden gate
Of the holy heaven to which you are gone,
  Wait, my darling, wait.

AFTER A SHADOW.

BY ALICE CARY.

Stop, my merry-eyed little one
Fluttering over the grass in the sun,
With hair a-tumble before and behind,
As if 'twere play-fellow of the wind.
And head as brown as a honey bee,
And smile that it makes one smile to see.
Stop your chase, so glad and gay,
And tell me truly, whither away!

Never an answer! but I know
Why your cheek has the ruddy glow,
And why your smile is so bright to see,
And why your hand is as brown as a bee,
And why your foot is so lightly set
On dewy daisy and violet,
And why you flutter away, away,
Fleet as a butterfly, all the day!

Never stopping to catch the note
Trilled by the bird with the speckled throat
And the golden topknot on his head,
Never picking the rose so red,
Nor blowing tunes on the hollow reeds,
Nor stringing the brier-buds like beads;
Ah, my child, I have found you out,
Busy, chasing your shadow about.

And let me tell you, my pretty one,
Fluttering over the grass in the sun,
When your hair, with the light now lit,
Shall come to have only frost in it,
And you put it away from care-worn face
As thought goes back to this childish race
You will marvel to see that women and men
Are chasing shadows, as you were then.

RELIGIOUS POEMS.

THE GOLDEN MEAN.

Lest to evil ways I run
  When I go abroad,
Shine about me, like the sun,
  O my gracious Lord!
Make the clouds, with silver glowing,
Like a mist of lilies blowing
  O'er the summer sward;
And mine eyes keep Thou from being
Ever satisfied with seeing,
  O my light, my Lord!

Lest my thoughts on discontent
  Should in sleep be fed,
Make the darkness like a tent
  Round about my bed;
Sweet as honey to the taster,
Make my dreams be, O my Master,
Sweet as honey, ere it loses
  Spice of meadow-blooms,
While the taster tastes the roses
  In the golden combs.

Lest I live in lowly ease,
  Or in lofty scorn,

Make me like the strawberries
  That run among the corn;
Grateful in the shadows keeping,
Of the broad leaves o'er me sweeping;
In the gold crop's stead, to render
Some small berries, red and tender,
  Like the blushing morn.

Lest that pain to pain be placed —
  Weary day to day,
Let me sit at good men's feasts
  When the house is gay:
Let my heart beat up to measures
Of all comfortable pleasures,
  Till the morning gray,
O'er the eastern hill-tops glancing,
Sets the woodlands all to dancing,
  And scares night away.

Lest that I in vain pretense
  Careless live and move,
Heart and mind, and soul and sense,
  Quicken Thou with love!
Fold its music over, under,
Breath of flute and boom of thunder,
Nor make satisfied my hearing,
As I go on, nearing, nearing,
  Him whose name is Love.

THE FIRE BY THE SEA.

THERE were seven fishers, with nets in their hands,
And they walked and talked by the sea-side sands;
Yet sweet as the sweet dew-fall
The words they spake, though they spake so low,
Across the long, dim centuries flow,
And we know them, one and all —
Aye! know them and love them all.

Seven sad men in the days of old,
And one was gentle, and one was bold,
And they walked with downward eyes;
The bold was Peter, the gentle was John,
And they all were sad, for the Lord was gone,
And they knew not if He would rise —
Knew not if the dead would rise.

The livelong night, 'till the moon went out
In the drowning waters, they beat about;
Beat slow through the fog their way;
And the sails drooped down with wringing wet,
And no man drew but an empty net,
And now 'twas the break of the day —
The great, glad break of the day.

"Cast in your nets on the other side!"
('Twas Jesus speaking across the tide;)
And they cast and were dragging hard;
But that disciple whom Jesus loved
Cried straightway out, for his heart was moved:
"It is our risen Lord —
Our Master, and our Lord!"

Then Simon, girding his fisher's coat,
Went over the nets and out of the boat —
Aye! first of them all was he;
Repenting sore the denial past,
He feared no longer his heart to cast
Like an anchor into the sea —
Down deep in the hungry sea.

And the others, through the mists so dim,
In a little ship came after him,
Dragging their net through the tide;
And when they had gotten close to the land
They saw a fire of coals on the sand,
And, with arms of love so wide,
Jesus, the crucified!

'Tis long, and long, and long ago
Since the rosy lights began to flow
O'er the hills of Galilee;
And with eager eyes and lifted hands
The seven fishers saw on the sands
The fire of coals by the sea —
On the wet, wild sands by the sea.

'Tis long ago, yet faith in our souls
Is kindled just by that fire of coals
That streamed o'er the mists of the sea;
Where Peter, girding his fisher's coat,
Went over the nets and out of the boat,
To answer, "Lov'st thou me?"
Thrice over, "Lov'st thou me?"

THE SURE WITNESS.

THE solemn wood had spread
Shadows around my head;
"Curtains they are," I said,
"Hung dim and still about the house of prayer."
Softly among the limbs,
Turning the leaves of hymns,
I heard the winds, and asked if God were there.
No voice replied, but while I listening stood,
Sweet peace made holy hushes through the wood.

With ruddy, open hand,
I saw the wild rose stand
Beside the green gate of the summer hills;
And pulling at her dress,
I cried, "Sweet hermitess,
Hast thou beheld Him who the dew distills?"
No voice replied, but while I listening bent,
Her gracious beauty made my heart content.

The moon in splendor shone;
"She walketh heaven alone,
And seeth all things," to myself I mused;
"Hast thou beheld Him, then,
Who hides Himself from men
In that great power through nature interfused?"
No speech made answer, and no sign appeared,
But in the silence I was soothed and cheered.

Waking one time, strange awe
Thrilling my soul, I saw

A kingly splendor round about the night;
Such cunning work the hand
Of spinner never planned, —
The finest wool may not be washed so white.
"Hast thou come out of heaven?" I asked; and lo!
The snow was all the answer of the snow.

Then my heart said, "Give o'er;
Question no more, no more!
The wind, the snow-storm, the wild hermit flower,
The illuminated air,
The pleasure after prayer,
Proclaim the unoriginated Power!
The mystery that hides Him here and there,
Bears the sure witness He is everywhere."

ONE DUST.

THOU, under Satan's fierce control,
Shall Heaven its final rest bestow?
I know not, but I know a soul
That might have fallen as darkly low.

I judge thee not, what depths of ill
Soe'er thy feet have found, or trod;
I know a spirit and a will
As weak, but for the grace of God.

Shalt thou with full-day laborers stand,
Who hardly canst have pruned one vine?
I know not, but I know a hand
With an infirmity like thine.

Shalt thou who hast with scoffers part,
  E'er wear the crown the Christian wears?
I know not, but I know a heart
  As flinty, but for tears and prayers.

Have mercy, O Thou Crucified!
  For even while I name thy name,
I know a tongue that might have lied
  Like Peter's, and am bowed with shame.

MY CREED

I HOLD that Christian grace abounds
  Where charity is seen; that when
We climb to heaven, 'tis on the rounds
  Of love to men.

I hold all else, named piety,
  A selfish scheme, a vain pretense;
Where centre is not, can there be
  Circumference?

This I moreover hold, and dare
  Affirm where'er my rhyme may go:
Whatever things be sweet or fair,
  Love makes them so.

Whether it be the lullabies
  That charm to rest the nursling bird,
Or that sweet confidence of sighs
  And blushes, made without a word.

Whether the dazzling and the flush
  Of softly sumptous garden bowers,
Or by some cabin door, a bush
  Of ragged flowers.

'Tis not the wide phylactery,
  Nor stubborn fast, nor stated prayers,
That make us saints ; we judge the tree
  By what it bears.

And when a man can live apart
  From works, on theologic trust,
I know the blood about his heart
  Is dry as dust.

LAST POEMS.

SPENT AND MISSPENT.

STAY yet a little longer in the sky,
  O golden color of the evening sun!
Let not the sweet day in its sweetness die,
  While my day's work is only just begun.

Counting the happy chances strewn about
  Thick as the leaves, and saying which was best,
The rosy lights of morning all went out,
  And it was burning noon, and time to rest.

Then leaning low upon a piece of shade,
  Fringed round with violets and pansies sweet,
My heart and I, I said, will be delayed,
  And plan our work while cools the sultry heat.

Deep in the hills, and out of silence vast,
  A waterfall played up his silver tune;
My plans lost purpose, fell to dreams at last,
  And held me late into the afternoon.

But when the idle pleasure ceased to please,
  And I awoke, and not a plan was planned,
Just as a drowning man at what he sees
  Catches for life, I caught the thing at hand.

And so life's little work-day hour has all
  Been spent and misspent doing what I could,
And in regrets and efforts to recall
  The chance of having, being, what I would.

And so sometimes I cannot choose but cry,
  Seeing my late-sown flowers are hardly set—
O darkening color of the evening sky,
  Spare me the day a little longer yet!

LAST AND BEST.

SOMETIMES, when rude, cold shadows run
  Across whatever light I see;
When all the work that I have done,
  Or can do, seems but vanity;

I strive, nor vainly strive, to get
  Some little heart's-ease from the day
When all the weariness and fret
  Shall vanish from my life away;

For I, with grandeur clothed upon,
  Shall lie in state and take my rest,
And all my household, strangers grown,
  Shall hold me for an honored guest.

But ere that day when all is set
  In order, very still and grand,
And while my feet are lingering yet
  Along this troubled border-land,

What things will be the first to fade,
 And down to utter darkness sink?
The treasures that my hands have laid
 Where moth and rust corrupt, I think.

And Love will be the last to wait
 And light my gloom with gracious gleams;
For Love lies nearer heaven's glad gate,
 Than all imagination dreams.

Aye, when my soul its mask shall drop,
 The twain to be no more at one,
Love, with its prayers, shall bear me up
 Beyond the lark's wings, and the sun.

IN THE DARK.

Has the Spring come back, my darling,
Has the long and soaking rain
Been moulded into the tender leaves
Of the gay and growing grain —
The leaves so sweet of barley and wheat
All moulded out of the rain?
O, and I would I could see them grow,
O, and I would I could see them blow,
All over field and plain —
The billows sweet of barley and wheat
All moulded out of the rain.

Are the flowers dressed out, my darling,
In their kerchiefs plain or bright —

The groundwort gay, and the lady of May,
In her petticoat pink and white?
The fair little flowers, the rare little flowers,
Taking and making the light?
O, and I would I could see them all,
The little and low, the proud and tall,
In their kerchiefs brave and bright,
Stealing out of the morns and eves,
To braid embroidery round their leaves,
The gold and scarlet light.

Have the birds come back, my darling,
The birds from over the sea?
Are they cooing and courting together
In bush and bower and tree?
The mad little birds, the glad little birds,
The birds from over the sea!
O, and I would I could hear them sing,
O, and I would I could see them swing
In the top of our garden tree!
The mad little birds, the glad little birds,
The birds from över the sea!

Are they building their nests, my darling,
In the stubble, brittle and brown?
Are they gathering threads, and silken shreds,
And wisps of wool and down,
With their silver throats and speckled coats,
And eyes so bright and so brown?
O, and I would I could see them make
And line their nests for love's sweet sake,
With shreds of wool and down,
With their eyes so bright and brown!

AN INVALID'S PLEA.

O Summer! my beautiful, beautiful Summer!
  I look in thy face, and I long so to live;
But ah! hast thou room for an idle new-comer,
  With all things to take, and with nothing to give?
With all things to take of thy dear loving-kindness,
  The wine of thy sunshine, the dew of thy air;
And with nothing to give but the deafness and blindness
  Begot in the depths of an utter despair?

As if the gay harvester meant but to screen her,
  The black spider sits in her low loom, and weaves:
A lesson of trust to the tender-eyed gleaner
  That bears in her brown arms the gold of the sheaves.
The blue-bird that trills her low lay in the bushes
  Provokes from the robin a merrier glee;
The rose pays the sun for his kiss with her blushes,
  And all things pay tithes to thee — all things but me

At even, the fire-flies trim with their glimmers
  The wild, weedy skirts of the field and the wood;
At morning, those dear little yellow-winged swimmers
  The butterflies, hasten to make their place good.
The violet, alway so white and so saintly;
  The cardinal, warming the frost with her blaze;
The ant, keeping house at her sand-hearth so quaintly
  Reproaches my idle and indolent ways.

When o'er the high east the red morning is breaking,
  And driving the amber of starlight behind,

The land of enchantment I leave, on awaking,
  Is not so enchanted as that which I find.
And when the low west by the sunset is flattered,
  And locust and katydid sing up their best,
Peace comes to my thoughts, that were used to be flut-
      tered,
  Like doves when an eagle's wing darkens their nest.

The green little grasshopper, weak as we deem her,
  Chirps, day in and out, for the sweet right to live;
And canst thou, O Summer! make room for a dreamer,
  With all things to take, and with nothing to give?
Room only to wrap her hot cheeks in thy shadows,
  And all on thy daisy-fringed pillows to lie,
And dream of the gates of the glorious meadows,
  Where never a rose of the roses shall die!

THE GREAT QUESTION.

"How are the dead raised up, and with what body do they come?"

The waves, they are wildly heaving,
  And bearing me out from the shore,
And I know of the things I am leaving,
  But not of the things before.
O Lord of Love, whom the shape of a dove
  Came down and hovered o'er,
Descend to-night with heavenly light,
  And show me the farther shore.

There is midnight darkness o'er me,
  And 'tis light, more light, I crave;

The billows behind and before me
  Are gaping, each with a grave:
Descend to-night, O Lord of might,
  Who died our souls to save;
Descend to-night, my Lord, my Light,
  And walk with me on the wave!

My heart is heavy to breaking
  Because of the mourners' sighs,
For they cannot see the awak'ning,
  Nor the body with which we arise.
Thou, who for sake of men didst break
  The awful seal of the tomb —
Show them the way into life, I pray,
  And the body with which we come!

Comfort their pain and pining
  For the nearly wasted sands,
With the many mansions shining
  In the house not made with hands:
And help them by faith to see through death
  To that brighter and better shore,
Where they never shall weep who are fallen asleep,
  And never be sick any more.

A PENITENT'S PLEA.

Like a child that is lost
  From its home in the night,
I grope through the darkness
  And cry for the light;

Yea, all that is in me
  Cries out for the day—
Come Jesus, my Master,
  Illumine my way!

In the conflicts that pass
  'Twixt my soul and my God,
I walk as one walketh
  A fire-path, unshod;
And in my despairing
  Sit dumb by the way—
Come Jesus, my Master,
  And heal me, I pray!

I know the fierce flames
  Will not cease to uproll,
Till Thou rainest the dew
  Of thy love on my soul;
And I know the dumb spirit
  Will never depart,
Till Thou comest and makest
  Thy house in my heart.

My thoughts lie within me
  As waste as the sands;
O make them be musical
  Strings in thy hands!
My sins, red as scarlet,
  Wash white as a fleece—
Come Jesus, my Master,
  And give me thy peace!

PUTTING OFF THE ARMOR

WHY weep ye for the falling
  Of the transient twilight gloom?
I am weary of the journey,
  And have come in sight of home.

I can see a white procession
  Sweep melodiously along,
And I would not have your mourning
  Drown the sweetness of their song.

The battle-strife is ended;
  I have scaled the hindering wall,
And am putting off the armor
  Of the soldier — that is all!

Would you hide me from my pleasures?
  Would you hold me from my rest?
From my serving and my waiting
  I am called to be a guest!

Of its heavy, hurtful burdens
  Now my spirit is released:
I am done with fasts and scourges,
  And am bidden to the feast.

While you see the sun descending,
  While you lose me in the night,
Lo, the heavenly morn is breaking,
  And my soul is in the light.

I from faith to sight am rising
  While in deeps of doubt you sink;
'Tis the glory that divides us,
  Not the darkness, as you think.

Then lift up your drooping eyelids,
  And take heart of better cheer;
'Tis the cloud of coming spirits
  Makes the shadows that ye fear.

O, they come to bear me upward
  To the mansion of the sky,
And to change as I am changing
  Is to live, and not to die;

Is to leave the pain, the sickness,
  And the smiting of the rod,
And to dwell among the angels,
  In the City of our God.

LATER POEMS BY PHŒBE CARY

BALLADS.

THE CHRISTMAS SHEAF.

"Now, good-wife, bring your precious hoard,"
  The Norland farmer cried;
"And heap the hearth, and heap the board,
  For the blessèd Christmas-tide.

"And bid the children fetch," he said,
  "The last ripe sheaf of wheat,
And set it on the roof o'erhead,
  That the birds may come and eat.

"And this we do for his dear sake,
  The Master kind and good,
Who, of the loaves He blest and brake,
  Fed all the multitude."

Then Fredrica, and Franz, and Paul,
  When they heard their father's words,
Put up the sheaf, and one and all
  Seemed merry as the birds.

Till suddenly the maiden sighed,
  The boys were hushed in fear,
As, covering all her face, she cried,
  "If Hansei were but here!"

And when, at dark, about the hearth
  They gathered still and slow,
You heard no more the childish mirth
  So loud an hour ago.

And on their tender cheeks the tears
  Shone in the flickering light;
For they were four in other years
  Who are but three to-night.

And tears are in the mother's tone;
  As she speaks, she trembles, too:
"Come, children, come, for the supper's done,
  And your father waits for you."

Then Fredrica, and Franz, and Paul,
  Stood each beside his chair;
The boys were comely lads, and tall,
  The girl was good and fair.

The father's hand was raised to crave
  A grace before the meat,
When the daughter spake; her words were brave
  But her voice was low and sweet:

"Dear father, should we give the wheat
  To all the birds of the air?
Shall we let the kite and the raven eat
  Such choice and dainty fare?

"For if to-morrow from our store
  We drive them not away,
The good little birds will get no more
  Than the evil birds of prey."

"Nay, nay, my child," he gravely said,
  "You have spoken to your shame,
For the good, good Father overhead,
  "Feeds all the birds the same.

"He hears the ravens when they cry,
  He keeps the fowls of the air;
And a single sparrow cannot lie
  On the ground without his care."

"Yea, father, yea; and tell me this," —
  Her words came fast and wild, —
"Are not a thousand sparrows less
  To Him than a single child?

"Even though it sinned and strayed from home?"
  The father groaned in pain
As she cried, "O, let our Hansei come
  And live with us again!

"I know he did what was not right" —
  Sadly he shook his head;
"If he knew I longed for him to-night,
  He would not come," he said.

"He went from me in wrath and pride;
  God! shield him tenderly!
For I hear the wild wind cry outside,
  Like a soul in agony."

"Nay, it is a soul!" O, eagerly
  The maiden answered then;
"And, father, what if it should be he,
  Come back to us again!"

She stops — the portal open flies;
Her fear is turned to joy:
'Hansei!" the startled father cries;
And the mother sobs, "My boy!"

'Tis a bowed and humbled man they greet,
With loving lips and eyes,
Who fain would kneel at his father's feet,
But he softly bids him rise;

And he says, "I bless thee, O mine own;
Yea, and thou shalt be blest!"
While the happy mother holds her son
Like a baby on her breast.

Their house and love again to share
The Prodigal has come!
And now there will be no empty chair,
Nor empty heart in their home.

And they think, as they see their joy and pride
Safe back in the sheltering fold,
Of the child that was born at Christmas-tide
In Bethlehem of old.

And all the hours glide swift away
With loving, hopeful words,
Till the Christmas sheaf at break of day
Is alive with happy birds!

[NOTE. — In Norway the last sheaf from the harvest-field is never threshed, but it is always reserved till Christmas Eve, when it is set up on the roof as a feast for the hungry birds.]

LITTLE GOTTLIEB.

A CHRISTMAS STORY.

ACROSS the German Ocean,
  In a country far from our own,
Once, a poor little boy, named Gottlieb,
  Lived with his mother alone.

They dwelt in the part of a village
  Where the houses were poor and small,
But the home of little Gottlieb
  Was the poorest one of all.

He was not large enough to work,
  And his mother could do no more
(Though she scarcely laid her knitting down),
  Than keep the wolf from the door.

She had to take their threadbare clothes,
  And turn, and patch, and darn;
For never any women yet
  Grew rich by knitting yarn.

And oft at night, beside her chair,
  Would Gottlieb sit, and plan
The wonderful things he would do for her,
  When he grew to be a man.

One night she sat and knitted,
  And Gottlieb sat and dreamed,
When a happy fancy all at once
  Upon his vision beamed.

'Twas only a week till Christmas,
And Gottlieb knew that then
The Christ-child, who was born that day,
Sent down good gifts to men.

But he said, "He will never find us,
Our home is so mean and small.
And we, who have most need of them,
Will get no gifts at all."

When all at once, a happy light
Came into his eyes so blue,
And lighted up his face with smiles,
As he thought what he could do.

Next day when the postman's letters
Came from all over the land;
Came one for the Christ-child, written
In a child's poor, trembling hand.

You may think he was sorely puzzled
What in the world to do;
So he went to the Burgomaster,
As the wisest man he knew.

And when they opened the letter,
They stood almost dismayed
That such a little child should dare
To ask the Lord for aid.

Then the Burgomaster stammered,
And scarce knew what to speak,
And hastily he brushed aside
A drop, like a tear, from his cheek.

Then up he spoke right gruffly,
  And turned himself about:
"This must be a very foolish boy,
  And a small one, too, no doubt."

But when six rosy children
  That night about him pressed,
Poor, trusting little Gottlieb
  Stood near him, with the rest.

And he heard his simple, touching prayer,
  Through all their noisy play;
Though he tried his very best to put
  The thought of him away.

A wise and learned man was he,
  Men called him good and just;
But his wisdom seemed like foolishness,
  By that weak child's simple trust.

Now when the morn of Christmas came,
  And the long, long week was done,
Poor Gottlieb, who scarce could sleep,
  Rose up before the sun,

And hastened to his mother,
  But he scarce might speak for fear,
When he saw her wondering look, and saw
  The Burgomaster near.

He wasn't afraid of the Holy Babe,
  Nor his mother, meek and mild;
But he felt as if so great a man
  Had never been a child.

Amazed the poor child looked, to find
  The hearth was piled with wood,
And the table, never full before,
  Was heaped with dainty food.

Then half to hide from himself the truth,
  The Burgomaster said,
While the mother blessed him on her knees,
  And Gottlieb shook for dread :

"Nay, give no thanks, my good dame,
  To such as me for aid,
Be grateful to your little son,
  And the Lord to whom he prayed!"

Then turning round to Gottlieb,
  "Your written prayer, you see,
Came not to whom it was addressed,
  It only came to me!

"'Twas but a foolish thing you did,
  As you must understand;
For though the gifts are yours, you know,
  You have them from my hand."

Then Gottlieb answered fearlessly,
  Where he humbly stood apart,
"But the Christ-child sent them all the same,
  He put the thought in your heart!"

RELIGIOUS POEMS.

CHRISTMAS.

THIS happy day, whose risen sun
  Shall set not through eternity,
This holy day when Christ, the Lord,
  Took on Him our humanity,

For little children everywhere
  A joyous season still we make;
We bring our precious gifts to them,
  Even for the dear child Jesus' sake.

The glory from the manger shed,
  Wherein the lowly Saviour lay,
Shines as a halo round the head
  Of every human child to-day.

And each unconscious infant sleeps
  Entrusted to his guardian care;
Hears his dear name in cradle hymns,
  And lisps it in its earliest prayer.

Thou blessed Babe of Bethlehem!
  Whose life we love, whose name we laud;
Thou Brother, through whose poverty,
  We have become the heirs of God;

Thou sorrowful, yet sinless Man —
 Tempted in all things like as we,
Treading with tender, human feet,
 The sharp, rough way of Calvary;

We do remember how, by Thee,
 The sick were healed, the halting led;
How Thou didst take the little ones
 And pour thy blessings on their head.

We know for what unworthy men
 Thou once didst deign to toil and live;
What weak and sinful women Thou
 Didst love, and pity, and forgive.

And, Lord, if to the sick and poor
 We go with generous hearts to-day,
Or in forbidden places seek
 For such as wander from the way;

And by our loving words or deeds
 Make this a hallowed time to them;
Though we ourselves be found unmeet,
 For sin, to touch thy garment's hem;

Wilt Thou not, for thy wondrous grace,
 And for thy tender charity,
Accept the good we do to these,
 As we had done it unto Thee?

And for the precious little ones,
 Here from their native heaven astray
Strong in their very helplessness,
 To lead us in the better way;

If we shall make thy natal day
  A season of delight to these,
A season always crowded full
  Of sweet and pleasant memories;

Wilt Thou not grant us to forget
  Awhile our weight of care and pain,
And in their joys, bring back their joy
  Of early innocence again?

O holy Child, about whose bed
  The virgin mother softly trod;
Dead once, yet living evermore,
  O Son of Mary, and of God!

If any act that we can do,
  If any thought of ours is right,
If any prayer we lift to Thee,
  May find acceptance in thy sight,

Hear us, and give to us, to-day,
  In answer to our earnest cries,
Some portion of that sacred love,
  That drew Thee to us from the skies!

PRODIGALS.

AGAIN, in the Book of Books, to-day
I read of that Prodigal, far away
    In the centuries agone,
Who took the portion that to him fell,
And went from friends and home to dwell
    In a distant land alone.

And when his riotous living was done,
And his course of foolish pleasure run,
And a fearful famine rose,
He fain would have fed with the very swine,
And no man gave him bread nor wine,
For his friends were changed to foes.

And I thought, when at last his state he knew
What a little thing he had to do,
To win again his place:
Only the madness of sin to learn,
To come to himself, repent, and turn,
And seek his Father's face.

Then I thought however vile we are,
Not one of us hath strayed so far
From the things that are good and pure,
But if to gain his home he tried
He would find the portal open wide,
And find his welcome sure.

My fellow-sinners, though you dwell
In haunts where the feet take hold on hell,
Where the downward way is plain;
Think, who is waiting for you at home,
Repent, and come to yourself, and come
To your Father's house again!

Say, out of the depths of humility,
"I have lost the claim of a child on Thee,
I would serve Thee with the least!"
And He will a royal robe prepare,
He will call you son, and call you heir;
And seat you at the feast.

Yea, fellow-sinner, rise to-day,
And run till He meets you on the way,
Till you hear the glad words said, —
"*Let joy through all the heavens resound*
For this, my son, who was lost is found,
And he lives who once was dead."

ST. BERNARD OF CLAIRVAUX.

In the shade of the cloister, long ago —
They are dead and buried for centuries —
The pious monks walked to and fro,
Talking of holy mysteries.

By a blameless life and penance hard,
Each brother there had proved his call;
But the one we name the St. Bernard
Was the sweetest soul among them all.

And oft as a silence on them fell,
He would pause, and listen, and whisper low,
"There is One who waits for me in my cell;
I hear Him calling, and I must go!"

No charm of human fellowship
His soul from its dearest love can bind;
With a "*Jesu Dulcis*" on his lip,
He leaves all else that is sweet behind.

The only hand that he longs to take,
Pierced, from the cross is reaching down;

And the head he loves, for his dear sake
  Was wounded once with a thorny crown.

Ah ! men and brethren, He whose call
  Drew that holy monk with a power divine,
Was the One who is calling for us all,
  Was the Friend of sinners — yours and mine !

From the sleep of the cradle to the grave,
  From the first low cry till the lip is dumb
Ready to help us, and strong to save,
  He is calling, and waiting till we come.

Lord ! teach us always thy voice to know,
  And to turn to Thee from the world beside,
Prepared when our time has come to go,
  Whether at morn or eventide.

And to say when the heavens are rent in twain,
  When suns are darkened, and stars shall flee,
Lo ! Thou hast not called for us in vain,
  And we shall not call in vain for Thee !

OLD PICTURES.

Old pictures, faded long, to-night
  Come out revealed by memory's gleam;
And years of checkered dark and light
  Vanish behind me like a dream.

I see the cottage, brown and low,
  The rustic porch, the roof-tree's shade,
And all the place where long ago
  A group of happy children played.

I see the brother, bravest, best,
  The prompt to act, the bold to speak;
The baby, dear and honored guest!
  The timid sister, shy and meek.

I see her loving face who oft
  Watched, that their slumbers might be sweet;
And his whose dear hand made so soft
  The path for all their tender feet.

I see, far off, the woods whose screen
  Bounded the little world we knew;
And near, in fairy rings of green,
  The grass that round the door-stones grew.

I watch at morn the oxen come,
  And bow their meek necks to the yoke;
Or stand at noontide, patient, dumb,
  In the great shadow of the oak.

The barn with crowded mows of hay,
  And roof upheld by golden sheaves;
Its rows of doves, at close of day,
  Cooing together on the eaves.

I see, above the garden-beds,
  The bee at work with laden wings;
The dandelions' yellow heads
  Crowding about the orchard spring;

The little, sweet-voiced, homely thrush;
  The field-lark, with her speckled breast,
The finches in the currant-bush;
  And where the blue-birds hid their nest.

I see the comely apple-trees,
  In spring, a-blush with blossoms sweet;
Or, bending with the autumn breeze,
  Shake down their ripe fruits at our feet.

I see, when hurtling through the air
  The arrows of the winter fly,
And all the frozen earth lies bare,
  A group about the hearth draw nigh,

Of little ones that never tire
  Of stories told and told again;
I see the pictures in the fire,
  The firelight pictures in the pane.

I almost feel the stir and buzz
  Of day; the evening's holy calm;
Yea, all that made me what I was,
  And helped to make me what I am.

Then lo! it dies, as died our youth;
  And things so strange about me seem,
I know not what should be the truth,
  Nor whether I would wake or dream.

I have not found to-day so vain,
  Nor yesterday so fair and good,
That I would have my life again,
  And live it over if I could.

Not every hope for me has proved
  A house on weak foundation built;
I have not seen the feet I loved
  Caught in the awful snares of guilt.

But when I see the paths so hard
  Kept soft and smooth in days gone by;
The lives that years have made or marred,
  Out of my loneliness I cry :

O, for the friends that made so bright
  The days, alas! too soon to wane!
O, but to be one hour to-night
  Set in their midst, a child again!

THE PLAYMATES.

Two careless, happy children,
  Up when the east was red,
And never tired and never still
  Till the sun had gone to bed;
Helping the winds in winter
  To toss the snows about;
Gathering the early flowers,
  When spring-time called them out;
Playing among the windrows
  Where the mowers mowed the hay;
Finding the place where the skylark
  Had hidden her nest away;
Treading the cool, damp furrows
  Behind the shining plough;

Up in the barn with the swallows,
  And sliding over the mow;
Pleased with the same old stories,
  Heard a thousand times;
Believing all the wonders
  Written in tales or rhymes;
Counting the hours in summer
  When even a day seemed long;
Counting the hours in winter
  Till the time of leaves and song.
Thinking it took forever
  For little children to grow,
And that seventy years of a life-time
  Never could come and go.
O, I know they were happier children
  Than the world again may see,
For one was my little playmate
  And one, ah! one was me!

A sad-faced man and woman,
  Leagues and leagues apart,
Doing their work as best they may
  With weary hand and heart;
Shrinking from winter's tempests,
  And summer's burning heat;
Thinking that skies were brighter
  And flowers were once more sweet;
Wondering why the skylark
  So early tries his wings;
And if green fields are hidden
  Beyond the gate where he sings!
Feeling that time is slipping
  Faster and faster away;

That a day is but as a moment,
  And the years of life as a day;
Seeing the heights and places
  Others have reached and won;
Sighing o'er things accomplished,
  And things that are left undone;
And yet still trusting, somehow,
  In his own good time to become
Again as little children,
  In their Heavenly Father's home;
One crowding memories backward,
  In the busy, restless mart,
One pondering on them ever,
  And keeping them in her heart;
Going on by their separate pathways
  To the same eternity —
And one of these is my playmate,
  And one, alas! is me!

"THE BAREFOOT BOY."

Ah! "Barefoot Boy!" you have led me back
  O'er the waste of years profound,
To the still, sweet spots, which memory
  Hath kept as haunted ground.
You have led me back to the western hills,
  Where I played through the summer hours;
And called my little playmate up,
  To stand among the flowers.

We are hand in hand in the fields again,
  We are treading through the dew!
And not the poet's "barefoot boy,"
  Nor him the artist drew,
Is half so brave and bold and good,
  Though bright their colors glow,
As the darling playmate that I had
  And lost, so long ago!

I touch the spring-time's tender grass,
  I find the daisy buds;
I feel the shadows deep and cool,
  In the heart of the summer woods;
I see the ripened autumn nuts,
  Like thick hail strew the earth;
I catch the fall of the winter snow,
  And the glow of the cheerful hearth!

But alas! my playmate, loved and lost,
  My heart is full of tears,
For the dead and buried hopes, that are more
  Than our dead and buried years:
And I cannot see the poet's rhymes,
  Nor the lines the artist drew,
But only the boy that held my hand,
  And led my feet through the dew!

LOVE POEMS.

AMY'S LOVE-LETTER.

TURNING some papers carelessly
  That were hid away in a desk unused,
I came upon something yesterday
  O'er which I pondered and mused:

A letter, faded now and dim,
  And stained in places, as if by tears;
And yet I had hardly thought of him
  Who traced its pages for years.

Though once the happy tears made dim
  My eyes, and my blushing cheeks grew hot,
To have but a single word from him,
  Fond or foolish, no matter what.

If he ever quoted another's rhymes,
  Poor in themselves and commonplace,
I said them over a thousand times,
  As if he had lent them a grace.

The single color that pleased his taste
  Was the only one I would have, or wear,
Even in the girdle about my waist
  Or the ribbon that bound my hair.

Then my flowers were the self-same kind and hue;
And yet how strangely one forgets —
I cannot think which one of the two
It was, or roses or violets!

But O, the visions I knew and nursed,
While I walked in a world unseen before!
For my world began when I knew him first,
And must end when he came no more.

We would have died for each other's sake;
Would have given all else in the world below;
And we said and thought that our hearts would break
When we parted, years ago.

How the pain as well as the rapture seems
A shadowy thing I scarce recall,
Passed wholly out of my life and dreams,
As though it had never been at all.

And is this the end, and is here the grave
Of our steadfast love and our changeless faith
About which the poets sing and rave,
Naming it strong as death?

At least 'tis what mine has come to at last,
Stript of all charm and all disguise;
And I wonder if, when he thinks of the past,
He thinks we were foolish or wise?

Well, I am content, so it matters not;
And, speaking about him, some one said —
I wish I could only remember what —
But he's either married or dead.

DO YOU BLAME HER?

NE'ER lover spake in tenderer words,
  While mine were calm, unbroken;
Though I suffered all the pain I gave
  In the No, so firmly spoken.

I marvel what he would think of me,
  Who called it a cruel sentence,
If he knew I had almost learned to-day
  What it is to feel repentance.

For it seems like a strange perversity,
  And blind beyond excusing,
To lose the thing we could have kept,
  And after, mourn the losing.

And this, the prize I might have won,
  Was worth a queen's obtaining;
And one, if far beyond my reach,
  I had sighed, perchance, for gaining.

And I know — ah! no one knows so well,
  Though my heart is far from breaking —
'Twas a loving heart, and an honest hand,
  I might have had for the taking.

And yet, though never one beside
  Has place in my thought above him,
I only like him when he is by,
  'Tis when he is gone I love him.

Sadly of absence poets sing,
  And timid lovers fear it;

But an idol has been worshipped less
Sometimes when we came too near it.

And for him my fancy throws to-day
A thousand graces o'er him;
For he seems a god when he stands afar
And I kneel in my thought before him.

But if he were here, and knelt to me
With a lover's fond persistence,
Would the halo brighten to my eyes
That crowns him now in the distance?

Could I change the words I have said, and say
Till one of us two shall perish,
Forsaking others, I take this man
Alone, to love and to cherish?

Alas! whatever beside to-day
I might dream like a fond romancer,
I know my heart so well that I know
I should give him the self-same answer.

SONG.

LAUGH out, O stream, from your bed of green,
Where you lie in the sun's embrace;
And talk to the reeds that o'er you lean
To touch your dimpled face;
But let your talk be sweet as it will,
And your laughter be as gay,

You cannot laugh as I laugh in my heart,
  For my lover will come to-day!

Sing sweet, little bird, sing out to your mate
  That hides in the leafy grove;
Sing clear and tell him for him you wait,
  And tell him of all your love;
But though you sing till you shake the buds
  And the tender leaves of May,
My spirit thrills with a sweeter song,
  For my lover must come to-day!

Come up, O winds, come up from the south
  With eager hurrying feet,
And kiss your red rose on her mouth
  In the bower where she blushes sweet;
But you cannot kiss your darling flower,
  Though you clasp her as you may,
As I kiss in my thought the lover dear
  I shall hold in my arms to-day!

SOMEBODY'S LOVERS.

Too meek by half was he who came
  A-wooing me one morn,
For he thought so little of himself
  I learned to share his scorn.

At night I had a suitor, vain
  As the vainest in the land;
Almost he seemed to condescend
  In the offer of his hand.

In one who pressed his suit I missed
  Courage and manly pride;
And how could I think of such a one
  As a leader and a guide?

And then there came a worshipper
  With such undoubting trust,
That when he knelt he seemed not worth
  Upraising from the dust.

The next was never in the wrong,
  Was not too smooth nor rough;
So faultless and so good was he,
  That that was fault enough.

But one, the last of all who came,
  I know not how to paint;
No angel do I seem to him —
  He scarcely calls me saint!

He hath such sins and weaknesses
  As mortal man befall;
He hath a thousand faults, and yet
  I love him with them all!

He never asked me yea nor nay,
  Nor knelt to me one hour;
But he took my heart, and holds my heart
  With a lover's tender power.

And I bow, as needs I must, and say,
  In proud humility,
Love's might is right, and I yield at last
  To manhood's royalty!

LAST POEMS.

NOBODY'S CHILD.

ONLY a newsboy, under the light
  Of the lamp-post plying his trade in vain:
Men are too busy to stop to-night,
  Hurrying home through the sleet and rain.
Never since dark a paper sold;
  Where shall he sleep, or how be fed?
He thinks as he shivers there in the cold,
  While happy children are safe abed.

Is it strange if he turns about
  With angry words, then comes to blows,
When his little neighbor, just sold out,
  Tossing his pennies, past him goes?
"Stop!" — some one looks at him, sweet and mild,
  And the voice that speaks is a tender one:
"You should not strike such a little child,
  And you should not use such words, my son!"

Is it his anger or his fears
  That have hushed his voice and stopped his arm?
"Don't tremble," these are the words he hears;
  "Do you think that I would do you harm?"

"It isn't that," and the hand drops down;
"I wouldn't care for kicks and blows;
But nobody ever called me son,
Because I'm nobody's child, I s'pose."

O men! as ye careless pass along,
Remember the love that has cared for you;
And blush for the awful shame and wrong
Of a world where such a thing could be true!
Think what the child at your knee had been
If thus on life's lonely billows tossed;
And who shall bear the weight of the sin,
If one of these "little ones" be lost!

JOHN G. WHITTIER.

GREAT master of the poet's art!
Surely the sources of thy powers
Lie in that true and tender heart
Whose every utterance touches ours.

For, better than thy words, that glow
With sunset dyes or noontide heat,
That count the treasures of the snow,
Or paint the blossoms at our feet,

Are those that teach the sorrowing how
To lay aside their fear and doubt,
And in submissive love to bow
To love that passeth finding out.

And thou for such hast come to be
  In every home an honored guest —
Even from the cities by the sea
  To the broad prairies of the West.

Thy lays have cheered the humble home
  Where men who prayed for freedom knelt;
And women, in their anguish dumb,
  Have heard thee utter what they felt.

And thou hast battled for the right
  With many a brave and trenchant word,
And shown us how the pen may fight
  A mightier battle than the sword.

And therefore men in coming years
  Shall chant thy praises loud and long;
And women name thee through their tears
  A poet greater than his song.

But not thy strains, with courage rife,
  Nor holiest hymns, shall rank above
The rhythmic beauty of thy life,
  Itself a canticle of love!

THOU KNOWEST

Lord, with what body do they come
  Who in corruption here are sown,
When, with humiliation done,
  They wear the likeness of thine own?

Lord, of what manner didst Thou make
  The fruits upon life's healing tree?
Where flows that water we may take
  And thirst not through eternity?

Where lie the beds of lilies prest
  By virgins whiter than their snow?
What can we liken to the rest
  Thy well-belovèd yet shall know?

And where no moon shall shine by night,
  No sun shall rise and take his place,
How shall we look upon the light,
  O, Lamb of God, that lights thy face?

How shall we speak our joy that day
  We stand upon the peaceful shore,
Where blest inhabitants shall say,
  Lo! we are sick and sad no more?

What anthems shall they raise to Thee,
  The host upon the other side?
What will our depths of rapture be
  When heart and soul are satisfied?

How will life seem when fear, nor dread,
  Nor mortal weakness chains our powers;
When sin is crushed, and death is dead,
  And all eternity is ours?

When, with our lover and our Spouse,
  We shall as angels be above,
And plight no troths and breathe no vows,
  How shall we tell and prove our love?

How can we take in faith thy hand,
  And walk the way that we must tread?
How can we trust and understand
  That Christ will raise us from the dead?

We cannot see nor know to-day,
  For He hath made us of the dust;
We can but wait his time, and say,
  Even though He slay me, will I trust!

Swift to the dead we hasten now,
  And know not even the way we go;
Yet quick and dead are thine, and Thou —
  Thou knowest all we do not know!

LIGHT.

While I hid mine eyes, I feared;
  The heavens in wrath seemed bowed;
I look, and the sun with a smile breaks forth,
  And a rainbow spans the cloud.

I thought the winter was here,
  That the earth was cold and bare,
But I feel the coming of birds and flowers,
  And the spring-time in the air.

I said that all the lips
  I ever had kissed were dumb;
That my dearest ones were dead and gone,
  And never a friend would come.

But I hear a voice as sweet
  As the fall of summer showers;
And the grave that yawned at my very feet
  Is filled to the top with flowers!

As if 'twere the midnight hour,
  I sat with gloom oppressed;
When a light was breaking out of the east,
  And shining unto the west.

I heard the angels call
  Across from the beautiful shore;
And I saw a look in my darling's eyes,
  That never was there before.

Transfigured, lost to me,
  She had slipped from my embrace;
Now lo! I hold her fast once more,
  With the light of God on her face!

WAITING THE CHANGE.

I HAVE no moan to make,
  No bitter tears to shed;
No heart, that for rebellious grief,
  Will not be comforted.

There is no friend of mine
  Laid in the earth to sleep;
No grave, or green or heaped afresh,
  By which I stand and weep.

Though some, whose presence once
  Sweet comfort round me shed,
Here in the body walk no more
  The way that I must tread,

Not they, but what they wore
  Went to the house of fear;
They were the incorruptible,
  They left corruption here.

The veil of flesh that hid
  Is softly drawn aside;
More clearly I behold them now
  Than those who never died.

Who died! what means that word
  Of men so much abhorred?
Caught up in clouds of heaven to be
  Forever with the Lord!

To give this body, racked
  With mortal ills and cares,
For one as glorious and as fair,
  As our Redeemer wears;

To leave our shame and sin,
  Our hunger and disgrace;
To come unto ourselves, to turn
  And find our Father's face;

To run, to leap, to walk,
  To quit our beds of pain,
And live where the inhabitants
  Are never sick again;

To sit no longer dumb,
  Nor halt, nor blind; to rise —
To praise the Healer with our tongue,
  And see Him with our eyes;

To leave cold winter snows,
  And burning summer heats,
And walk in soft, white, tender light,
  About the golden streets.

Thank God! for all my loved,
  That out of pain and care,
Have safely reached the heavenly heights,
  And stay to meet me there!

Not these I mourn; I know
  Their joy by faith sublime —
But for myself, that still below
  Must wait my appointed time.

THOU AND I.

STRANGE, strange for thee and me,
    Sadly afar;
Thou safe beyond, above,
    I 'neath the star;
Thou where flowers deathless spring,
    I where they fade;
Thou in God's paradise,
    I 'mid time's shade!

Thou where each gale breathes balm,
I tempest-tossed;
Thou where true joy is found,
I where 'tis lost;
Thou counting ages thine,
I not the morrow;
Thou learning more of bliss,
I more of sorrow.

Thou in eternal peace,
I 'mid earth's strife;
Thou where care hath no name,
I where 'tis life;
Thou without need of hope,
I where 'tis vain;
Thou with wings dropping light,
I with time's chain.

Strange, strange for thee and me
Loved, loving ever;
Thou by Life's deathless fount,
I near Death's river;
Thou winning Wisdom's love,
I strength to trust;
Thou 'mid the seraphim,
I in the dust!

SPRING FLOWERS.[1]

O SWEET and charitable friend,
Your gift of fragrant bloom
Has brought the spring-time and the woods,
To cheer my lonesome room.

It rests my weary, aching eyes,
And soothes my heart and brain;
To see the tender green of the leaves,
And the blossoms wet with rain.

I know not which I love the most,
Nor which the comeliest shows,
The timid, bashful violet,
Or the royal-hearted rose:

The pansy in her purple dress,
The pink with cheek of red,
Or the faint, fair heliotrope, who hangs,
Like a bashful maid, her head.

For I love and prize you one and all,
From the least low bloom of spring
To the lily fair, whose clothes outshine
The raiment of a king.

And when my soul considers these,
The sweet, the grand, the gay,
I marvel how we shall be clothed
With fairer robes than they;

[1] The last poem written by Phœbe Cary.

www.ingramcontent.com/pod-product-compliance
Lightning Source LLC
LaVergne TN
LVHW010142110826
845151LV00002B/400

* 9 7 8 1 4 2 5 5 3 8 4 3 9 *